To Lorna and Don Blake

Thank you sincerely for being such kind and caring neighbors to my mother.

June 25, 2025
with deep gratitude
Claire Lyu.

A SUN WITHIN A SUN

A SUN
WITHIN
A SUN

The Power and Elegance of Poetry

Claire Chi-ah Lyu

UNIVERSITY OF PITTSBURGH PRESS

Published by the University of Pittsburgh Press, Pittsburgh, PA 15260
Copyright © 2006, Claire Chi-ah Lyu
All rights reserved
Manufactured in the United States of America
Printed on acid-free paper
10 9 8 7 6 5 4 3 2 1

Library of Congress Cataloging-in-Publication Data
Lyu, Claire Chi-ah.
  A sun within a sun : the power and elegance of poetry / Claire Chi-ah Lyu.
    p. cm.
  Includes bibliographical references and index.
  ISBN 0-8229-4277-1 (cloth : alk. paper)
  1. Poetry, Modern—19th century—History and criticism. 2. Poetry, Modern—20th century—History and criticism. I. Title.
PN1261.L98 2004
808.1—dc22

2005026404

The following texts have been included with permission:

  Two lines from "The Voyage," from *Selected Poems: Charles Baudelaire*, translated by Carol Clark (Penguin Classics, 1995). Translation copyright © Carol Clark, 1995. Reproduced by permission of Penguin Books Ltd.

  Excerpts from "On Some Motifs in Baudelaire" and "The Work of Art in the Age of Mechanical Reproduction," from *Illuminations* by Walter Benjamin, copyright © 1995 by Suhrkamp Verlag, Frankfurt a.M., English translation by Harry Zohn copyright © 1968 and renewed 1996 by Harcourt, Inc., reprinted by permission of Harcourt, Inc.

  Excerpts from *Difference and Repetition* by Gilles Deleuze, translated by Paul Patton. Copyright © 1994 Athlone Press. Reprinted with permission of the publisher. Excerpts from *Difference and Repetition* by Gilles Deleuze, translated by Paul Patton. Copyright © 1994 Columbia University Press. Reprinted with permission of the publisher.

  Excerpts from "Preface to *La Presse*, 1862," from *The Parisian Prowler: Le Spleen de Paris. Petits Poèmes en prose* by Charles Baudelaire, translated by Edward K. Kaplan. Copyright © 1989, 1997 by Edward K. Kaplan. Reprinted by permission of the University of Georgia Press.

  "Rose, O pure . . ." from *Uncollected Poems* by Rainer Maria Rilke, translated by Edward Snow. Translation copyright © 1996 by Edward Snow. Reprinted by permission of North Point Press, a division of Farrar, Strauss and Giroux, LLC.

  Seven lines from "The First Elegy," copyright © 1982 by Stephen Mitchell, from *The Selected Poetry of Rainer Maria Rilke* by Rainer Maria Rilke, translated by Stephen Mitchell. Used by permission of Random House, Inc.

  "The Panther," from *The Best of Rilke* by Rainer Maria Rilke, translated by Walter Arndt. Copyright © University Press of New England, Hanover, NH. Reprinted with permission.

  Excerpt from "Three Songs," from *West Wind: Poems and Prose Poems* by Mary Oliver. Copyright © 1997 by Mary Oliver. Reprinted by Permission of Houghton Mifflin Company. All rights reserved.

  Two earlier and shorter versions of chapter 2 appeared as Claire Lyu, "Stéphane Mallarmé as Miss Satin: The Texture of Fashion and Poetry," *Esprit Créateur* 40:3 (Fall 2000): 61–71; and Claire Lyu, "Mallarmé's Fashion," *figurationen. gender literatur kultur* 2 (Winter 2000): 29–50.

To My Grandmother

Mother

Father

And

The Fullness of Summer 2004

What can be this drunkenness of love,
already so powerful in its natural state,
when it is enclosed in the other drunkenness,
like a sun within a sun?

> Charles Baudelaire, "Le poème du hachisch"

Now, in these times of *our* modernity,
when knowledge no longer reckons with poetry . . .
in what way can the practice of poetry,
reading and writing,
interest our *savoir-vivre* . . . ?

> Michel Deguy, "To Spear It on the Mark,
> of Mystical Nature"

Poetry—unique source.

> Stéphane Mallarmé, "Observation relative au poème
> *Un coup de dés jamais n'abolira le hasard*"

CONTENTS

Acknowledgments ... xi

Prologue: "A Sun within a Sun" ... 1

1 Surrender of Freedom and Surrender to Freedom: Hashish and Poetry ... 9

2 The "Frivolous" Other and the "Authentic" Self: Fashion and Poetry ... 42

3 "Vise of Stone" and Open Air: "The Weight of Living" and "The Search for Lightness" ... 73

4 Beyond Hell and Paradise: The Poet and the Critic ... 95

5 Quantum Elegance: Content and Form in Science, Fashion, Poetry ... 131

6 The Eternal Enigma of Beauty ... 151

Epilogue: "Emotion-in-Syntax" ... 178

Notes ... 187

Index ... 215

ACKNOWLEDGMENTS

"A blank sheet of paper becomes lighter when someone holds it with you," a Korean proverb says. So it has been with the pages of this book. Many people have held them with me, bearing together the weight and the lightness of writing. I thank all those who have accompanied me on the journey I embarked on to make sense of life, asking the question "how should I live?" and inquiring whether and how we can live in a poetic relationship to the world.

The Woodrow Wilson National Fellowship Foundation and the Andrew W. Mellon Foundation offered me a Career Enhancement Fellowship, and the Office of the Vice Provost for Research and the Dean of Arts and Sciences at the University of Virginia gave me Faculty Summer Grants and the Sesquicentennial Associateship. These grants allowed me to explore deeper and wider horizons in thinking and writing.

I thank Lew Purifoy, George Crafts, and Charles Rice at the University of Virginia's Alderman Library for all the books they obtained through express delivery; and Cynthia Miller, Deborah Meade, Carol Sickman-Garner, Ann Walston, Chiquita Babb, Lowell Britson, and David Baumann at the University of Pittsburgh Press for their expertise and care.

Friends, colleagues, and teachers at the University of Virginia and elsewhere have encouraged me, lending support, holding not only the pages but also so much more: Amy Ogden, Michelle Amt, Janet Horne, Mary McKinley, Elisabeth Arnould-Bloomfield, Eleanor Kaufman, Janet Beizer, Sophie Rosenfeld, Kandioura Dramé, John Lyons, Cheryl Krueger, Elisabeth Ladenson, Vincent Descombes, Richard Terdiman, Suzanne Guerlac, Werner Hamacher, Rainer Nägele, Jean-Xavier Ridon, Tal Brewer, Dick Holway, Matthew Affron, Philippe Roger, Edward Kaplan, Kevin Newmark, Terri Smith, Jessica Wood, Tony Zanella, and Nickolas Knightly. Their friendship, in which poetry, reading, and thinking merge and emerge naturally, illuminates daily life.

Jeannette Hopkins has held every single page, and many more, being with me every step of the way. Without her clarity, exactitude, and generosity, this book simply would not be. I thank her for seeing the book I was yet to write and for helping me see it myself and bring it into being for others to see.

Bill Stephens, Sharon Beckman-Brindley, and Lisa Stendig have been a source of luminous presence with the clarity of their hearts. Their deep listening and openness hold anything and everything, showing me that it is possible to hold the universe within the self, and the self within the universe. Eileen Stephens, Catherine Boston, Victoria Doughty, Jeanne Manis, Gail Todter, and David Dyer, too, have been inspiring friends and guides, without whom I would not be where I am today.

I am grateful to Shadow and Piaf for summer 2004; to my mother, father, and brothers; and to my grandmother with whom it all began—I mean my love of poetry.

A SUN WITHIN A SUN

PROLOGUE

"A Sun within a Sun"

*And burned by the love of the beautiful . . .
my consumed eyes see only [m]emories of suns.*

Charles Baudelaire, "Les plaintes d'un Icare"

ACCORDING TO THE STORY, Daedalus and his young son, Icarus, were trapped in the Labyrinth on the island of Crete. To escape, Daedalus, a skilled artist, sculptor, architect, and engineer, designed and built wings for himself and his son and attached them to their shoulders with wax. Together they flew out of the Labyrinth, but as they took flight, Daedalus warned Icarus not to fly too high or too low: if he flew too high, the sun might melt the wax; if too low, the water might weigh down the feathers. Daedalus went ahead, keeping the middle course, but Icarus, ignoring his father's words, flew high into the sky toward the sun. The wax melted, and with his wings detached, Icarus plunged into the ocean that now bears his name.

Icarus is considered by some an imprudent fool—Pierre Grimal's *Dictionary of Classical Mythology* calls him "a foolish youth" who "did not listen to his father's advice"—by others a brave soul who had the courage to take risks for a higher ideal.[1] In a sonnet, Philippe Desportes, a French poet of the sixteenth century, praises Icarus: he "died pursuing a great adventure," burned by "the most beautiful of stars" (Il mourut poursuivant une haute aventure; Il eut pour le brûler des astres le plus beau). "The sky was his desire, the Sea his sepulcher / Is there a more beautiful purpose, or richer tomb?" (Le ciel fut son désir, la Mer sa sépulture: / Est-il plus beau dessein, ou plus riche tombeau?).[2] Charles Baudelaire, in the nineteenth century, gives Icarus a voice in "Les plaintes d'un Icare" ("The Laments of an Icarus"):

> The lovers of prostitutes
> Are happy, rested, and sated;
> As for me, my arms are broken
> For having embraced clouds.
>
> It is thanks to the matchless stars,
> That blaze in the depths of sky,
> That my consumed eyes see only
> Memories of suns.
>
> In vain I wanted of space
> To find the end and the middle;
> Under some fiery eye I know not
> I feel my wing breaking;
>
> And burned by the love of the beautiful,
> I shall not have the sublime honor
> Of giving my name to the abyss
> That will serve as my tomb.
>
> *(Les amants des prostituées*
> *Sont heureux, dispos et repus;*
> *Quant à moi, mes bras sont rompus*
> *Pour avoir étreint des nuées.*
>
> *C'est grâce aux astres nonpareils,*
> *Qui tout au fond du ciel flamboient,*

*Que mes yeux consumés ne voient
Que des souvenirs de soleils*

*En vain j'ai voulu de l'espace
Trouver la fin et le milieu;
Sous je ne sais quel œil de feu
Je sens mon aile qui se casse;*

*Et brûlé par l'amour du beau,
Je n'aurai pas l'honneur sublime
De donner mon nom à l'abîme
Qui me servira de tombeau.)*

[1: 143]³

    Neither a complete fool who fails pitifully nor a pure hero who succeeds gloriously, Baudelaire's Icarus speaks of opening up simultaneously to the brilliance and beauty of "the matchless stars" and to the darkness and terror of the abyssal "tomb." He does not claim the "sublime honor / Of giving [his] name to the abyss" but tells of his "arms . . . broken / For having embraced clouds," of his "consumed eyes see[ing] only / Memories of suns," and of his entire being "burned by the love of the beautiful." He accepts the wound the world inflicts on and inscribes in him in a movement of complete opening of the self to the world and its risks for the sake of the "love of the beautiful." He takes the risk of wings knowing that he might be consumed by the sun, lamenting that those who take no risks of flight, "The lovers of prostitutes / Are happy, rested, and sated; / As for me, my arms are broken / For having embraced clouds." *Repus* (sated) and *rompus* (broken) rhyme in French, emphasizing a relationship, but one of opposition, between holding tight onto easy pleasure, possession, and certainty, on the one hand, and poetry's move that lets go of certainties, breaks open and free, on the other.

    "The poem is the answer's absence," Maurice Blanchot writes. "The poet is one who, through his sacrifice, keeps the question open in his work."⁴ Icarus is the figure of the poet who risks sacrificing himself to "the love of the beautiful," willing to be "broken" by and open himself to love and

Beauty, and thereby opens—and leaves open—the question of love, Beauty, and risk. For poetry is clear perception, or realization, that only "broken" arms can hold the whole universe and, as Rabbi Nahman of Bratzlav said, that "no heart is as whole as a broken heart."[5] In breaking out of the secure closure of the answer and migrating into the uncertain openness of the question, poetry is pure, lucid, and rigorous in its surrendering to all of life's possibilities. Poetry is language that explores "how much risk one can take in allowing one's words to be modified by the world," to borrow Bruno Latour's statement regarding scientific discourse.[6] Risk is the willingness "to be modified." Poetry takes, and depends on, essential risks of not holding back from deep intimacy with the open, the self, and the other.

> *Every species forces the natural historian*
> *to take as much risk to account for its evolution*
> *through an innovative form of narration*
> *as it took the species to survive.*
>
> Bruno Latour, foreword to
> *Power and Invention*, by Isabelle Stengers

The historian of science Isabelle Stengers proposes to scientists that we "take, accept, and learn to measure the risks," warning against the "sterility" of the "least risky approach," which she calls "easy critique."[7] In his foreword to Stengers' book, Latour agrees that science must acknowledge "risky construction" that "takes risk as its cornerstone," indeed, that even the discourse and narration of science—"the words"—must take risks.[8] He might as well have been speaking about poetry: "There are constructions where neither the world nor the word, neither the cosmos nor the scientists take any risk. These are badly constructed propositions and should be weeded out of science and society. . . . On the other hand, there exist propositions where the world and the scientists are both at risk. Those are well constructed, that is, reality constructing, reality making, and they should be included in science and society."[9]

He rejects "most critical thinking" that reproduces "exactly at the outcome what was expected from the beginning . . . because the writer incurred no risk in being kicked out of his or her standpoint in writing them. . . . The equation is simple, although very hard to carry out: no risk, no good construction, no invention, thus no good science."[10]

"No risk, no good construction, no invention, thus no good poetry," one could also say. Or, no science or poetry at all, because both good science and good poetry would be tautologies. Poetry, like science, seeks to produce what Stengers terms *"astringent effects"* that stop *"thought from just turning in self-satisfying circles."*[11] It insists that we abandon and awaken from the deceptive comforts of habit and addiction. Risk is the willingness to open up the limited and limiting circle of the familiar and the easy so as "to be modified." To receive the power of poetry, reader, critic, and teacher of poetry alike must "be modified," for the poet takes the risk of language that is "modified by the world," that eschews preconception. Poetry is a venture, an exploration, not a resort to doctrine or established hierarchy. It is a way of seeing that leaves nothing out and yet selects and concentrates what it has seen to the essential, which Stengers calls "the singularity of an object or situation."[12] It condenses language as embodiment of thought and feeling to its core of active and creative principle. It activates the potential play of meaning with a heightened energy that strikes those who read it with a kinetic force. It stuns the reader with the intensity of "a sun within a sun," to use Baudelaire's words from "Le poème du hachisch": "What can be this drunkenness of love, already so powerful in its natural state, when it is enclosed in the other drunkenness, like a sun within a sun?" (Que peut être cette ivresse de l'amour, déjà si puissante à son état naturel, quand elle est enfermée dans l'autre ivresse, comme un soleil dans un soleil?) [1: 433].

Baudelaire writes that people who have never taken hashish often imagine naively that hashish intoxication enhances love's pleasure as if to the second power—"like a sun within a sun." The poet's answer is clear. Intoxication and addiction, in destroying freedom, lead only to lethargy and dissipation. Hashish's "sun" is a false lure. Only poetry, as the incomparable force of concentration and intensification, opens to authentic experiences of love and freedom, and hence to the true intensity of "a sun within a sun." I follow Baudelaire's move of celebrating poetry by reading "a sun within a sun" as pertaining, ultimately, to poetry's power.

A Sun within a Sun explores poetry's "risky construction": its experiment and experience that open language to its infinite possibility and hence to the creative potential of Beauty. If understanding the meaning of Reality is the ideal and the consequence of science, Beauty is the ideal and the consequence of poetry, each an enigma in that each requires an opening toward and an acceptance of the unknown and unknowable other. Wisdom is the fruit of both.

Poets answer Beauty's call to risk and freedom—the risk of freedom—through language, but not language as routine and familiar. Paul Valéry calls verse a "strange/foreign [étrange] discourse," a *"language within a language."*[13] Poetry risks creating a "foreign language" within the familiar discourse, transforming language by compelling it to speak of what is outside its bounds. Poetry takes the risk of wounding us as we approach the sun in order to heighten our awareness of life's beauty and terror, joy and sorrow, fragility and perishability. It demands also that we live as we read, intensely and openly —in risk—for the sake of deeper meaning, willing to encounter peril and to transform it into Beauty. Beauty and poetry—the beauty of poetry—invite us to move closer to our selves, to live in intimate proximity to our own deep original strangeness/foreignness. Poetry is an "invitation to depths" (invitation des profondeurs), to borrow Blanchot's words.[14]

For to read poetry is only the beginning. Poetry insists that we refuse to live in denial. Baudelaire warns the reader against hypocrisy in his poem "Au lecteur" ("To the Reader") and insists, in "Le voyage," that the reader "plunge into the depths of the abyss, Hell or Heaven, what does it matter? / To the depths of the Unknown to find something *new!*"(Plonger au fond du gouffre, Enfer ou Ciel, qu'importe? / Au fond de l'Inconnu pour trouver du *nouveau!*) [1: 134, original emphasis].[15] Poetry demands of those who read the constant practice of clear-sightedness, critical intelligence, and responsibility. Only such a commitment will bring the power and freedom to create for ourselves and to live in a poetic relationship to the world and to ourselves. Writing, reading, writing (about), and teaching poetry require that we acknowledge and accept the shock of poetry and respond to its imperative to explore the unknown, not to hoard and guard the known, to create and open possibilities, not to narrow our options to probabilities or certainties. Certainties can be a hindrance to life, just as dogma is to science.

To risk is to take chances. Chance, according to *The Oxford English Dictionary*, is a "possibility . . . of anything happening: as distinct from a certainty." To act when there is certainty of failure would be foolish; to act when there is certainty of success would be logical. Neither case involves risk, for risk, as chance, is the possibility of "*anything* happening." To take risks is to act and engage when nothing guarantees success; it is to accept as truthfully and as courageously as possible anything and everything that life brings our way. We habitually avoid risks in our daily life, hoping to reduce the chances of failure and loss, forgetting that doing so limits, too, the opportunities for growth and joy. Henry Miller writes that "the test of a man's humanity lies in his acceptance of life, all aspects of life, not just those which correspond with his own limited viewpoint."[16] To live with a larger perspective that opens up the world and life to their fullest and richest potential—risk means maximum living that awakens us to our deeper "humanity"; it is the openness, the truth, and the fact of life.

In taking risks poetry takes responsibilities, which, in Miller's words, is "to bear the consequences which a pure act always involves."[17] Poetry is a "pure act" of language and hence must "*always*" "bear [its own] consequences." Poetry's purity is the aesthetic and ascetic practice of language, awakening us from anesthesia, whose power of concentration does not block out risks but puts the world and words at risk in order to create maximum possibilities of life and hence give life its chance. Chance, as "the way in which things fall out," comes from the Latin *cadere*, "to fall." *Cadentia*, the "action or mode of falling, sinking down," gives rise to *cadence*—the flow, rhythm, and measure—in music, verse, and poetry. *Cadere*, cadence, chance, risk—falling is poetry's way; and risk is poetry's very measure, construction, and cornerstone. Poetry, like science, *means* to "take, accept, and learn to measure the risks."[18] Icarus, the falling body, is the figure—the corpus—indeed, if doomed, of poetry.

Forgetting the law of the father in his own ecstatic flight, Icarus says "Yes" to the fatally beautiful and all-consuming sun. His "Yes" celebrates

Beauty as pure living and dying. It is a hymn honoring the intensive and extensive luminescence of poetic language that opens a world gleaming with possibilities authentic and new. To say "Yes" to the profound gravity of infinite risk with joy, innocence, and lightness—that is the demand of poetry: to bear and to bare the pure weight of the soul, falling freely into "a sun within a sun."

CHAPTER ONE

Surrender of Freedom and

Surrender to Freedom

Hashish and Poetry

IN THE ENTIRE WORK OF BAUDELAIRE, Orpheus appears only once. In "Le poème du hachisch," the first part of *Les paradis artificiels: Opium et hachisch*, published in 1860, the poet frees himself from hashish intoxication and becomes like "Orpheus conqueror of Hell" (des Orphées vainqueurs de l'Enfer) [1: 428].[1] Deliverance from addiction is a poetic act par excellence. Poetry, as the power of concentration, resists the pleasure of intoxication as the dangerous lure of dissipation leading to fatal consequences. The last section of "Le poème du hachisch," "Morale," pronounces a severe sentence on the crowd of addicts who wallow in the poisonous delights of a numbing life.

For Baudelaire, poetry is not a drug. It does not put people to sleep, does not induce states of narcissistic indulgence or debilitating torpor; it does not kill. Poetry, accused of being a poison at the trial of Baudelaire's

Les fleurs du mal (*The Flowers of Evil*), is the opposite of a poison.[2] It awakens those who hear its call to a state of lucidity that sees *what is;* it nourishes the capacity to open to a life authentic in all its pain as well as all its joy. Baudelaire's law of poetry states a subtle yet stark reality: attraction to a poetic ideal, in contrast to addiction to hashish or any other addictive, is an act of surrender *to* freedom. *Addiction is attraction without freedom.*

Baudelaire's firm stance against hashish seems at odds with his poetic persona. He is best known as the poet of scandalous excess, urging us to inebriate ourselves as in the prose poem "Enivrez-vous" ("Get High") [1: 337]. Yet, Orpheus's appearance in "Le poème du hachisch" at the precise moment of passage from intoxication/addiction to sobriety/freedom requires us to reevaluate the relationship between poetry and intoxication in Baudelaire. It makes possible another reading of Baudelaire.

The attention I give to the opposition between poetry and addiction in Baudelaire differs from the focus of recent modes of reading, which tend to search primarily for disjunctures between the manifest content of a text and its subtending rhetoric, where binary oppositions break down.[3] I take the risk of difference, the risk of taking at face value that opposition, and the risk of thinking and speaking critically "in the interest of poetry," to borrow Michel Deguy's words.[4] I approach poetic criticism from the side of poetry.[5] I share the view of Michel Butor, expressed in his essay "Les paradis artificiels," written almost half a century ago, that "Le poème du hachisch" is a "defense" of poetry, in which hashish is not "condemned ... by the rules of bourgeois morality" but "vanquished by poetry, more powerful than hashish."[6]

Orpheus emerges at the end of "Le poème du hachisch" to honor poetic experience. He embodies the higher law of poetic inspiration, that a poet can write about experience, as of intoxication and addiction, without becoming intoxicated or addicted himself. It is a poetics of sobriety and purity consonant with what Gilles Deleuze sees as fundamental in the writings of both William Burroughs and Henry Miller. Deleuze identifies the central question in Burroughs: "can you harness the power of drugs without their taking over, without turning into a dazed zombie?"[7] He refers to Miller's "experimentation," his attempts "to get high without using drugs, to get drunk on pure water."[8] For Deleuze, "We are trying to extract from alcohol the life that it contains, without drinking. . . . To do without alcohol, drugs . . . this is the becoming, the becoming-sober, for a life that is more and more rich."[9]

Les paradis artificiels is the only book of Baudelaire's other than *Les fleurs du mal* that Baudelaire published during his lifetime. More than any other pieces Baudelaire wrote, the poet identified himself as the author of *Les fleurs* and *Les paradis*. In his letter of December 11, 1861, requesting admission to the French Academy, Baudelaire presents himself as the author of *Les fleurs du mal*, "*a book of poetry*"; of "*a translation*" of Poe's works; of *Les paradis artificiels*, "a severe and minute *study* of the jouissances and dangers *Stimulants* possess" (*une étude* sévère et minutieuse sur les jouissances et dangers contenus dans les *Excitants*) [*Corr* 2: 193, original emphasis]; and of "a great number of brochures and articles." In letters of August 3, 1863, to two ministers, Maréchal Vaillant and Victor Dupuy, asking for funds for a lecture tour to Belgium, Baudelaire writes: "I am the author of *Les Fleurs du mal*, of *Les Paradis artificiels*, etc., etc., and the translator of works by *Edgar Poe*" [*Corr* 2: 309–10, original emphasis]. Baudelaire was satisfied with *Les paradis artificiels* all his life: we learn from his letter of February 3, 1865, to Julien Lemer, editor, literary agent, and director of a Parisian bookstore, that he found *Les paradis artificiels* "good as it is" and would "not add anything to" or "subtract anything from" it (Je trouve le livre bon comme il est, je n'y ajouterai rien, je n'en retrancherai rien) [*Corr* 2: 442]. "Le poème du hachisch," the first part of *Les paradis artificiels*, appeared two years before the book itself in *La revue contemporaine* of September 1858.

In "Le poème du hachisch," Baudelaire insists on distinguishing his voice, the voice of poetry, from the voices of intoxication:

> Today, I shall speak only of hashish, and I shall do so by drawing on copious and detailed information, extracted from notes or confidences of intelligent men who have given themselves over to hashish for a long

time. But I shall meld these diverse documents in a sort of monograph, choosing a soul, easy to explain and define as suited to an experience of this nature.

(Aujourd'hui, je ne parlerai que du hachisch, et j'en parlerai suivant des renseignements nombreux et minutieux, extraits des notes ou des confidences d'hommes intelligents qui s'y étaient adonnés longtemps. Seulement, je fondrai ces documents variés en une sorte de monographie, choisissant une âme, facile d'ailleurs à expliquer et à définir, comme type propre aux expériences de cette nature.) [404]

Although it is not certain whether Baudelaire was one of these "intelligent men who have given themselves over to hashish," the poet's voice is sober at least at the moment of writing. Its distinct sobriety amid others' experiences of intoxication brings out the double meaning of *expérience* in French, as both experience and experiment. The poet's function is not to "feel the poetic state," which is "a private issue," but "to create it in others," Paul Valéry writes.[10] For Baudelaire, too, the poet's function is less to experience passively and more to experiment actively. The poet experiments with experience.

The poetic experiment turns chemical in the section "Qu'est-ce que le hachisch?" ("What Is Hashish?"), which is the second of five. Detailed descriptions appear of chemical procedures for isolating hashish's active ingredient, on the one hand, and for preparing the pure principal substance for oral consumption, on the other. Poetic alchemy of the projected "Epilogue" for the 1861 edition of *Les fleurs du mal*—"I have extracted the quintessence from every single thing, / You have given me your mud and I have turned it into gold" (j'ai de chaque chose extrait la quintessence, / Tu m'as donné ta boue et j'en ai fait de l'or) [1: 192]—meets poetic chemistry in "Le poème du hachisch."

The intoxicated voices dwell in a textual space different from that occupied by the poetic voice. The voices of addiction are confined to the middle section, "Le théâtre de Séraphin," which has been set up explicitly as the center stage of the piece, on which the voices appear as "a tableau of artificial voluptuousness" (un tableau de voluptés artificielles) [399]. By its nature hashish spreads like smoke or vapor. During its harvesting, a kind of "vertiginous spirit" (esprit vertigineux) "ascends maliciously" (monte maliciéusement) to the brains of the harvesters, creating "whirlwinds" (tourbillons) in their heads, weakening their limbs [388]. When hashish is ingested in the form of "green jam" (confiture verte), "a great languor takes over" and "spreads through your faculties, like a fog on a landscape" (Une grande langueur... s'empare de vore esprit et se répand à travers vos facultés, comme un brouillard dans un paysage) [409, 426]. The idea and sensation of evaporation, for one addict, took over with an intensity so overwhelming that he felt as if the pipe were smoking him [420]. The four anecdotes of intoxication Baudelaire sets up on stage seem to evaporate into thin air as the poet warns that they are "trickery and puppets, born of the *smoke* of childish brains" (jonglerie et... marionnettes, nées de la *fumée* des cerveaux enfantins) [426, my emphasis]. Hashish possesses a "conquering and invading humor" (l'humeur conquérante et envahissante) [411] that desolidifies, dissipates, and vaporizes all it touches with an insidious insistence. It acts like a slow poison that leaves the addict, "for several hours, incapable of work, action, and energy" (pour quelques heures encore, incapable de travail, d'action et d'énergie) [426].[11] It is, Baudelaire writes, "the punishment for the impious prodigality with which you have wasted your nervous fluid. You have disseminated your personality to the four celestial winds, and now, what trouble you will have to reassemble it and concentrate it!" (C'est la punition de la prodigalité impie avec laquelle vous avez dépensé le fluide nerveux. Vous avez disséminé votre personnalité aux quatre vents du ciel, et, maintenant, quelle peine n'éprouvez-vous pas à la rassembler et à la concentrer!) [426].

The poet assembles and confines the invasive vapor of intoxication to the stage of "Le théâtre de Séraphin" as if to prevent its spilling off stage and contaminating the space of sobriety. Stories of intoxication, in Baudelaire's telling, are kept inside quotation marks, between the opening and the closing of curtains, and recounted as anecdotes that remain separate from, and subordinated to, the central narrative led by the poetic voice. They are quarantined, as if to find an antidote to each is a necessity. The segregation between the stage of intoxication and the off-stage sobriety is also at work at a larger textual level. In the middle section, the hashish voices are free to speak, in contrast to the other four sections of "Le poème du hachisch." The middle section opposes itself to the others, where the poet writes his "monograph of inebriation" (la monographie de l'ivresse), as theater and illusion are opposed to real life. "Le poème du hachisch" presents itself as the writing process of this monograph, from the collecting of raw data from people's experiences of intoxication, to the gathering, the melding, and the compiling into a written piece.

The opposition is clear. Intoxicated voices are staged; the poetic voice stages. Intoxicated voices are passive, experiencing, and multiple; the poetic voice is active, experimenting, sober, and single. Hashish is *voice* that vaporizes and disperses in smoke; poetry is *writing* that concentrates, condenses, and intensifies into a *mono-graph*. The opposition between intoxication and poetry embodies the famous Baudelairian double postulation: "Of vaporization and centralization of the *Self*. That is the key" (De la vaporisation et de la centralisation du *Moi*. Tout est là) [*Mon cœur mis à nu* (*My Heart Laid Bare*) 1: 676, original emphasis]. Closer, still, is the sentence Baudelaire quotes from Emerson, "The one prudence in life is concentration; the one evil is dissipation" (English in the original).[12]

"The taste for productive concentration must replace, in a mature man, the taste for destructive dispersal/waste," writes Baudelaire (Le goût de la concentration productive doit remplacer, chez un homme mûr, le goût de la déperdition) [*Fusées* 1: 649]. Hashish, as the expansive force of disorder that turns productive energy into unproductive, and even destructive, lethargy, is the law of entropy incarnate. Poetry's alchemy and chemistry fight that addictive thermodynamics. Poetic alchemy experiences the pull of the diminishing second law of thermodynamics. Mud is not always turned into gold. And gold can always turn into iron, as in the poem "Alchimie de la douleur" ("Alchemy of Suffering"): "You make me equal to Midas, / The saddest of alchemists; / By you I change gold to iron / And paradise to hell" (Tu me rends l'égal de Midas, / Le plus triste des alchimistes; / Par toi je change l'or en fer / Et le paradis en enfer) [1: 77].

Writing and intoxication are mutually exclusive. Baudelaire compares hashish intoxication to a "fantastic novel" that is "alive" instead of "being written" (un roman fantastique . . . vivant au lieu d'être écrit) [420]. Intoxication's dangerous lure offers wondrous visions, ones seemingly poetic. It promises equally rich manifestation in writing, but, in reality, it delivers fatigue, inertia, addiction, and, therefore, a loss of freedom and the capacity to write.

"Orgy is not the sister of inspiration: we have broken this adulterous relationship" (L'orgie n'est pas la sœur de l'inspiration: nous avons cassé cette parenté adultère), Baudelaire writes in an early piece published in April 1846, *Conseils aux jeunes littérateurs* (Advice to Young Men of Letters):

> Inspiration is decidedly the sister of daily work. . . . Inspiration submits, like hunger, like digestion, like sleep. There is no doubt a sort of celestial mechanism in the spirit, of which one shouldn't be ashamed, but of whose most glorious part one should take advantage, just as doctors do of corporeal mechanism.
>
> *(L'inspiration est décidément la sœur du travail journalier. . . . L'inspiration obéit, comme la faim, comme la digestion, comme le sommeil. Il y a sans doute dans l'esprit une espèce de mécanique céleste, dont il ne faut pas être honteux, mais tirer le parti le plus glorieux, comme les médecins de la mécanique du corps.)* [2: 18]

"Le poème du hachisch"'s revelation of the anatomy of the orgy demonstrates its incompatibility with the anatomy of the creative corpus. For Baudelaire, Wagner and Delacroix embody creativity in its highest form. The poet discovers in them an astounding energy in which concentration, not dissipation, is the law, and which harnesses, converts, and enhances available energy for production. Creativity, or productivity, generates and multiplies energy necessary for useful work, precisely counter to the inexorable law of entropy that drains all systems, diminishing energy by dissipating it as heat, pure waste. It replaces *passive experience*, which costs energy, with *active experiment*, which creates it: "Pleasure wears us out. Work fortifies us. Let's choose" (Le plaisir nous use. Le travail nous fortifie. Choisissons) [*Hygiène* 1: 669]. "Le poème du hachisch" makes the choice.

"*Willpower, desire, concentration, nervous intensity, explosion*" (*volonté, désir, concentration, intensité nerveuse, explosion*) characterize Wagner's music [*Richard Wagner et Tannhäuser à Paris* 2: 807, original emphasis]. A creative system emits energy as "explosion," not as dissipation. "What marks most visibly the style of Delacroix," Baudelaire writes in his piece on his favorite painter, "is the concision and a sort of intensity without ostentation, the habitual result of concentration of all spiritual forces toward a given point. '*The hero is he who is immovably centered*' [English in the original], says the moralist from overseas Emerson" (Ce qui marque le plus visiblement le style de Delacroix, c'est la concision et une espèce d'intensité sans ostentation, résultat habituel de la concentration de toutes les forces spirituelles vers un point donné. "*The hero is he who is immovably centered*," dit le moraliste d'outre-mer Emerson) [*L'œuvre et la vie d'Eugène Delacroix* (*The Life and Work of Eugène Delacroix*) 2: 754–55, original emphasis]. Emerson's maxim for "the conduct of life" "can also apply to the domain of poetry and art," in Baudelaire's words: "*The literary hero, that is, the true writer, is he who is immutably concentrated*" (La maxime que [Emerson] ... applique à la conduite de la vie ... peut également s'appliquer au domaine de la poésie et de l'art.... "*Le héros littéraire, c'est-à-dire le véritable écrivain, est celui qui est immuablement concentré*") [2: 755, original emphasis].

The law of "con-centration" of artistic creation is the synergetic merging of the two centers, of "celestial mechanism" and "corporeal mechanism," of body and work, into a single corpus. Hashish, a "fantastic novel" that is "alive" but not "written," separates body and work. There is no converging, no centering "toward a given point," no concentration: no body *of* work, or corpus. In the intoxicated body, the two corpora fight and cancel each other out. The system dwindles to a state of waste. In the poetic body, the two corpora enter into a relation of supportive containment: corpus within a corpus, "celestial mechanism" within "corporeal mechanism," "the infinite within the finite" (l'infini dans le fini) [*Salon de 1859* 2: 636], "a sun within a sun" (un soleil dans un soleil) [433]. Each intensifies the other: "corporeal mechanism" is elevated to the power of "celestial mechanism." "Great poets," writes Baudelaire, citing Barbereau, a philosopher and theoretician of music, in an earlier version of "Le poème du hachisch," are able "by the pure and free exercise of their willpower to attain a state in which they are both cause and effect, subject and object, mesmerizer and the sleepwalker" (Les grands poètes ... sont des êtres qui par le pur et libre exercice de la volonté parviennent à un état où ils sont à la fois cause et effet, sujet et objet, magnétiseur et somnambule) ["Du vin et du hachisch" 1: 398].

The synergy between the "celestial" and "corporeal mechanisms" in the artistic corpus is nowhere better demonstrated than in Baudelaire's seminal essay *Le peintre de la vie moderne* (*The Painter of Modern Life*) [2: 683–724].[13] The artistic creation is depicted as a comprehensive bodily activity, a masterful choreography of inner processes (optical, neural, cerebral, and digestive) and outer movements (painting is like the art of fencing). Metaphors of ingestion and digestion describe the process of creation exemplified by M.G., or "the painter of modern life." The "modern beautiful" is a "divine cake" (divin gâteau) [685] M.G. devours with enormous appetite. He is curious about—hungry for—the entire universe, hunting and swooping from sunrise to sunset with the unerring precision of a bird of prey, eating with his eyes (he has the *"eye of eagle"* [*œil d'aigle*] [693, original emphasis]), soaking up with his skin and nerves all the intense jolts that emanate from the "immense reservoir of electricity" (immense réservoir de l'électricité) [692] of the pulsating streets of Paris. Baudelaire writes that "M.G. absorbs [the fantastic real] ceaselessly; his memory and eyes are filled" (M.G. l'absorbe sans cesse; il en a la mémoire et les yeux pleins) [697]. And yet, he can never have enough of the world; he is a *"self* insatiable of *non-self"* (un *moi* insatiable du *non-moi*) [692, original emphasis].

Baudelaire describes M.G.'s body as that of a convalescent and a child, thus in an altered corporeal and mental state that functions outside the healthy adult body. Far from being a negative state marked by weakness and lack, this is a privileged state with an enhanced capacity for ingestion and digestion: "Nothing resembles more what is called inspiration than the joy with which the child absorbs form and color" (Rien ne ressemble plus à ce qu'on appelle l'inspiration, que la joie avec laquelle l'enfant absorbe la forme et la couleur) [690]. And convalescence "is like a return to childhood" (est comme un retour vers l'enfance), notes Baudelaire. "The convalescent delights to the highest degree, like a child, in the faculty of being vividly interested in things, even the most trivial in appearance" (Le convalescent jouit au plus haut degré, comme l'enfant, de la faculté de s'intéresser vivement aux choses, même les plus triviales en apparence) [690]. Baudelaire continues: "Having returned recently from the shadows of death, he breathes in with delectation all the seeds and emanations from life; as he was on the verge of forgetting everything, he remembers and wants, with ardor, to remember everything" (Revenu récemment des ombres de la mort, il aspire avec délice tous les germes et tous les effluves de la vie; comme il a été sur le point de tout oublier, il se souvient et veut avec ardeur se souvenir de tout) [690]. The convalescent and the child are dynamic bodies, the convalescent recovering, the child growing. The body has inherent receptivity and openness to the maximum intake of nutrients for repair, stimulation, and growth. At the same time, it possesses a drive to renew and transform itself into a state of superior strength.[14]

The body of the artist opens up to outside stimuli that "penetrate" (pénétrer), "possess" (posséder), and "take over" (s'emparer de) [691]. The impact of the external world reaches deep into the body of the artist, up to the brain center and out from sense to sense through the process of synesthesia. It is as though a dual system of vertical and horizontal "Correspondances" of Baudelaire's poetics has mapped itself onto the poet's body as a vertical and horizontal channeling of the nerves. The poetic corpus is thoroughly wired for maximum receptivity and resonance between outside and inside, between "celestial mechanism" and "corporeal mechanism." For this hypersensitive body, "no aspect of life is *dulled*" (aucun aspect de la vie n'est *émoussé*) [691, original emphasis], and perception is so sharp (perception aigüe) [694] that it almost hurts. The universe makes deep incisions into the body. "Celestial mechanism" slices into "corporeal mechanism." The artistic corpus experiences and experiments with cutting, becoming both object and subject, as the eyes wounded by a sharp perception shoot out glances like darts ("darting out . . . glances" [dardant . . . le regard] [693]). Creation becomes like fencing ("fencing with his pencil, his pen, his brush" [s'escrimant avec son crayon, sa plume, son pinceau] [693]). In the poem

"Le soleil" ("The Sun"), the speaker-poet engages in "fantastic fencing" (fantasque escrime), "stumbling over" (trébuchant) and "knocking against" (heurtant) "rhyme" and "verses" [1: 83]. The poet carves, incises, and inscribes words and dreams.[15] Inspiration is thus in-scription of the body.

"I dare push further," Baudelaire writes. "I affirm that inspiration has some rapport with *congestion*, and that all sublime thought is accompanied by a nervous jolt, more or less strong, with repercussions in the cerebellum" (J'oserai pousser plus loin; j'affirme que l'inspiration a quelque rapport avec la *congestion*, et que toute pensée sublime est accompagnée d'une secousse nerveuse, plus ou moins forte, qui retentit jusque dans le cervelet) [690, original emphasis]. *Congestion*, from the Latin *con-gerere*, "to carry," or bring together, is the movement of convergence. It is corporeal concentration. To be inspired is to open up to the outside world with such power of reception, amassment, and concentration as to come to the edge of congestion, or cerebral stroke.[16] An inspired body is necessarily a congested body, and congestion runs the risk of trauma.[17]

In convergence and concentration, health and sickness, no longer opposites, support each other as states of sheer corporeal intensity—*absolute intensity*, one might say, as one says *absolute value* in mathematics. In this state of absolute corporeal intensity, positive and negative do not negate each other but are modes of living—experiencing and experimenting—a state of intensity. A different arithmetic holds: entropy is reduced, negative opens up to positive, object to subject, "the sleepwalker" to "the mesmerizer," experience to experiment, physical body to body of work, and "corporeal mechanism" to "celestial mechanism." It is a "*real* state of emergency" that lays out its *own* norm, to borrow Walter Benjamin's formulation.[18]

Baudelaire compares the "ideal execution" (l'exécution idéale) of the work to the process of digestion [699], which maintains the body's life and growth.[19] If producing work is like digestion, the body of the artist sustains and grows through achieving work. Work turns truly vital. M.G. in painting becomes animated with a life force from within, "fencing with his pencil, his pen, his brush, splashing water from the glass to the ceiling, wiping his pen on his shirt, hurrying, violent, active . . . quarrelling all alone, and jostling with himself" (s'escrimant avec son crayon, sa plume, son pinceau, faisant jaillir l'eau du verre au plafond, essuyant sa plume sur sa chemise, pressé, violent, actif . . . querelleur quoique seul, et se bousculant lui-même) [693]. Congestion, excessive accumulation of bodily fluid clogging one area, is countered by digestion. Di-gestion undoes con-gestion by restoring the flow that has been blocked. Baudelaire claims that "ideal execution" must become "as *flowing* as . . . digestion" (aussi *coulante* que l'est la digestion) [699, original emphasis]. Creative work is a visceral response to, an experiential and experimental passage through, and a vital recovery and growth from a state of corporeal emergency. The dangerous intensity of *mal* is converted into creative energy. *Flowers* of convalescence blossom from *pains of the body*.

Genius, as "*childhood regained* at will, childhood endowed, now, to express itself, with virile organs and analytic spirit that allow him to order the sum of materials involuntarily accumulated," follows the same corporeal flow (*l'enfance retrouvée* à volonté, l'enfance douée maintenant, pour s'exprimer, d'organes virils et de l'esprit analytique qui lui permet d'ordonner la somme de matériaux involontairement amassée) [690, original emphasis]. The "sum of materials involuntarily accumulated" that con-gests the body is di-gested, that is, carried apart and away into a flow. Creation is the flow from an involuntary stasis (congestion) to a willed dynamism (digestion), a state of corporeal intensity emerging from birth (child) and returning from the "shadows of death" (convalescent). The genius has digested his own birth and death, turning the two extreme points of life (stasis) into a force of life unfolding from within (dynamism) that entails harnessing the power of childhood and convalescence without being helpless or remaining sick.

M.G., the child-convalescent, paints at night. While others "drink up" (boire la coupe de l'oubli) [693], M.G. chooses work, satisfies thirst from a different *coupe*, which in French means not only "cup" but also "a cut, a form, a contour." M.G. paints, cutting out forms, drinking not from a "coupe de l'oubli" (cup of forgetfulness and dissipation) but from a *coupe* of remembered contour and form: "At the last moment, the contour of objects is definitively encircled with ink" (Au dernier moment, le contour des objets est définitivement cerné par de l'encre) [699]. M.G. "encircles" a contour, traces a circle, a *coupe* not of dissipation but of concentration. M.G.'s drawings have concentrated "the bitter or heady flavor of the wine of Life" (la saveur amère ou capiteuse du vin de la Vie) [724]; he works, in "inebriation of the pencil, of the brush, almost akin to fury" (une ivresse de crayon, de pinceau, ressemblant presqu'à une fureur) [699]. The execution of work, that is, the active experiment, generates an experience of inebriation, a "cut/cup" of intoxication. Poetry contains and generates its intoxication from within. "As others seek the secret for debauchery, [Delacroix] seeks the secret of inspiration," writes Baudelaire, "and he gave himself up to true drunken bouts of work" (Comme d'autres cherchent le secret pour la débauche, [Delacroix] cherche le secret de l'inspiration, et il s'y livrait à de véritables ribotes de travail) [2: 761]. Baudelaire's ideal artists of modernity create the high without drugs. They have no need for hashish—the source of "artificial voluptuousness" (voluptés artificielles) [1: 399]—and they generate *"perpetual voluptuousness"* from the very source of daily "torment": work (de faire ma *perpétuelle volupté* de mon tourment ordinaire, c'est-à-dire du Travail!) [*Hygiène* 1: 668, original emphasis]. *Flowers* of voluptuousness blossom from *pains of the work*.[20]

Baudelaire's construction of the "monograph of inebriation" in "Le poème du hachsich" follows the creative method of the painter of modern life. Like M.G., dashing to fill his vision during the day in order to paint at night, the poet gathers raw data from anecdotes of intoxication in order to produce, in the last two sections of "Le poème du hachsich," a "monograph of inebriation": "To abbreviate my task and make my analysis clearer, instead of collecting scattered anecdotes, I will amass in one fictive persona a large number of observations" (pour abréger ma tâche et rendre mon analyse plus claire, au lieu de rassembler des anecdotes éparses, j'accumulerai sur un seul personnage fictif une masse d'observations) [429]. Poetic writing is not a mere "collecting [of] *scattered* anecdotes," but an act of concision ("to abbreviate") and condensation into one ("amass"). Like M.G.'s painting—which "at the last moment encircle[s] definitely the contour of objects with ink" [2: 699]—the poet's writing culminates in a circle, a soul, the very figure, and literally so, of concentration/centralization. Baudelaire explicitly gives the form of the circle to his monograph: "In order to idealize my subject matter, I must concentrate all the rays into a single circle, I must polarize them; and the tragic circle in which I shall assemble them will be, as I said, a soul of my choosing" (Pour idéaliser mon sujet, je dois en concentrer tous les rayons dans un cercle unique, je dois les polariser; et le cercle tragique où je les vais rassembler sera, comme je l'ai dit, une âme de mon choix) [429].[21] Completion of the poetic work coincides with the tracing of a full circle, as Baudelaire writes at the end; to conclude "is to close a circle" (Conclure, c'est fermer un cercle) [440].

"Le poème du hachsich" narrates the passage from dissipation of anecdotes to concentration of monograph and puts to practice the maxim "The taste for productive concentration must replace, in a mature man, the taste for destructive waste/loss" (Le goût de la concentration productive doit remplacer, chez un homme mûr, le goût de la déperdition) [*Fusées* 1: 649]. "Le poème du hachsich" performs the process of poetic maturation ("the maturation of dream" and "poetic childbirth" [cette maturation du rêve et cet enfantement poétique] [421]) by steering toward sober concentration the unquenchable "taste of/for the infinite"—the title and subject of its opening section—that seduces us toward narcotic dissipation. Poetry itself approaches the infinite through "concentration of all spiritual forces toward a given point" (concentration de toutes les forces spirituelles vers un point donné) [2: 754–55], not through the haze of a foggy daze. Not vagueness but focus gives rise to the experience of the vast infinite, as expressed in the prose poem "Le *confiteor* de l'artiste": "there is no sharper point than that of the Infinite" (il n'est pas de pointe plus acérée que celle de l'Infini) [1: 278].

Yet the opposition between hashish as vaporization and poetry as concentration/circle needs further articulation, since hashish, too, is presented as a circle. But it is a "vicious circle." Baudelaire encapsulates the risks and dangers of the use of hashish:

> This hope [to make positive use of hashish by turning it into a thinking machine, or a productive instrument] is a vicious circle: let us say

for a moment that hashish gives, or at least enhances, genius; they [the hashish eaters] forget that it is hashish's nature to decrease the will, and therefore it grants on one hand what it takes away on the other, that is, the imagination without the faculty to profit from it.

(Cette espérance est un cercle vicieux: admettons un instant que le hachisch donne, ou du moins augmente le génie; ils oublient qu'il est de la nature du hachisch de diminuer la volonté, et qu'ainsi il accorde d'un côté ce qu'il retire de l'autre, c'est-à-dire l'imagination sans la faculté d'en profiter.) [440][22]

A vicious circle is a flawed reasoning, a sophism in which the conclusion rests on a premise that depends on its own conclusion. To Baudelaire the "sophisms" of hashish are "numerous and admirable" [432]. By extension, it is a situation in which one is locked or trapped, a prison from which one seldom escapes.

Hashish has a highly circular dynamic and topology. The proverb Baudelaire employs as a metaphor for the way people seek any means—even dangerous—to attain that false state of bliss is *"All roads lead to Rome"* (*Tout chemin mène à Rome*) [403, original emphasis]. With hashish it doesn't matter how we get there; any means is as good as any other. Why not take me, I'm so easy. This seemingly benign and open way to Rome—or paradise, albeit artificial—closes up as a trap once we enter its space. The circle contracts. We are inevitably led to Rome, but Rome becomes the only center there is. What has appeared as striking an incredibly good bargain—an easy way to get to paradise, an excellent deal—turns out to be the most expensive way of all. We pay with our will, our freedom, and our soul. It is to hell, not to paradise, that addiction leads. The circle is vicious because it is a lie: paradise turns out to be a "secondhand paradise" (*paradis d'occasion*) that ultimately leads to hell (*l'enfer*) [441]. The centripetal force hides behind centrifugal vaporization. It erases itself.

Poetry takes on the task not only of resisting vaporization by concentration but also of competing with the vicious circle of addiction by splitting it open. Baudelaire writes in the beginning of "Le poème du hachisch": "One could take in a metaphorical sense the common proverb *All roads lead to Rome* and apply it to the moral domain: everything leads to reward or punishment, two forms of eternity" (On pourrait prendre dans un sens métaphorique le vulgaire proverbe: *Tout chemin mène à Rome*, et l'appliquer au monde moral; tout mène à la récompense ou au châtiment, deux formes d'éternité) [402–03, original emphasis]. The "common proverb" (vulgaire proverbe) describes a centripetal situation in which Rome is the only destination and center, and all roads are infallible and identical. It is "common" in that it is what people want, simply to go to Rome/to get high. With *"All roads lead[ing] to Rome,"* and everyone going to Rome, Rome is "con-gested." To split Rome open is to "di-gest" a Rome that has become "involuntarily" amassed. The poet shatters the nondiscriminating, single-minded, and involuntary universe of the "common proverb" by splitting Rome, the unique center, into extreme opposites: "reward or punishment." It matters profoundly which road we take. The poet introduces the possibility of failure ("punishment"), and thus the possibility of a true success ("reward"), into the "infallible" universe.

For it is the "infallibility" of hashish—that it works "always well" (à coup sûr) [439] and "at one go" (d'un seul coup) [402, 441]—that for Baudelaire "constitutes its immorality." "We call a crook, a player who has found the means to win all the time," he writes. "It is the very infallibility of the means that constitutes [hashish's] immorality" (Nous appelons escroc le joueur qui a trouvé le moyen de jouer à coup sûr. . . . C'est l'infaillibilité même du moyen qui en constitue l'immoralité) [439–40]. If infallibility implies immorality, then morality implies fallibility. The poet's gesture that splits Rome open in the first section of "Le poème du hachisch" and introduces fallibility bears direct relation to the last section, "Morale." Rome is no longer the single destination or the sole principle of the journey's direction and orientation. A new *sens*—direction, orientation, sensation, and meaning—emerges within the once one-way street, its metaphor: to split Rome open is to "take in a metaphorical sense the common proverb" [402–03]. Metaphor shakes and liberates sense from the stricture and habit of commonplace and unilateral use that results from lack of reflection and imagination. The people are stuck to the literal meaning: to go *only* to Rome, to ingest happiness *literally* in the form of "green jam," to take the rhetoric of hashish *at face value*.[23] "Common" use is unfree use trapped in the daily pull and stickiness. In their obsession with going only to Rome, the people fail to realize that the true problem is never being able to leave.

Intoxication does not offer the experience it seems to promise of freedom from the confines of everyday life: "In hashish inebriation, . . . we will not go out of a dream that is natural" (Dans l'ivresse du hachisch, . . . nous ne sortirons pas du rêve naturel) [409]; "the brain and organism on which hashish operates yield only their ordinary, individual phenomena, increased, it is true, in number and energy, but faithful always to their origin" (le cerveau et l'organisme sur lesquels opère le hachisch ne donneront que leurs phénomènes ordinaires, individuels, augmentés, il est vrai, quant au nombre et à l'énergie, mais toujours fidèles à leur origine) [409]. Hashish vision is "the son of its father" (le fils de son père) [409], its "root in the ambient milieu and in the present" (racine dans le milieu ambiant et dans le temps présent) [421]. It "derive[s] from earth rather than from heaven and owes a large part of [its] beauty to the nervous agitation, the avidity with which the spirit throws itself into [hallucination]" (Elles tiennent de la terre plutôt que du ciel, et doivent une grande partie de leur beauté à l'agitation nerveuse, à l'avidité avec laquelle l'esprit se jette sur elles) [440].

The metaphorical sense of poetry creates a way out, a liberation and a possibility of true trans-port out of Rome, escaping the pull of gravity that habit exerts. Freedom offers alternatives and the responsibility to choose: "Pleasure wears us out. Work fortifies us. Let's choose" (Le plaisir nous use. Le travail nous fortifie. Choisissons) [*Hygiène* 1: 669]. Poetry demands that we practice responsibility. It understands that freedom and responsibility are necessarily connected and inscribes this lucidity in language. Poetry is free and responsible use of language.

The mind stupefied by hashish, on the other hand, takes enslavement for freedom, failure for success, Rome for heaven though it is stuck there as in hell, never to leave. The addict never leaves the self, however much he may be "augmented in number and in energy." He is "subjugated," but "only by himself" (il est subjugué; mais . . . il ne l'est que par lui-même) [409]. Intoxication induces the addict to believe in his own centrality ("all these things have been created *for me, for me, for me!*" [toutes ces choses ont été créées *pour moi, pour moi, pour moi!*] [437, original emphasis]) and divinity ("*I have become God!*" [*Je suis devenu Dieu!*] [437, original emphasis]).²⁴ The "high" state is, in reality, a "low" state, since the addict, "playing God," has, in fact, "*become an animal*" (*il est devenu une bête*) [409, original emphasis]. The addict lives in total delusion, thinking he is in heaven and is God when he is, instead, in hell and enslaved.

Poetry, a lucidity that corrects this stupidity, faces failure for what it is, aware that the most ambitious and idealized program of transport, or "correspondances," may lead to failure. As Walter Benjamin points out, "the *Fleurs du mal* would not be what it is if all it contained were this success [of poetic transport in the sonnet "Correspondances"]. It is unique because it was able to wrest from the inefficacy of the same consolation, the breakdown of the same fervor, the failure of the same effort poems that are in no way inferior to those in which the *correspondances* celebrate their triumphs."²⁵ Paul de Man's reading of the sonnet "Correspondances" [1: 11] reveals, at the high point of poetic transport, the stuttering failure of the metaphor to "transport," or cross over to the other, from one sense to another or from senses to spirit, merely proliferating, going nowhere, trapped within the same. Poetry's transport, like "truth" in de Man's essay, fights "not [the] error but [the] stupidity" of hashish's "belief that [it] is right when [it] is in fact in the wrong."²⁶

Poetry is an "agency of clear-sightedness," as Ross Chambers has said, that "keep[s] alive the sense of pain," that counters the "moral numbness" of "Ennui," or "boredom."²⁷ Baudelaire compares hashish to the anesthetizing "ether and chloroform" and to "all modern inventions that tend to diminish human freedom and indispensable *pain*" (toutes les inventions modernes qui tendent à diminuer la liberté humaine et l'indispensable *douleur*) [439, my emphasis], "pain" that the speaker-poet of the poem "Bénédiction" knows to be "the unique nobleness / that earth and hells will never corrode" (la noblesse unique / où ne morderont jamais la terre et les enfers) [1: 6–9]. Poetry, as Chambers writes, is an "expression of pain and the sign of a critical intelligence that puts lucidity above pleasure."²⁸

In "Le poème du hachisch," poetry becomes the practice of lucidity and sobriety that faces the painful disconnection and contradiction that lie at the heart of our life. Baudelaire calls "Le poème du hachisch" a philosophical study [440]. The most philosophical of his pieces, *De l'essence du rire* (*On the Essence of Laughter*) [2: 525–43], sees laughter that runs through and shakes us like a lightning bolt as the expression of the immense contradiction arising from our fallen state: "since laughter is essentially human, it is essentially contradictory, that is, it is a sign of both infinite grandeur and infinite misery, infinite misery relative to the Absolute Being of which it possesses only the conception, and infinite grandeur relative to animals. It is from the perpetual shock of these two infinites that laughter emanates" (comme le rire est essentiellement humain, il est essentiellement contradictoire, c'est-à-dire qu'il est à la fois signe d'une grandeur infinie et d'une misère infinie, misère infinie relativement à l'Etre absolu dont il possède la conception, grandeur infinie relatvement aux animaux. C'est du choc perpétuel de ces deux infinis que se dégage le rire) [2: 532]. Poetry, too, emanates from "the perpetual shock of the two infinites." It expresses the experience of contradiction and shock in the "jolts/somersaults of consciousness" (sou-bresauts de la conscience) ["A Arsène Houssaye" 1: 276]. "Baudelaire placed the shock experience at the very center of his artistic work," Benjamin writes.[29]

Intoxication, on the contrary, "erases all contradictions" (Toute contradiction s'efface) [434]. The "infinite grandeur" comes no longer as a "perpetual shock" to the "infinite misery" but as readily accessible. Hashish dampens shock and numbs pain. The most "convenient and handy" (le plus commode et le plus sous la main) [403] of intoxicants, it seemingly provides instant gratification and "the means to escape" the "filthy dwelling-place" and "'carry off paradise at one go'" (les moyens de fuir ... son habitacle de fange ... et ... "d'emporter le paradis d'un seul coup") [402]. The instantaneousness in time corresponds to proximity in space: it brings everything close, within reach. The most dangerous of hashish's "sophisms" is to "transform desire into reality" [432]. It delivers happiness on demand in one's own living room. A "spoonful of green jam" reproduces the "exceptional state of spirit and senses," that state of "paradisiacal" bliss, "so rare and fleeting," "intermittent," and unforeseeable in our daily lives [401].

Baudelaire's analysis and critique of the demand of the "common" mass not only to go to Rome at one go but even to bring Rome home trace a similar distinction as Benjamin's in "The Work of Art in the Age of Mechanical Reproduction," an essay that refers back to Baudelaire's own differentiation and hierarchization between photography and painting in the *Salon de 1859*.[30] Photography, the modern invention, according to Benjamin, works "by making many reproductions," "substitut[ing] a plurality of copies for a unique existence" [221], aligning itself with hashish. "Poetry in the Age of Narcotic Reproduction" would be an appropriate subtitle to "Le poème du hachisch."[31] In both Benjamin and Baudelaire, photography and hashish, on the one hand, and painting and poetry, on the other, refer less to specific art forms or to drugs in a literal way, than to opposing *modes* of relating to the play of distance and proximity. "The desire of contemporary masses to bring things 'closer' spatially and humanly," writes Benjamin, "is just as ardent as their bent toward overcoming the uniqueness of every reality by accepting its reproduction. Every day the urge grows stronger to get hold of an object at very close range by way of its likeness, its reproduction" [223]. Hashish is a way to "get hold of" the experience of "infinite grandeur" "at very close range by way of its likeness, its reproduction." The opposition between dissipation and concentration finds an echo in Benjamin, for whom "distraction and concentration," too, "form polar opposites which may be stated as follows: A man who concentrates before a work of art is absorbed by it. . . . In contrast, the distracted mass absorbs the work of art" [239]. Baudelaire's "distracted mass absorbs" the "green jam" and brings Rome into the living room.

For both Benjamin and Baudelaire, art and poetry have to do with "aura," "the unique phenomenon of a distance, however close it may be" [222]. Poetry is the art of the distant. It embraces the vast space that separates us from our dream, and dream as the phenomenon of distance itself.[32] Poetry takes the object of desire on its own terms, in its very inapproachability. It lets dream—distance—remain distant: "And love you the more, beautiful one, the more you flee me, / And seem, ornament of my nights, /

The more ironically to accumulate the leagues / That separate my arms from the blue immensities" (Et t'aime d'autant plus, belle, que tu me fuis, / Et que tu me parais, ornement de mes nuits, / Plus ironiquement accumuler les lieues / Qui séparent mes bras des immensités bleues) [XXIV 1: 27]. The poet leaps into the void, arms stretched out, more to give out than to take in: "The lovers of prostitutes / Are happy, rested, and sated; / As for me, my arms are broken / For having embraced clouds" (Les amants des prostituées / Sont heureux, dispos et repus; / Quant à moi, mes bras sont rompus / Pour avoir étreint des nuées), cries out Icarus in Baudelaire's poem "Les plaintes d'un Icare" ("The Laments of an Icarus") [1: 143]. Icarus the poet tries to embrace, and does embrace, the vast sky and sun without exhausting either the sky/sun or his own desire. His burning desire becomes the burning sun: "a sun within a sun." But hashish eaters are like "sated lovers": they take possession avidly, forcing distance into proximity in an instant gratification that in destroying distance exhausts desire.[33]

Benjamin, quoting Valéry, locates the fundamental property of a work of art in such a phenomenon of inexhaustible desire:

> "We recognize a work of art by the fact that no idea it inspires in us, no mode of behavior that it suggests we adopt could exhaust it or dispose of it. We may inhale the smell of a flower whose fragrance is agreeable to us for as long as we like; it is impossible for us to rid ourselves of the fragrance by which our senses have been aroused, and no recollection, no thought, no mode of behavior can obliterate its effects or release us from the hold it has on us. He who has set himself the task of creating a work of art aims at the same effect." According to this view [of Valéry], the painting we look at reflects back at us that of which our eyes will never have their fill. What it contains that fulfills the original desire would be the very same stuff on which the desire continuously feeds. What distinguishes photography from painting is therefore clear . . . : to the eyes that will never have their fill of a painting, photography is rather like food for the hungry or drink for the thirsty. [186–87]

In temporal terms, inexhaustibility extends into the perpetuity of "daily work." When Baudelaire writes that "orgy is not the sister of inspiration," but that "inspiration is decidedly the sister of daily work," and when he opposes, in "Le poème du hachisch," the temporality of the easy ("à coup sûr") and quick ("d'un seul coup") of intoxication to the temporality of daily perseverance of poetic work ("the daily exercise of our will" [l'exercice journalier de notre volonté] [402]; "assiduous and good intention" [bonne intention assidue] [439]; "successive work" [le travail successif] [441]; "assiduous exercise of will and permanent nobleness of intention" [l'exercice assidu de la volonté et la noblesse permanente de l'intention] [441]), he makes the never-ending "daily"-"assiduous"-"successive"-"permanent" into the site of inexhaustibility and inspiration.

Icarus's "broken arms" speak of the openness of desire, the movement toward the open and the movement of the opening itself. Ovid writes that Icarus was "led by a desire for the heavens" (caelique cupidine tractus).[34] Baudelaire's Icarus—"burned by the love of the beautiful" (brûlé par l'amour du beau), whose eyes "see only / Memories of suns" (ne voient / Que des souvenirs de soleils), having been "consumed" (consumés) by the blazing and "matchless stars" (astres nonpareils), and whose arms "are broken / For having embraced clouds" (rompus / Pour avoir étreint des nuées)—opens to the sky ["Les plaintes d'un Icare" 1: 143]. "Corporeal mechanism" opens to "celestial mechanism," health to trauma, and the "child-convalescent" to the state of corporeal intensity of the sun. It is body elevated to the experience and experiment of celestial bodies, thereby body inscribed—broken into—by the open sky as eyes are by "memories of suns" and arms by "clouds." It is body "modified by the world"—a body at risk.[35]

The failure of "corporeal mechanism" ("In vain I wanted of space / To find the end and the middle" [En vain j'ai voulu de l'espace / Trouver la fin et le milieu] [1: 143]) is the very mechanism through which "celestial" measure is reached and embraced; the failure of poetic transport becomes itself the inexhaustible movement of desire both painful and joyful. Ovid portrays Icarus as "rejoicing" in his flight ("puer audaci coepit gaudere volatu") [8.223]. The fatal forgetting of the law of the father, with its painful consequence, is at the same time the movement of joyful inspiration. Baudelaire, too, defines inspiration not only as pain (akin to the trauma of a cerebral stroke) but also as joy: "Nothing resembles more what is called inspiration than the *joy* with which the child absorbs form and color" (Rien ne ressemble plus à ce qu'on appelle inspiration, que la *joie* avec laquelle l'enfant absorbe la forme et la couleur) [2: 690, my emphasis]. Icarus leaping into the sky and absorbing, and being absorbed by, the sun and clouds is like the inspired child in Baudelaire, a body, as Chambers has said, that speaks about "what it's like to be a desiring subject."[36] "Unhappy perhaps the man, but happy the artist torn by desire!" (Malheureux peut-être l'homme, mais heureux l'artiste que le désir déchire!) the prose poem "Le désir de peindre" begins [1: 340].

Intoxication's circle tightens and closes down; inspiration's circle unlooses and opens up. The circumference of the encircling poetic embrace far exceeds, and even breaks open, the closure and measure of the embracing arms. In embracing openness, poetry's circle opens the embrace. What the poet, in the prose poem "Le désir de peindre," desires to paint is the laughter that bursts forth from the mouth of the woman, "an explosion in darkness" (une explosion dans les ténèbres) that makes us "dream of the miracle of a splendid flower blossoming in a volcanic ground" (rêver au miracle d'une superbe fleur éclose dans un terrain volcanique). To encircle the contour of the mouth in "red and white" is to open it to a burst of sonority that exceeds the order of color, the lines of the lips, and the measure of speech.[37] God, the "common and inexhaustible reservoir of love" (le réservoir commun, inépuisable de l'amour), and therefore the most "prostituted" of beings (l'être le plus prostitué), according to Baudelaire [*Mon cœur mis à nu* 1: 692], has been thought of traditionally as a circle/sphere "whose center is everywhere and whose circumference is nowhere."[38] Icarus's and poetry's arms encompass the divine, or celestial, immensity. The last section of *Les fleurs du mal*, on death, entitled "La mort," ends with the poem "Le voyage" [1: 129–34]. Death, the closure and measure of "corporeal mechanism," opens to the measurelessness of "celestial mechanism." Ultimate closure opens as departure.[39] *Les fleurs du mal*, or the "dream of the miracle of a splendid flower blossoming in a volcanic ground," is measurelessness blossoming from measure and opening from closure.[40]

It may be the immensity of this open embrace that Baudelaire traces when, near the end of "Le poème du hachisch," he writes: "In philosophical studies, the human spirit, imitating the motion of the stars, must follow a curve that brings it back to its point of departure. To conclude is to close a circle. At the beginning, I have spoken of this marvelous state, which man's spirit sometimes finds itself thrown into as if by a special grace" (Dans les études philosophiques, l'esprit humain, imitant la marche des astres, doit suivre une courbe qui le ramène à son point de départ. Conclure, c'est fermer un cercle. Au commencement j'ai parlé de cet état merveilleux, où l'esprit de l'homme se trouvait quelquefois jeté comme par une grâce spéciale) [440–41]. Poetry's metaphor is a circle that closes by opening itself through joining—"imitating the motions of"—the stars of the sky. Poetry's metaphorical move splits open the constricting circle of hashish's Rome, drawing its own circle by tracing the measureless circumference of the starry immensity.

"Baudelaire insists on the magic of distance," according to Benjamin, who writes that "the law of [Baudelaire's] poetry . . . shines in the sky of the Second Empire as 'a star without atmosphere.'"[41] Benjamin links distance, experience, and the stars in positing "wish" as "a kind of experience," quoting Goethe: "What one wishes for in one's youth, one has in abundance in old age." In *Hygiène*, Baudelaire quotes the same passage he came across while taking notes from Emerson's *The Conduct of Life* [1: 673]. Benjamin continues: "The earlier in life one makes a wish, the greater one's chances that it will be fulfilled. The further a wish reaches out in time, the greater the hopes for its fulfillment. But it is experience that accompanies one to the far reaches of time, that fills and divides time. Thus a wish fulfilled is the crowning of experience. In folk symbolism, distance in space can take the place of distance in time; that is why the shooting star, which plunges into the infinite distance of space, has become the symbol of a fulfilled wish."[42]

Benjamin saw in Baudelaire the magic of the shooting stars in which distance, the very measure of inapproachability and impossibility of fulfillment, functions at the same time as the figure of fulfillment. Icarus's open embrace traverses the sky of "Le poème du hachisch" like a shooting star, "crowning" not only experience but also experiment. Experience transported to and merging with experiment is the wish fulfilled at the closing of "Le poème du hachisch."

Benjamin contrasts the proximity of the "*next* card" and the "*next* compartment," into which, in gambling, the "ivory ball ... rolls," to the distance of the shooting stars.[43] Baudelaire compares the hashish eater to a gambler who has found a way to win a sure hand and subjects everything to close proximity. Hashish comes to us—Baudelaire presents it to us: "Here is the drug in front of your eyes: a bit of green jam, the size of a nut. . . . Here thus is happiness!" (Voici la drogue sous vos yeux: un peu de confiture verte, gros comme une noix. . . . Voilà donc le bonheur!) [409–10]—and it "incorporates itself into" us. It is a "poem," but one that "come[s] into [our] brain" [431].[44] Proximity in space translates into proximity in time of the instantaneous *coup* (blow/strike), which is, according to Benjamin, the measure of hellish time in Baudelaire, where the merciless hand of the clock strikes each second in the poem "L'horloge" ("The Clock") [1: 81]. The distant falling star is "the antithesis of time in hell," Benjamin writes. Hashish's instant gratification falls short of the stars. It fails to fulfill.

With the stars, "Le poème du hachisch" goes back to its beginning, to the dedication, and to the woman "who turns now her gaze to the Sky, this place of all transfigurations" (qui tourne maintenant tous ses regards vers le Ciel, ce lieu de toutes les transfigurations) [400]. The poet's gaze follows the woman's gaze into the night and to the stars of the night. In this movement toward woman and night, Orpheus finally emerges in "Le poème du hachisch":

> In this last section, I want to define and analyze the moral havoc caused by this dangerous and delicious gymnastics, havoc so great and danger so profound, that those who return from the battle [against hashish] only lightly scathed, seem to me like brave escapees from the cavern of a multiform Proteus, Orpheus conqueror of Hell.
>
> (*Je veux, dans cette dernière partie, définir et analyser le ravage moral causé par cette dangereuse et délicieuse gymnastique, ravage si grand, danger si profond, que ceux qui ne*

reviennent du combat que légèrement avariés, m'apparaissent comme des braves échappés de la caverne d'un Protée multiforme, des Orphées vainqueurs de l'Enfer.) [428]

Orpheus, the figure of the poet par excellence, appears at the moment of liberation from hashish addiction. To escape from the vicious circle of intoxication in which one is *"enchained, fettered, enslaved"* [427, English and emphasis in the original] is to become "Orpheus conqueror of Hell." Poetry emerges in the moving away and *as* the moving away from the force that binds in a movement of freedom.

Orpheus goes down to Hell to bring back Eurydice, who had fallen dead, "smitten in the ankle by a serpent's tooth," Ovid writes [10.10]. Orpheus implores the gods of the underworld: "I beg of you, unravel the fates of my Eurydice, too quickly run. We are totally pledged to you, and though we tarry on earth a little while, slow or swift we speed to one abode. Hither we all make our way; this is our final home; yours is the longest sway over the human race. She also shall be yours to rule when of ripe age she shall have lived out her allotted years. I ask the enjoyment of her as a boon; but if the fates deny this privilege for my wife, I am resolved not to return. Rejoice in the death of two" [10.31–39].

The deadly poison spreading inside Eurydice's body acts as a centripetal force that draws her down and binds her to Hell, the "one abode," "the final home" to which "we all make our way." Orpheus's request to the gods to reverse her fate ("I beg of you, unravel the fates of my Eurydice, too quickly run" [Eurydices, oro, properata retexite fata] [10.31]) and allow her to cross back with him from the netherworld asks that the one-way street to Hell that only closes down be opened up. Just as poetry strikes open, in Baudelaire, the constricting circle of Rome, Orpheus the poet asks, in Ovid, for an exception—an alternative—to the most "common" and "infallible" of roads "all leading to Rome." In both stories, Orpheus and poetry face a centripetal configuration out of which no one escapes and introduce a new *sens* that pulls away from, and undoes, the force that binds.

The Latin *retexere*, for "unravel," means "to unweave," an appropriate term for a request to reverse fate, since fate, from *fatum* (*fari*, "to speak"), meaning the word of a god, has a "textile" representation in Greek mythology. Fates are "three old women, spinning out men's destinies like thread: one drew them out, one measured them, and one cut them off."[45] Orpheus's song touches the gods of the underworld. They become willing to reverse their words and unravel Eurydice's fate on condition that Orpheus not turn back until they reach the earth, "or else the gift would be in vain" (aut inrita dona futura) [10.52]. The texts (textile-textual) of poetry (poem), of the gods (words), and of Eurydice (fate) start to interweave, unweaving Eurydice's destiny and reweaving the text of Orpheus and Eurydice. In the new text that poetry weaves, the centripetal topology of Hell opens up, and Eurydice is permitted to follow Orpheus back up to the world of the living. The song of Orpheus, a true antidote to the serpent's poison that killed Eurydice, generates a new direction, or *sens*, as it spins out the thread that guides Eurydice out of Hell—the labyrinth of death—like the thread of Ariadne:

> [Orpheus and Eurydice] took the up-sloping path through places of utter silence, a steep path, indistinct and clouded in pitchy darkness. And now they were nearing the margin of the upper earth, when he, afraid that she might fail him, eager for sight of her, turned back his longing eyes; and instantly she slipped into the depths. He stretched out his arms, eager to catch her or to feel her clasp; but, unhappy one, he clasped nothing but the yielding air. And now, dying a second time, she made no complaint against her husband; for of what could she complain save that she was beloved? She spake one last "farewell" which scarcely reached her husband's ears, and fell back again to the place whence she had come. [10.53–63]

In love, impatient, and apprehensive, Orpheus disobeys the law of the gods and looks back. His glance cuts the thread that guides Eurydice. As his "longing eyes" turn, his arms "stretch out" as if to prolong, or become, the thread he has just severed, but to no avail. In plunging Eurydice back to the darkness of night—and this time, forever—Orpheus undoes the work of *retexere* his song had begun. He fails irremediably. But the prefix *re* in *re-texere* marks repetition in more than one way, as "back," "again," and "against." The weaving, reweaving, and unweaving blend so that the work of weaving the text becomes its own undoing. Failure resides within the work of the poetic text, and measureless unwinding, at the heart of the measure of the song. Orpheus's drawing out the thread with the measure and measurelessness of his song and his cutting of it amount to the work of the three Fates. And isn't this what he went down to Hell for: to ask to recast Eurydice's fate? He asked for a choice in a universe that has none (Hell) and received what he asked for. The gods bestowed upon him the privilege of deciding between obeying their law and keeping Eurydice or disobeying their law and losing her. Orpheus chooses; the "gift" becomes "in vain."

Of this fatal look, Maurice Blanchot writes: "To look at Eurydice, without regard for the song, in the impatience and imprudence of desire which forgets the law: *that is inspiration*": "Not to look would be infidelity to the measureless, imprudent force of his movement, which does not want Eurydice in her daytime truth and her everyday appeal, but wants her in her nocturnal obscurity, in her distance, with her closed body and sealed face —wants to see her not when she is visible, but when she is invisible, and not as the intimacy of a familiar life, but as the foreignness of what excludes all intimacy, and wants, not to make her live, but to have living in her the plenitude of her death."[46]

Eurydice, wrapped in "nocturnal obscurity," follows Orpheus [172]. She and the night are, as Blanchot sees it, "enclosed" and "bound": they "follow," "maintained within the song's limits and its measured space" [175]. Icarus, too, follows within measure: "I warn you, Icarus," Daedalus has said, "to fly in a middle course, lest, if you go too low, the water may weigh your wings; if you go too high, the fire may burn them. Fly between the two . . . fly where I shall lead" [Ovid 8.203–08]. The middle course within limits is measured space, obedient following, prudent movement. Like Orpheus, Icarus, too, "forgets" the law of the father in a moment of boldness that is both courageous and imprudent.[47] The desire of both Orpheus and Icarus is to be free from the measure and safety of boundary and obedience. Orpheus's work, in *re-texere*, looses the text from its constricting weave, frees it, and leaves it open, just as Icarus's measure of the arms breaks open to encompass the measureless open sky.

Blanchot writes: "Everything is risked, then, in the decision to look" [175]. He asserts: "Everything proceeds as if, by disobeying the law, by looking at Eurydice, Orpheus had only obeyed the deep demand of the work—as if, by this inspired movement, he had indeed captured from Hell the obscure shade and had, unknowingly, led it back into the broad daylight of the work" [173]. Orpheus's gaze, Blanchot writes, is "the moment when he frees himself from himself and, still more important, frees the work from his concern, frees the sacred contained in the work, *gives* the sacred to itself, to the freedom of its essence, to its essence which is freedom" [175, original emphasis]. To break open the limits and bring the text to the openness of *sens*, this is Orpheus's, or poetry's, work. "*The Open is the poem*," Blanchot writes in an essay on poetry and Orpheus in Rilke: "*The Open is the poem*. The space where everything returns to deep being, where there is infinite passage between the two domains [of the visible and the invisible], where everything dies but where death is the learned companion of life, where horror is ravishing joy, where celebration laments and lamentation praises—the very space toward which 'all worlds hasten as toward their nearest and truest reality,' this space of the mightiest circulation and of ceaseless metamorphosis—this is the poem's space. This is the Orphic space."[48]

Orpheus—in Ovid, Baudelaire, Rilke, and Blanchot—migrates toward the open. Freed from the centripetal pull of Hell/Rome, the "one abode," "the final home" to which "we all make our way" [Ovid 10.33–34] and to which all roads lead, Orpheus enters the space of poetry. There "everything returns to deep being." The poet moves according to a different—a more authentic—law of gravity, a law that attracts and draws but to unbind and free, a law of gravity that is also a law of levity. Orpheus's gaze "by no means has the weight or the gravity of a profanation," but "its substance is all levity, unconcern, innocence" [175]. The law of inspiration, deep and grave, gives rise, in Blanchot's words, to the failure so immense and yet so "insouciant, weightless [of the] gaze of Orpheus" [176].

Poetry opens the "Orphic space," "the very space toward which 'all worlds hasten as toward their nearest and truest reality.'" If worlds, then words, too. *Words,* unhinged from the "common" groove, migrate toward their "nearest and truest reality," to the "source of all authenticity" [174], and to their "deep being": they drop into their own center of gravity. Words are drawn not by the law of addiction that clutches tight to take possession but by the law of attraction—with arms stretching out—that frees, lets go, and gives. "This is why inspiration is the gift par excellence" [175] and why "Orpheus's gaze is Orpheus's ultimate gift to the work. It is a gift whereby he refuses, whereby he sacrifices the work" [174]. The "gift" (*dona*) that has become "vain" (*inrita*) is freed from the bonds of exchange and possession. It is the gift given finally to itself in an act of infinite generosity.

In Ovid, Eurydice falls back into the night with a "last 'farewell'" that "scarcely reached her husband's ears" [10.62–63]. Icarus falls into the sea, and "his lips, calling to the last upon his father's name, were drowned in the dark blue sea" [8.229–30]. Words fall. In falling they may give name: Ovid tells us that the sea "took its name from [Icarus]" [8.230]. But they may also "become invisible" in a "sudden eclipse" and fail to give name: Icarus laments, in Baudelaire, "I shall not have the sublime honor / Of giving my name to the abyss / That will serve as my tomb" (Je n'aurai pas l'honneur sublime / De donner mon nom à l'abîme / Qui me servira de tombeau) ["Les plaintes d'un Icare" 1: 143]. Words plunging, but with lightness and in *free* fall, shining like shooting stars yet eclipsing, traverse the space of poetry, fulfilling the wish, yielding to the law of attraction. Words falling to their own center of gravity, following their own *sens*, opening to the sky and to the stars, "this space of the mightiest circle and of ceaseless metamorphosis—this is the poem's space. This is the Orphic space."[49] It is the "deep" and boundless circle of metaphor in Baudelaire.

In "Le poème du hachisch," where metaphor splits Rome open and introduces the possibility of loss and failure, to take the road of the metaphor is to refuse the safety of "all roads leading to Rome." The certainty of the decision to abide by the law of inspiration gives only, "as compensation, the work's uncertainty, for is there ever a work?" Blanchot asks. "Before the most convincing masterpiece, where the brilliance and the resolution of the beginning shine, it can also happen that we confront something extinguished: a work suddenly become invisible again, which is no longer there, has never been there. This sudden eclipse is the distant memory of Orpheus's gaze; it is the nostalgic return to the uncertainty of the origin" [174]. There is not necessarily work, or word, at the end of a persevering effort to write.

Orpheus's look, Blanchot tells us, is "the point of extreme uncertainty" [174] and "the extreme moment of liberty" [175]. Liberty, uncertainty, extremity: risk—"Everything is risked, then, in the decision to look" [175]. When "extreme point" and "extreme moment" impose as *central* concern, when points of extreme instability attract with the force of gravity of the center, when the extreme becomes the true center that "displaces itself, while remaining the same and becoming always more central, more hidden, more uncertain and more imperious,"[50] there is the experience and experiment of profound risk: the risk of "deep" open space.

Poetry, with the song of Orpheus, becomes the song from the depths, the "invitation des profondeurs" that "open[s] an abyss in every utterance and powerfully entice[s] whoever hear[s] it to disappear into that abyss."[51] "Le poème du hachisch" invites us not to avoid but to take risks—*profound* risks, risks of reaching depths, of yielding to a force of attraction deeper and greater: "We, we infinitely risked"; we "risk being" and "risk language."[52] "Le poème du hachisch" demands that we take the infinite risk that is the risk of the infinite, but not in the form of hashish, because hashish is the safe and cowardly way. For the infinite does not lie at the end of risk: it is risk itself, the very opening to it.

Baudelaire states that the "man who, having given himself over to opium or hashish for a long time, has managed, enfeebled as he was by the habit of his bondage, to find the necessary energy to free himself" is "an escaped prisoner" who inspires "more admiration than the prudent man who has never succumbed, having always been careful to avoid temptation" (L'homme qui, s'étant livré longtemps à l'opium ou au hachisch, a pu trouver, affaibli comme il l'était par l'habitude de son servage, l'énergie nécessaire pour se délivrer, m'apparaît comme un prisonnier évadé. Il m'inspire plus d'admiration que l'homme prudent qui n'a jamais failli, ayant toujours eu soin d'éviter la tentation) [427]. The "prudent man who has never succumbed" and the addict who never severs the bond of enslavement both dwell in safety, but also in complacency and indulgence. The "prudent man" who has "*always* been careful to avoid temptation" is as bound as the addict; he is bound to fear. Both grab onto and hold tight the known and familiar, indulging in and settling for acquisition, guarantees, and certainties. Neither takes risks.

In "Le poème du hachisch," poetry's trajectory, through the descent and return of Orpheus, coincides with the journey of fall and return from temptation and danger. What touches Baudelaire the most in De Quincey's *Confessions of an English Opium Eater*—the second part of *Les paradis artificiels* is Baudelaire's own translation/adaptation of De Quincey's book—is the work's "most dramatic part," where De Quincey speaks of "the superhuman efforts of willpower he had to deploy in order to escape the damnation to which he had brashly doomed himself" (des efforts surhumains de volonté qu'il lui a fallu déployer pour échapper à la damnation à laquelle il s'était imprudemment voué lui-même) [404].

The hashish eater is like Ulysses, who, advised by Circe, found a way to hear the Sirens' song without risking his life. Stopping the ears of his crew with wax and binding himself to the mast of his ship, he listened to the deadly song without paying its price. "It is true, Ulysses did overcome [the Sirens], but how did he do it? Ulysses—the stubbornness and caution of Ulysses, the treachery by which he took pleasure in the spectacle of the Sirens without risking anything and without accepting the consequences; this cowardly, mediocre and tranquil pleasure, this moderate pleasure," Blanchot writes.[53] Ulysses employed the "power of technology, which will always claim to trifle in safety with unreal (inspired) powers."[54] He tied himself. The hashish eaters, too, "trifle in safety" with the power of the infinite by means of a "mechanical reproduction" within easy and safe reach.

Orpheus, to the contrary, untied himself in front of the "inspired powers," as Michel Foucault writes:

> Orpheus may have succeeded in quieting barking dogs and outmaneuvering sinister forces, but on the return trip he should have been chained like Ulysses or as unperceiving as his sailors; in fact, he was the hero and his crew combined in a single character: he was seized by the forbidden desire and untied himself with his own hands, letting the invisi-

ble face disappear into the shadows, just as Ulysses let the song he did not hear vanish in the waves. Each of their voices is then freed: Ulysses' with his salvation and the possibility of telling the tale of his marvelous adventure; Orpheus's with his absolute loss and never-ending lament. But it is possible that behind Ulysses' triumphant narrative there prevails the inaudible lament of not having listened better and longer, of not having ventured as close as possible to the wondrous voice that might have finished the song. And that behind Orpheus's laments shines the glory of having seen, however fleetingly, the unattainable face at the very instant it turned away and returned to darkness: a nameless, placeless hymn to the light.[55]

"Everything is risked, then, in the decision to look."[56] Poetry is this decision to risk everything.

Orpheus unties himself and looks back, facing the unknown. *Les fleurs du mal* closes with such a call: "To plunge into the depths of the abyss . . . / To the depths of the Unknown to find something *new!*" (Plonger au fond du gouffre . . . / Au fond de l'Inconnu pour trouver du *nouveau!*) ["Le voyage" 1: 134, original emphasis].[57]

And so, too, does "Le poème du hachisch," whose last word is "license." Poetic license in its purest discipline and highest form is freedom, power, and responsibility to create and live in a poetic relationship to the world, to "plunge into the depths," the "unknown," and the "*new.*"[58] It is to live, following Blanchot's words on Orpheus, "as if to renounce failure were much graver than to renounce success, as if what we call the insignificant, the inessential, error, could, to one who accepts the risk and surrenders to it without restraint, reveal itself as the source of all authenticity."[59] In the depth of sky of *Les paradis artificiels,* poetry conquers the addictive law of entropy with the gaze of Orpheus that *turns* to open and "surrender . . . without restraint" to infinite risk. In that deep open space, the law of Baudelaire's poetic en-tropy ("the turning of energy," from *energy* and *trope*) and poetic license shines still—quiet and absolute: "a star without atmosphere."[60]

CHAPTER TWO

The "Frivolous" Other and the "Authentic" Self

Fashion and Poetry

LA DERNIÈRE MODE, *gazette du monde et de la famille* (The Latest Fashion, Gazette of the World and of the Family), the fashion magazine Stéphane Mallarmé published between September and December of 1874, has always been considered a surprising and curious enterprise.[1] There is Mallarmé the Poëte, whose quintessentially "pure" and "obscure" verses are read and praised by a select elite, and there is Mallarmé the fashion journalist, who talks to bourgeois ladies about dresses, jewels, hats, fashionable vacation destinations, lunch and dinner menus. Mallarmé himself made a clear distinction between journalistic language and poetic language, between "universal *reporting*" (l'universel *reportage*) and "literature," between the "double state of the word, raw and immediate on the one hand, on the other, essential"[2] (le double état de la parole, brut ou immédiat ici, là essentiel) ["Crise de vers" 2: 212, original emphasis], that justifies and even imposes the opposition between the "frivolous" fashion journalistic writings and the "serious" pure poetic writings.

Most critics have either given little importance to *La dernière mode*, excluding it from what they consider the essential Mallarméan corpus, or reabsorbed it completely into the poetic writings as embodying all the elements of Mallarmé's pure poetics. With the growing interest in the subject of fashion within the fields of art and literature has come a desire to reread and to reevaluate *La dernière mode*. One cannot simply dismiss *La dernière mode* as a mere *ouvrage alimentaire*. If Mallarmé the poet condemns journalistic writings, from what authorial position does he write *La dernière mode*? What, if any, is the relation between poetry and fashion? In short, how are we to read Mallarmé's *La dernière mode*?

Both critical gestures—complete exclusion as well as complete inclusion of the fashion magazine with respect to the poetic corpus—bypass a crucial issue: the question in poetry of the other, and of the other genre. How does poetry relate to the Other it seems to exclude? *La dernière mode*—both its writing and its reading—raises the very question of the other, of another writing/reading of Mallarmé, and even perhaps of another Mallarmé.

On November 16, 1885, eleven years after the brief publication of *La dernière mode*, Mallarmé wrote a letter to Paul Verlaine providing some biographical information about himself to be included in *Les hommes d'aujourd'hui*, a brief study of contemporary writers Verlaine was editing at the time. After a long section devoted to the explanation of "le Livre" (the Book), his dream book of poetry, Mallarmé speaks about *La dernière mode*:

> I had to do work in moments of financial difficulty or to buy ruinous boats and that is all (*Ancient Gods, English Words*) of which it is suitable not to speak: but apart from these, concessions to necessities and to pleasures alike have not been frequent. If at one moment, however, despairing of the despotic book I myself had let go, after a few articles peddled from here and there, I have attempted alone to write on toilette, jewelry, furniture, and even of theater and of dinner menus, a periodical, *The Latest Fashion*, whose eight or ten issues, when I dust them, still make me dream for a long time.

> (*J'ai dû faire, dans des moments de gêne ou pour acheter de ruineux canots, des besognes propres et voilà tout* [Dieux Antiques, Mots Anglais] *dont il sied de ne pas parler: mais à part cela, les concessions aux nécessités comme aux plaisirs n'ont pas été fréquentes. Si à un moment, pourtant, désespérant du despotique bouquin lâché de Moi-même, j'ai après quelques articles colportés d'ici et de là, tenté de rédiger tout seul, toilettes, bijoux, mobilier, et jusqu'aux théâtres et aux menus de dîner, un journal* La Dernière Mode, *dont les huit ou dix numéros parus servent encore quand je les dévêts de leur poussière à me faire longtemps rêver.)* [1: 789]

In this passage, Mallarmé marks *La dernière mode* with an otherness that is double. *La dernière mode* is other than the Book of pure poetry: he wrote it at a time when he had temporarily abandoned the "despotic" poetic project. The magazine is other, too, than circumstantial works produced out of sheer economic necessities: it escapes from the silence Mallarmé prefers to observe about his work of "besognes propres," such as *Les dieux antiques* and *Les mots anglais*, "of which it is suitable not to speak." It is not clear whether *La dernière mode* is a "concession to necessity" (during "moments of financial difficulty") or to "pleasure" ("buy[ing] ruinous boats").

Mallarmé's lingering reminiscence speaks for its special status. Unlike the "besognes propres," *La dernière mode* still makes him dream. The terms *dream* and *to dream* appear only two other times in the letter, and both refer to the dream of the Book of poetry. Four paragraphs earlier, Mallarmé had written:

> I have always dreamed and attempted another thing, with the patience of an alchemist, ready to sacrifice all vanity and all satisfaction for it.... What? It is difficult to say: a book, simply, in many volumes, a book that is a book, architectural and premeditated.... The very rhythm of the book then impersonal and alive, up to its pagination, juxtaposes itself to equations of this dream, or Ode.
>
> ([*J*]*'ai toujours rêvé et tenté autre chose, avec une patience d'alchimiste, prêt à y sacrifier toute vanité et toute satisfaction.... Quoi? c'est difficile à dire: un livre, tout bonnement, en maints tomes, un livre qui soit un livre, architectural et prémédité....* [*L*]*e*

rythme même du livre alors impersonnel et vivant, jusque dans sa pagination, se juxtapose aux équations de ce rêve, ou Ode.) [1: 788]

Both *La dernière mode* and "le Livre" are objects of dreams. Even if distinctly other, fashion and poetry speak to Mallarmé and make Mallarmé speak in similar terms. The dream of poetry and the dream of fashion have a similar continuity in time: the dream of poetry has "always" (toujours) been with him, and the dream of fashion continues for a "long time" (longtemps). The two dreams further relate to each other temporally, fashion writing occurring at a moment of hiatus from poetic writing. They mingle in Mallarmé's memory in a play of time between permanence ("always"), continuity ("long time"), and pause/interruption.

Vastly different though these dreams may be, the writing of the fashion magazine and of the Book of poetry intersect in the use of terms common to both. The difficulty in placing *La dernière mode* within the Mallarméan corpus seems to stem from the ambiguous status of its otherness. It is doubly other (other than the "despotic book" of poetry; other, also, than the rest of the minor "besognes propres") and yet also the same (it participates in the same [use of the term] dream as poetic writing; it belongs to the same category as works of concession).

Toward the end of the letter, Mallarmé speaks of another reminiscence:

> I was forgetting my escapades, as soon as my spirit became too fatigued, on the bank of the Seine and the woods of Fontainebleau, to the same place for years: there, I appear to myself altogether different, in love with the sole fluvial navigation. I honor the river that lets entire days sink into its water with neither the impression of losing them nor the slightest remorse. A simple wanderer in a mahogany skiff, but a sailor with fury, very proud of his flotilla.
>
> *(J'oubliais mes fugues, aussitôt que pris de trop de fatigue d'esprit, sur le bord de la Seine et de la forêt de Fontainebleau, en un lieu le même depuis des années: là je m'apparais tout différent, épris de la seule navigation fluviale. J'honore la rivière, qui laisse s'engouffrer dans son eau des journées entières sans qu'on ait l'impression de les avoir perdues, ni*

une ombre de remords. Simple promeneur en yoles, d'acajou, mais voilier avec furie, très fier de sa flottille.) [1: 790]

The periodic escapades to Valvins, where Mallarmé had a small house and a boat, evoke the play of temporality of the "always" and "long time" of the two dreams. His delight in remembering and describing his trips to Valvins is reminiscent of the delight he takes in dusting the pages of the fashion magazine and lingering over them. The writing of *La dernière mode* and his visits to Valvins are both movements of flight away from ordeals: from the "despair" of the "despotic book" of poetry and from the tiresome life of Paris. Both provide respite and the pleasure of temporary escape.

In Mallarmé's account, various forms of escapades, or "fugue," as he calls them, punctuate his life. *Fugue* in French—from *fugere*, "to flee"—means both escapade/absence and a musical composition. In his reminiscence, the temporalities of "always," "long time," and "for years" mingle contrapuntally as in a fugue. Fashion writing and poetic writing seem to become part of the flow and rhythm of life. "Every soul is a rhythmic knot" (toute âme est un nœud rythmique) ["La musique et les lettres" 2: 64], Mallarmé writes. "There is rhythm as soon as style is emphasized" (rythme dès que style [s'accentue]) ["Crise de vers" 2: 205].[3] Poetry and fashion, both concerned with style, are about rhythm, "*Rhythmical Creations of Beauty*," to borrow Poe's definition of "the Poetry of words."[4]

Mallarmé writes that "all, in the world, exists to culminate in a book" (tout, au monde, existe pour aboutir à un livre) ["Le livre, instrument spirituel" 2: 224] and tells Verlaine that "the very rhythm of the book . . . impersonal and alive . . . juxtaposes itself to . . . this dream [of poetry]." It seems as though "all existed to culminate," too, in a larger rhythm, "impersonal and alive," of the book of life itself. In "the poetry of words" of Mallarmé's letter, life, writing, and dream, poetry and circumstantial writing, work and vacation echo each other rhythmically—the life of Mallarmé the poet becomes rhythmed.

"It is the difference that is rhythmic, not the repetition, which nevertheless produces it," Gilles Deleuze and Félix Guattari write. "To change milieus, taking them as you find them: Such is rhythm. Landing, splashdown, takeoff."[5] Mallarmé's escapades that "change milieus, taking them as [he] find[s] them," permeated by the rhythm of music—this is the Mallarméan *fugue*. On the bank of the Seine, in *fugue*, Mallarmé "appear[s] to [himself] altogether different." In *La dernière mode*, too, Mallarmé seems to "appear altogether different" and other.

La dernière mode had already been in circulation for about a year when Mallarmé assumed total control. He became its sole writer and editor during four months, replacing all but four of the usual illustrations with texts.[6] Each of the eight issues contained features, ranging from "Fashion" ("La mode"), "The Chronicle of Paris" ("Chronique de Paris"), "Advice about Education" ("Conseils sur l'éducation"), and "Correspondence with our Subscribers" ("Correspondance avec les abonnées"), to menu suggestions. All were written by Mallarmé himself and signed with various pseudonyms, the majority of them female: "Madame Marguerite de Ponty," "Miss Satin," "A Creole Lady" (Une Dame créole), "a Breton Chatelaine" (une Châtelaine bretonne), "an Ancestress" (une Aïeule), "Zizi, good mulatto of Surat" (Zizi, bonne mulâtre de Surate), "Olympia, the *Negress*" (Olympe, *Négresse* [original emphasis]), and "A Reader from Alsace" (une Lectrice Alsacienne).[7] The fewer male pseudonyms are "Ix," "Brébant's Chef de Bouche" (Le Chef de bouche chez Brébant), "Marliani, the *tapestry worker–decorater*" (Marliani, *Tapissier-décorateur* [original emphasis]), and "*Toussenel.*"

The only, and very significant, exception to the pseudonymic signature is in the literary section of poems and short stories commissioned from Mallarmé's male friends. Each is signed with the real name of the author: Banville, Coppée, Sully-Prudhomme, Valade, Daudet, d'Hervilly, des Essarts, Mendès, or Cladel. The literary section, with its distinct authorship, singles itself out as the only "authentic" part of the magazine. The opposition between journalistic writing and literary writing seems to play itself out.

The main fashion section, signed by "Madame Marguerite de Ponty" and "Miss Satin," could not be more opposed to the literary section. The female pseudonyms form a radical counterpart to the authentic male names.

A series of oppositions is established—authenticity versus pseudonymic disguise, truth versus simulation and travesty—that extends to the opposition between the two genres of writing—high versus low, literary versus journalistic, poetry versus fashion—which, in turn, is articulated in terms of gender division—male versus female. In this configuration, poetry is to fashion as authenticity is to travesty and as male is to female.

Can one take at face value this all-too-neat opposition between poetry-authenticity-male, on the one hand, and fashion-travesty-female, on the other? Apparently not. Mallarmé himself, *the* male author of our interest, is exclusively invested in the fashion section and conspicuously absent as author from the literary section, except for one instance. Mallarmé deliberately displaces his own identity as author through his escapade, or *fugue*, into the domain of fashion-travesty-female.

In the sixth issue, the magazine enacts literally the double meaning of the French term *fugue*, as fleeing/vacating/absence and also as musical composition. When Mallarmé took over the magazine, one of the first things he did was to change the rhythm of publication from the first and fifteenth days of each month to the first and third Sundays. The "Announcement" ("Avis") at the end of the sixth issue introduces the change of rhythm as one of the magazine's new directions:

> To await our Publication on the day of family reunion or at least of leisure, instead of being surprised by it at an inopportune moment of the week: this is the pleasure we provide to our Readers.
>
> *(Attendre notre Publication à ce jour des réunions de famille ou tout au moins du loisir, au lieu d'être surpris par elle à un moment inopportun de la semaine: voilà l'agrément que nous procurons à nos Lectrices.)* [610]

This new periodicity has "one inconvenience": "Which one? Once every Trimester, three weeks go by between one and the other monthly issues, in the month with five Sundays" (lequel? une fois par Trimestre, de laisser trois semaines s'écouler entre l'un et l'autre de nos Numéros mensuels, dans le mois aux cinq dimanches) [610].

The sixth and seventh issues are separated by three weeks instead of the usual two, and if *La dernière mode* had continued to be published, the same would have occurred every trimester. The newly established periodicity (two weeks) gives rise to two others (three weeks, trimester) and sets up a multiple periodic structure as in a fugue, where musical voices successively enter, one at a time, into a contrapuntal conversation.

The problem faced by the sixth issue is: how to wait, last, survive this extra week without going out of date? It is a pressing question since *La dernière mode*, "as much as it is a Fashion Magazine, aspires to be the magazine *in* fashion" (Notre journal qui, autant qu'un Recueil de Modes veut être le recueil *à* la mode) [549, my emphasis]. And being in fashion is all about being on time.

To counter the extra week that threatens to let it go out of fashion, the magazine, at the location of the "Gazette and Program of the Fortnight" ("Gazette et programme de la quinzaine"), prints a musical score—a song—a poem by Catulle Mendès put to music by Augusta Holmès:

> The faded Issue, as for the interest of the month, then stays a long time on the table of the drawing room: well but let it remain at the piano!
>
> A piece of music, new, by one of the notable composers of our time, will take hold of the attention during this lapse of time: laid aside, taken up again, read, played, sung by all lady musicians. In its favor, the issue confronts even forgetting.
>
> *(La Livraison défraîchie, quant à l'intérêt du moins, reste alors longtemps sur la table du salon: or, qu'elle demeure au piano!*
>
> *Un morceau de Musique, neuve, fait par un des compositeurs notables de l'époque, retiendra l'attention pendant ce laps de temps: quitté, repris, déchiffré, joué, chanté par toute musicienne. A sa faveur la Livraison affronte même l'oubli.)* [610]

The sixth issue thus offers not a dress but a musical score to hold the attention of readers during this in-between period. Music appears to fill the interval of absence in which periodicities and rhythms are generated and mingle and shift from one to the other. The extra week—the period of absence and vacancy—is the space of *fugue* in both senses of the word.⁸

Music simultaneously suspends time and makes time go by. It makes the "lapse of time" elapse and hence makes *La dernière mode* remain in time and in fashion. The appearance of a musical score at this point is noteworthy given the importance of music in Mallarmé's poetry. One thinks of Mallarmé's writings on Wagner, of his essay "La musique et les lettres," and of how he compared his final "grand poem," "Un coup de dés" ("A Throw of Dice"), to a musical score ("une partition").⁹

The first issue faces a similar temporal dilemma as the sixth. Dated August 1, its article "Fashion" opens as follows:

> Too late to talk about summer Fashions, too soon for winter's, or even autumn's (although many great Parisian houses are already busy, they tell us, with their "end-of-autumn" collection). Today, having nothing on hand even to begin an outfitting, we want to entertain our readers instead with its finishing touch: jewelry. A paradox? No. Isn't there, in jewelry, something permanent—don't you agree?—which makes it a suitable subject for a Fashion Magazine that has to wait between July and September?¹⁰

> (*Trop tard pour parler des Modes d'été et trop tôt pour parler de celles d'hiver [ou même de l'automne]: bien que plusieurs grandes maisons de Paris s'occupent déjà, à notre su, de leur assortiment pour l'arrière-saison. Aujourd'hui, n'ayant pas même, par le fait, sous la main les éléments nécessaires pour commencer une toilette, nous voulons entretenir nos lectrices d'objets utiles à l'achever: les Bijoux. Paradoxe? non: n'y a-t-il pas, dans les bijoux, quelque chose de permanent, et dont il sied de parler dans un courrier de Modes, destiné à attendre les Modes de juillet à septembre?*) [490]

Making its debut in the empty vacation month of August, the fashion's off-season time, the magazine is simultaneously belated and premature ("too late," "too soon"): there is no longer and not yet any fashion to talk about. From the impasse of its untimeliness it proposes a topic: jewelry, not because it "begin[s] an outfitting" (*commencer une toilette*) but because it is the "finishing touch" (achever). Marking the beginning as an end, jewelry is *untimely*, neither on nor in time, but outside. It is the symbol of timeless permanence rather than of ever-changing fashion. There is a threefold paradox —being late blurs into being early, beginning into ending, and transitoriness into permanence—quite strange for a fashion magazine whose essence is timeliness.

The first issue is to appear for the first time and to entertain— "entretenir"—its readers from July to September, but "isn't an entire month," Ix asks, "a period that is vaguer and less defined than eternity itself?" (tout un mois, n'est-ce pas une période plus vague et moins définie que ne l'est, elle-même, l'éternité?) [495]. It is a similar situation to that faced by the sixth issue: the necessity to occupy the readers, "tenir-entre" or "hold-(them)-between," and make elapse the "lapse of time." The jewelry of the first issue is like the music of the sixth: both appear during the period of a wait, suspension, a transition of in-between time and the "lapse of time." Just like music, so jewelry entertains a close affinity with poetry in Mallarmé. One needs only to think about the bejeweled Hérodiade embodying the ideal form and brilliance of pure poetry. *Or* (both "gold" and the locution "now"/"but then") and diamonds abound in his writings, and Villiers de l'Isle-Adam's letter of September 19, 1866, tells us that Mallarmé was working on a treatise on precious stones, which unfortunately would never come to be.[11] If we include all the crystalline images—glass, mirror, prism—and the brilliance of constellation, jewelry, in Mallarmé, has become pervasive.

Music is heard in the sixth issue with a new temporality. Jewelry shines when *La dernière mode* appears for the first time. In two crucial moments when the question of time, timing, and the creation of a periodic movement comes to the fore, fashion and poetry become permeable to each other. In Mallarmé, jewelry stands for the self-enclosed purity of poetry (as in the pure and sterile beauty of Hériodiade) and music for the absoluteness of poetry that is "the musicality of everything" (la musicalité de tout) ["La musique et les lettres" 2: 65]. And yet, what stands for the absolute purity of poetry opens poetry to the other. Fashion and poetry reflect each other in the brilliance of jewelry and echo each other in the rhythm of music.

Mallarmé's single exception to his absence from the literary section occurs in the fourth issue, where he contributes a poetic translation under his own name, "Stéphane Mallarmé." Yet what he contributes as a "genuine male author," in a move of reverse escapade, is not a poem or prose work of his own, but his French translation of Tennyson's English poem "Mariana" [2: 825–26]. As with his translations of Poe's poems, his French translation turns the original English poem into a prose poem.

Mallarmé's piece is the only translation to appear, all the other contributors having provided works of their own. It is the third literary piece; in all other issues there are only two. His translation is a surplus and hence cannot fit into the existing categories of the literary sections "Verse" ("Vers") and "Short Stories" ("Nouvelles"). The table of contents, instead of the usual divisions, now includes "Verse" and "Short Story and Translation" [557]. Mallarmé's contribution is neither just verse nor just short prose but transforms verse into prose. Neither one nor the other and at the same time both, it goes from one to the other, being, in a way, something in-between.

As a translator, and not the genuine author, Mallarmé does not quite belong to the circle of authentic literary male authors. As an author, he cannot be placed and has no place, and authorship itself does not take place.

A threefold doubling has occurred: a doubling of the author: Tennyson and Mallarmé; of language: English and French; and of form or genre: poem and prose poem. "Stéphane Mallarmé" signs and authorizes not so much poetic authenticity as doubling and the transposition of doubles, of the one to the other: of authorial signatures, languages, and genres in a movement of *fugue*. To author(ize) translations is to author(ize) transpositions.

This doubling goes hand in hand with a similar doubling in the main fashion section. In the same issue in which Mallarmé's translation appears, a new fashion reporter, Miss Satin, makes her debut, ending the reign of Madame de Ponty. Miss Satin becomes coauthor of the fashion column in all subsequent issues.

The two authors, Stéphane Mallarmé and Miss Satin, appearing at the same time are further linked through initials. Among all the pseudonyms, male or female, in *La dernière mode*, "Miss Satin" is the most distinct bearer of Mallarmé's own proper name, as her initials, "MS," form a mirror image of Mallarmé's own "SM."[12] The crisscrossing of initials in MS/SM creates a chiasmus and spells, in turn, another main pseudonym, "Ix," the most emblematic of all the pseudonyms. The coincidence between initials—in the structure of mirror-image reversal or crossing over—suggests that the author's identity and signature have a lot to do with anonymity and transvestism.[13] Miss Satin writes as Stéphane Mallarmé, and Stéphane Mallarmé dresses up as Miss Satin.

The enigmatic Ix is responsible for the "Chronicle of Paris (Theaters, Books, Fine-Arts; Echoes of the Salons and the Beach)" ("Chronique de Paris [Théâtres, livres, beaux-arts, echos des salons et de la plage]"). In the first issue, Ix explains the main objective of his "Chronicle of Paris":

> What each of these brief conversations aspires to, is indicated sufficiently by its place in the magazine, located between the Fashion Column and our literary section: to speak, of course, of the works of the mind, but always following the *goût du jour*. Here is a new collection of Poetry that contains the Poem our issue published or a selection of Short Stories our Program of the Fortnight brings to you first: these products of the latest hour (and others still), are they in Fashion or should they be?
>
> (*Ce que veut chacun de ces brefs entretiens, sa place, dans le journal, l'indique assez bien, choisie entre le Courrier de la Mode et notre partie littéraire: parler, certes, des œuvres de l'esprit, mais toujours selon le goût du jour. Voici un recueil nouveau de Poésie où se rencontre le Poëme publié par notre livraison; ou un choix de Nouvelles dont le Conte de quinzaine vous donne la primeur: ces produits de la dernière heure (et d'autres encore) sont-ils à la Mode ou doivent-ils l'être?*) [495]

Inserted between the fashion and the literary sections, the "Chronicle of Paris" bridges the two sections at the levels of both form and content with its goal to talk about literature according to the "goût du jour," the current taste and trend of "the latest fashion." Under Ix's pen, literary writing and fashion writing are both to be fashionable. In the "Chronicle of

Paris," fashion and literature intersect and intersect in Paris, the capital city of fashion.

Ix signs the crossing between fashion and literature and inscribes the *mode* of this crossing in the time and space of Paris. As suspected, he turns out to be closely involved with what goes on between MS/SM. He makes MS and SM come together and signs this contact/contract. "Ix" could be read as a pseudonym for the MS/SM couple, positioned vis-à-vis the MS/SM couple as is Mallarmé's translation vis-à-vis the "Vers/Nouvelle" category: neither one nor the other and yet also both and something in-between, a bridge.

Ix and Paris form the figure (Ix) and the place (Paris) of intersection between fashion and literature, the *mi-lieu*—the context and the middle terrain—of this intersection.

Written during the vacation months of August and September, the "Chronicle" and the "Gazette" of the first two issues insistently report that Paris is empty. Deserted Paris becomes a desert as Ix begins his "Chronicle" of the second issue: *"Rome is no longer in Rome* . . . Have you lived through those days that transform the city into a desert; no! into one of those ancient deserted cities, like Ecbatana, Tyre, Memphis" (*Rome n'est plus dans Rome* . . . Les avez-vous traversés, ces jours changeant la ville en désert, que dis-je? en cité antique du désert, pareille à Ecbatane, Tyr, Memphis) [523, original emphasis].[14] With *"Rome* . . . *no longer in Rome,"* Paris becomes remote in time and space (Paris is ancient Rome, or an "ancient deserted city"), and its remoteness recedes further into infinity as Rome is not even in Rome. Paris may be the capital center of fashion, but that center is empty, decentered, and elsewhere. The "Chronicle of Paris" portrays Paris as a space permeated by a movement of disappearance and a state of absence.

Paris is vacant, because Parisians, "avid for waves and foliage" (avides de vagues et du feuillage) [523], have gone on vacation:

> While from the four cardinal points the Traveler arrives, forgetting Alps and Saharas, totally given over to the obsession of having a look at the city . . . we who have always seen through the exotic lies and illusions of world tours . . . we simply go to the very edge of the Ocean,

where only a pale and blurred line can be seen, to behold what is beyond our usual dwelling place: the infinite and nothing.[15]

(Tandis que des quatre espaces cardinaux, arrive, oubliant Alpes et Saharas, avide et subjugué par l'idée fixe de voir la ville, le Voyageur; nous qui, de naissance, savons tous les mensonges exotiques et la déception des tours du monde . . . nous allons, simplement, au bord de l'Océan, où ne persiste plus qu'une ligne pâle et confuse, regarder ce qu'il y a au-delà de notre séjour ordinaire, c'est-à-dire l'infini et le rien.) [524]

Vacationing is presented as a quintessential Parisian move, and Ix ponders "if really there wasn't in the fact that we exiled ourselves the very hour of their [foreign tourists'] coming, something of the Parisian spirit" (si vraiment il n'y a pas de notre part dans ce fait de nous exiler à l'heure exacte de leur venue, quelque chose de cet esprit parisien) [524].[16] According to *La dernière mode*, to be fashionable is to vacate Paris in the summer and even in the winter, "to leave Paris, once or twice or even three times, in the winter, to enjoy a few hours of sun and azure" (quitter Paris, une fois ou deux ou trois même, dans l'hiver, pour goûter quelques heures de soleil et d'azur) [651]. Exiting Paris is a necessary condition of existing there. A fashionable life is one of periodic departure and return.

The movement of vacation frames the magazine. The magazine makes its debut during summer vacation and disappears during winter vacation, as Roger Dragonetti has remarked, and each issue appears on a Sunday—the "vacation" day of the week.[17] In each issue appears a list of seaside vacation destinations, along with details on train fares and train stations from which to depart. The section "Chronicle of Paris" has as its subtitle "Theaters, Books, Fine Arts, Echoes of the Salons and the *Beach*" (my emphasis). The "echoes of the beach" resonate through vacant Paris—as in an echo chamber —and the rhythm of the sea mingles ever so closely with the rhythm of the city as the call of the sea continues throughout the issues, from summer to fall and even into winter.

In the first "Chronicle of Paris," Ix writes, "appearing during this vacation season as if in its exact hour of appearance, the Magazine interposes itself between your reverie and the double azure of the sea and the sky" (apparu dans cette saison de vacance comme à son heure exacte d'apparaître, ce Journal s'interpose entre votre songerie et le double azur maritime et céleste) [499]. *La dernière mode* makes its debut exactly on time, and the "fashion magazine" becomes a "magazine *in* fashion," since is not fashion a way of being exactly on/in time? *La dernière mode* becomes truly fashionable when it becomes rhythmed by the sea.

In the "echoes of the beach" that the "double azure of the sea and the sky" give out, we start to hear the echo of the "dream," or the rhythm of the *fugue* to the river of Mallarmé's letter to Verlaine. The rhythm of seaside vacation mingles with the rhythm of riverside escapades, and fashion becomes permeable to poetry in its rhythmical structure.

Paris on vacation is a space that constantly opens up its boundaries, a place of transit, marked by two opposite and complementary movements: appearance and disappearance, the influx of foreign visitors and the outflux of Parisians. The "Gazette" of the first issue informs us that "Paris opens its doors on all horizons and leaves: the foreigner and the province take profit from this opening of doors to come ... admire ... the Parisian splendor" (Paris ouvre ses portes sur tous les horizons, et sort: l'étranger et la province profitent de cette ouverture de portes pour venir ... admirer ... la splendeur parisienne) [501]. In Ix's Paris, Parisians and foreigners participate in opening and crossing over, so that at the end, in the crossroads Paris has become, there is really no difference between a Parisian and a foreigner: "Let them leave, now, the foreigners, who are no longer foreigners/strangers" (Qu'ils partent, maintenant, les étrangers, qui ne sont plus des étrangers) [525].

It is no coincidence that the movement of opening and crossing over of fashionable Paris and Parisians comes to permeate the fashion and literary sections of the magazine in a fundamental way as well. In the fourth issue, the fashion section, which has hitherto been governed exclusively by the French Madame de Ponty, opens up to a foreign intrusion: Miss Satin, who is English. From then on, Miss Satin's column, "Fashion Gazette" ("Gazette de la fashion"), comes just after Madame de Ponty's "Fashion" ("La mode"), and the younger, unmarried, English "Miss" signs next to the older, (presumably) married, French "Madame." The English "fashion" rewrites the French "mode":

> A first chat! Three rather simple words and nonetheless there are a few hundred subscribers who are already agitated. They are those among you, Ladies, who don't care for novelties. "A first chat?" you ask. "So there will be several?" And, you continue: "Ah! what a pity! Our magazine was so complete, so artistic, and so well written!"—*The Latest Fashion* drops from your hands in the end when . . . you see a foreign name and you cry out: "An English Woman!"
>
> *(Une première causerie! Trois paroles fort simples et voilà pourtant quelques centaines d'abonnées déjà bien agitées. Ce sont celles d'entre vous, Mesdames, qui n'aiment pas les nouveautés. "Une première causerie?" demandez-vous. "Il y en aura donc plusieurs?". Puis, vous reprenez: "Ah! quel dommage! Notre journal était si complet, si artistique, si bien rédigé!"—La dernière Mode, enfin, vous tombe des mains, lorsque . . . vous voyez un nom étranger et vous vous écriez: "Une Anglaise!")* [562]

Miss Satin, "An English Woman" (Une Anglaise) with "a foreign name" (un nom étranger), appears suddenly in the fourth issue of *La dernière mode*, disrupting the familiarity of the magazine with her foreign identity. Acutely aware of her intrusion, Miss Satin explains the necessity of her presence:

> Ladies of the foreign colonies of Paris and Ladies of foreign countries of the entire world, all of them, were forgotten in your magazine.
> Preoccupied only with you, Ladies, it was as if the festivities of London, Moscow, Vienna didn't exist.
>
> *(On avait oublié, dans votre journal, les Dames de la colonie étrangère à Paris, et les Dames étrangères dans le monde entier; toutes.*
> *Préoccupés qu'on était de vous seules, Mesdames, c'était comme si les fêtes de Londres, de Moscou, de Vienne, n'existaient pas.)* [562]

Miss Satin presents herself as a spokeswoman for all the "foreigners" (étrangères). Her "Fashion Gazette," destined to "keep French Ladies well informed of what is going on abroad" (tenir les Dames Françaises au courant de ce qui se passe à l'Etranger) [563], recognizes the world outside of Paris and brings this outside world into Paris. Miss Satin introduces the foreign other. It can be no accident that her debut accompanies a proliferation of other "foreign names" in the magazine, all of them female: "A Creole Lady," "a Breton Chatelaine," "Zizi, good mulatto of Surat," "Olympia, the *Negress*," and "A Reader from Alsace." Miss Satin opens up the space and the culture of the center, Paris. If the stated overall objective of *La dernière mode* is to "provide necessary information so that even a person living far away from Paris may follow the Parisian customs in every regard" (fourn[ir] les renseignements nécessaires à une personne, même éloignée de Paris pour suivre de tous points les habitudes parisiennes),[18] that is, to export Parisian fashion, her "Fashion Gazette" traces the reverse movement of importing into Paris the outside, or foreign, world, symbolized by the importing of *female* pseudonyms into a magazine governed by male names and pseudonyms. Before Miss Satin appears, Madame de Ponty has been the only female reporter. Miss Satin shifts the gender balance.

The intrusion of Miss Satin, the "English woman" (Anglaise) with her "foreign name" (nom étranger), coincides precisely with Mallarmé's signed introduction of an "Anglais" (Tennyson) and his "poème étranger" ("Mariana") in the literary section.[19] Stéphane Mallarmé and Miss Satin make identical movements of cross-cultural import from England/English to France/French. They operate the quintessential Parisian move, to vacation or vacate, to open and cross over so as to let Parisians and foreigners come into contact. The three principal sections of the magazine—fashion, "Chronicle of Paris," and literary—engage in an opening and the concomitant two-way flux of importing/exporting, entering/exiting, and returning/departing. The magazine turns truly fashionable. In its opening to the other and to the foreign, the magazine becomes all the more Parisian and situates itself in the Parisian *mi-lieu*. It takes (its) place in Paris; it truly and finally takes place as if for the first time: "Fall has begun and the Magazine too, truly with this season" (L'Automne a commencé et le Journal véritablement avec cette saison) [559], observes Madame de Ponty at the beginning of the fourth issue.

Miss Satin, Ix, and Stéphane Mallarmé participate in the same activity. The correspondence between the chiasmic initials MS/SM and Ix not only signals the existence of this intimate community but also traces the very form of their common activity: crossing, the doubling and transposing between one and the other, inside and outside, center and periphery, familiar and foreign, Parisian and foreigner, male and female, and consequently between the two names, "Stéphane Mallarmé" and "Miss Satin." The chiasmus spells out the link between "Stéphane Mallarmé" and "Miss Satin" and also conceals it, as it traces the sign "X" of the unknowable and the forbidden. It exposes and yet dissimulates what goes on between the MS/SM(/Ix) couple.

The movement of crossing boundaries of all sorts comes to entertain a fundamental relation with a crossing that is essentially linguistic: translation across languages. The word *satin*, the same in both English and French, moves seamlessly across the two languages. If translation brings two languages, foreign to each other, into contact and crosses through their differences, then *satin* is an ideal term: a perfect crossing through a perfect contact.

Yet the noun is identical across the linguistic border. *Satin*, which is English, is already French. There is no need to transpose and thus no need to translate. Only in the title "Miss" does the foreign English identity reside. The sixth issue informs the reader that Miss Satin is not English but French, even "a known Parisian" (une Parisienne connue) [611]. Miss Satin may stand for the other, for all the "foreigners" (étrangères), but this "foreigner" is already in Paris and is, in fact, a Parisian herself. The "foreign name" turns out to be only a "foreign pseudonym (of a known Parisian)." The double identity of Madame de Ponty and Ix is also revealed. Madame de Ponty is introduced as "also a distinguished man of letters" (aussi un littérateur distingué) [610]. Madame de Ponty crosses over to the literary section. As for Ix, there is no revelation of his other hidden identity, but a reminder that he wears a masque: "behind his mask, . . . Ix, who will be recognized one day" (derrière son masque, . . . Ix, qu'on reconnaîtra quelque jour) [611].

Nonetheless, "Satin" is insistently marked with a certain foreignness, whether as a name or as a pseudonym. It is either a "foreign name" or a "foreign pseudonym." If the foreigner is a Parisian, then the Parisian is also already a foreigner. With her doubly shifting identity, "Satin" is at home in both English and French and yet is foreign to both.

According to its etymology, *satin* comes from China via the Arabic word *zaituni*; it is the name of a Chinese province, either Tsia-Toung or Quanzhou.[20] Mallarmé, in the section "Chinese and Japanese" of "Foreign Words," a chapter in *Les mots anglais* on English words with a foreign origin, writes, "Let us recognize SATIN, as our good" (Reconnaissons SATIN, comme notre bien) [2: 1084].[21] In its origin, *satin* literally names a foreign place, an exotic outside. This outside, however, has been so successfully imported and domesticated that it has become "*our* good" (my emphasis). *Satin* names a thorough relocation of a place, a complete displacement, a perfect transposition. It is a trans-position so perfect that it puts *satin* out of place—not only out of its own original place in China but also out of the very idea of place itself, since in both English and French, it no longer bears the meaning of a place. *Satin* goes from a *lieu* to a *non-lieu*, circulates freely, and hides the remote "otherness" of its origin in its "sameness" in English and French. A chameleon-like word, it dissimulates its foreignness while preserving it through the transparency of adaptation/translation across languages. It veils and yet names the difference between the familiar and the foreign, the inside and the outside, place and nonplace. It exhibits the logic of the Parisian *mi-lieu*, as it introduces the exotic outside (literally, England and China) and opens up the center to circulation. *Satin* is the exact *mi-lieu* that opens up to *lieu* and *non-lieu*.[22]

In *La dernière mode*, *satin* is a site of translation, where transpositions and circulations between languages, or tongues, take place. Miss Satin and her exotic female cohort propose an alternative not only to the French language but also to the French tongue through recipes for foreign dishes. In each issue, Brébant's Chef de Bouche suggests an elaborate menu (no recipe necessary) of French dishes. Starting with the fourth issue, four out of six "foreigners" provide menus for exotic meals, a precise counter-*langue* to the French *langue*. The "foreigners" of *La dernière mode* operate another translation, or change of *langue*, by shifting the emphasis from one experience and use of the *langue* to the other; from the speaking to the tasting *langue*. A Creole Lady provides a "gombo fevis" [567–68]; Zizi, good mulatto of Surat, offers the recipe for a "coconut jam" [607–08]; an Ancestress tells us how to make a "syrup to cure a cold" and an "ointment for frostbite" [608–09]; and finally Olympia, the *Negress*, gives a "Mulligatawny for New Year's Eve" [645–66]. Miss Satin, *the* figure of the exotic female, is the author of a translation as much as, if not more than, Stéphane Mallarmé.

Miss Satin's change of tongue goes hand in hand with a maternalization of signatures. The readers of *La dernière mode* are portrayed as women and mothers. From the very first issue, Ix proclaims, "it is said repeatedly, not without truth, that there are no longer male readers; I think as well, they are female readers" (On va répétant, non sans vérité, qu'il n'y a plus de lecteurs; je crois bien, ce sont des lectrices) [496]. Madame de Ponty writes in the seventh issue (in two passages among many where the readers of the magazine are identified as mothers):

> What to dream of when chiffons leave women idle: of children? But there are mothers who take care to beautify their family while they adorn themselves, they are the Readers of *The Latest Fashion*. Has not the magazine, from its first Issue, given the most beautiful page to Children and Adolescents' clothing, making the habitual image of charming beings appear amid the chronicle of Parisian things? . . .
>
> With what joy, equaled only by the inborn coquettishness of the little darling, the young woman prepares the layette of the newborn not even born yet, often making by herself inner vests and bonnets, which, from the memory of the ancestress, are invariably cut on the same pattern!

> *(A quoi songer quand les chiffons laissent désœuvrées les femmes: aux enfants? mais il est des mères qui s'occupent d'embellir leur famille en même temps que de se parer, ce sont les Lectrices de* la Dernière Mode. *Le journal n'a-t-il pas dès la première Livraison, donné sa plus belle page aux Costumes enfantins ou juvéniles, faisant apparaître, au milieu de la chronique des choses parisiennes, etc., l'image habituelle de charmants êtres? . . .*

> *Avec quelle joie, égalée seulement par la coquetterie native de ce mignon, la jeune femme ne prépare-t-elle pas la layette du nouveau-né même point encore né, souvent confectionnant elle-même les brassières et les bonnets de dessous qui, de mémoire d'aïeule, sont invariablement taillés sur le même patron!) [617–18]*

The female authors of the magazine give maternal advice to readers who are mothers on how to dress, feed, and educate their children, thus standing for the mother, the grandmother, or even an Arch-Mother: an Ancestress (une Aïeule). All of the exotic female pseudonyms indeed seem to merge into "une Aïeule"—a female ancestor and *the* figure of the Mother—who in the sixth issue provides instructions for concocting remedies against cold and frostbite.

Not only the female authors but female readers, too, become grandmothers in the sixth issue, where "une Aïeule" appears. Describing a "toilette for a ball," Madame de Ponty writes in the main fashion section:

> Very well for those of you, dear Readers, who are getting ready to dance, but I know of others, mothers in more than one way, whose good-willed satisfaction will be to attend to the triumph of a daughter, of a daughter-in-law, perhaps—who knows?—charming thing, of a granddaughter.
>
> *(Très bien, pour celles d'entre vous, chères Lectrices, qui s'apprêtent à danser, mais j'en sais d'autres, mères à plus d'un titre, dont la satisfaction bienveillante sera d'assister au triomphe d'une fille, d'une bru, qui sait peut-être? chose charmante, d'une petite-fille.) [601]*

Everyone seems to become "mothers in more than one way" (mères à plus d'un titre).

It is remarkable that the exemplary name of the mother, "une Aïeule," appears simultaneously with another female name: "Zizi, good mulatto of Surat." In the sixth issue, they appear side by side on opposite pages.[23] *Zizi* is a child's term for the male sex in French. It is as if the infinite motherhood or ancestry of "une Aïeule" has triggered a corresponding infantilization of language in the name. Together, "Zizi" and "une Aïeule" name *the* eternally missing object of desire: the maternal phallus, naming it as the name of the mother. "Satin," the site of the exotic females and the name of an elsewhere, or *ailleurs*, names "une Aïeule." The *ailleurs*, the outside, or the extra dimension "Satin" hides and reveals beneath its impenetrable surface, is the *lieu/non-lieu/mi-lieu* of the organ of the mother, or the tongue and the name of the mother. "Satin," or the *ailleurs*, is the place of the *langue maternelle*, or the m/other tongue, and this place is always *ailleurs/aïeule*, infinitely remote in place and time. The familiar mother tongue is also a foreign tongue that is other.

"Satin" functions as a perfect fetish, as its shiny impenetrable surface veils and unveils the maternal *langue* that is always missing and absent, always *ailleurs*. Through a series of transpositions, "Satin" comes to hide her exotic original *space* of China (geographical place) underneath her English or French *surface* (fabric with a shiny surface), hiding and revealing a three-dimensional space, volume, or depth within her two-dimensional impenetrable surface: "Satin" is a pure spatial structure of the fetish itself. "Satin," an exemplary structure of the *lieu/non-lieu/mi-lieu*, is the Mallarméan fetish par excellence. And it is the maternal space—exotic origin, infinite remoteness, and absence—that transpires and transappears through the satiny fabric.[24]

In the sixth issue, which summarizes earlier issues, the names of Stéphane Mallarmé and Tennyson are omitted from the list of literary collaborators that separates "poetry" from "tales/short stories." Could it be that the transposed genre—Tennyson's poem becomes a prose poem in Mallarmé's translation—escapes classification into one formal category? Why could there not be an adjustment—a category called "Translation," as in the fourth issue? Whatever the reason, Mallarmé has disappeared completely from the list of male authors; his name is nowhere. One cannot help seeing a resemblance, however remote, to the famous Mallarméan "elocutionary disappearance of the poet" (disparition élocutoire du poëte) ["Crise de vers" 2: 211]. As such, it seems to relate itself, in a certain way, to the poetic signature, or, more in tune with the logic of the magazine, to a gesture of pseudonymic poetic signature.

This disappearance of Mallarmé's name coincides with the appearance of "Zizi" and "une Aïeule," just as Mallarmé's contribution in the fourth issue coincided with Miss Satin's debut. It could be said that Mallarmé's absent name is inscribed *ailleurs*, at the place of the name of the mother, *in* the mother tongue, in "Zizi" and "une Aïeule." And is not this transposition of the name the most appropriate way of signing his change of tongue, his translation, the trans-position of his authorial identity, his *fugue*? In *La dernière mode*, Mallarmé's name appears and disappears in the name of the m/other. When Mallarmé chooses "Satin"—in which all other female pseudonyms are echoed—as the privileged site of his own signature, he posits writing in the space of an *ailleurs*, the space of the other gender, genre, and *langue*. Writing itself becomes the experience of transposition and translation and, as such, a relation to both mother tongue and foreign tongue. To write is to experience the mother tongue as an exotic foreign tongue, and vice versa. It is to turn all familiar words into "foreign names/words" and to make all foreign tongues familiar.[25]

The young mothers of *La dernière mode* prepare the layette of the newborn following the pattern that is "invariably" handed down by the Ancestress [618]. The maternal know-how and wisdom come to us and inhabit our memory. The figure of the Arch-Mother, "une Aïeule," stands for the presence of the mother in our memory and the presence of the mother tongue, an arch-language, in our language. The eternal rhyme between *mer* (sea) and *mère* (mother) runs throughout the magazine as an arch-rhyme. The horizon of the sea opens to "the horizon of maternal dreams" (l'horizon des rêves maternels) [617], and the rhythm of vacation coincides with the rhythm of the *mer/mère* (sea/mother). To say that writing has to do with the mother tongue is to say that we are forever, timelessly, rhythmed by the mother. The "musicality of everything" may come from that eternal rhythm.

The jewelry of the first issue is what a daughter inherits from her mother. Madame Marguerite de Ponty, herself a figure of the mother, talks about what jewelry an elegant mother might choose for her daughter as a wedding gift. She speaks not of clothing that goes out of date each season, but of what lasts through generations from mother to daughter:

Let's look for the Jewel itself alone. Where? everywhere; that is, *in a few places* on the surface of the globe, and *mostly* in Paris, for Paris provides the world with jewelry. What? doesn't every country, just as nature gives it flora, have a complete jewelry collection provided by human hands? The instinct for beauty and for the relation with diverse climates that determines, beneath every sky, the production of roses, tulips, and carnations, is this any different for the creation of earrings, rings, and bracelets? Flowers and gems: doesn't each kind have, as it were, its own soil?

(Cherchons le Bijou, isolé, en lui-même. Où? partout; c'est-à-dire un peu sur la surface du globe, et beaucoup à Paris: car Paris fournit le monde de bijoux. Quoi! toute contrée, comme, par sa nature, une flore, ne présente-elle pas, issue des mains de l'homme, un écrin complet? L'instinct de beauté et de relation avec les climats divers, qui règle, sous chaque ciel, la production des roses, des tulipes et des œillets, est-il étranger à celle des pendants d'oreilles, des bagues, des bracelets? Fleurs et joyaux: chaque espèce n'a-t-elle pas comme qui dirait son sol?) [490, original emphasis]

Flower and jewel mingle both in Ponty's column and in her own name: "Marguerite," the name of a flower, comes from the Latin *margarita*, or "pearl," from the perle-oyster, with a "cognate in Sanskrit, *manjari*, a pearl, but also a flower bud."[26] Marguerite de Ponty writes about flower and jewel, her own name, the name of the mother, and transmits them to the daughter as a "wedding gift" (corbeille de mariage): "all the delightful jewel box we have recounted stone by stone, pearl by pearl" (tout le délicieux écrin que nous avons, pierre à pierre ou perle à perle, raconté) [493]. "Stone by stone, pearl by pearl," she tells and transmits the story of the mother. The rhythm of the mother is the echo of the mother's name.

Madame de Ponty offers an elaborate description of a white wedding gown, the "feminine apparel par excellence, white and vaporous," "mundane and virginal" (vêtement féminin par excellence, blanc et vaporeux; mondain et virginal [561]). This wedding gown is made of satin, with a wide satin belt, and is lined entirely with satin [561]. Just after the appearance of the white satin wedding dress in Madame de Ponty's fashion column, Miss Satin and her "Fashion Gazette" make their debut.

Miss Satin associates herself with the white satin gown from the very start in an inevitable and ambiguous fashion. She names its fabric and from the fabric seems to become by metonymy the wedding dress and the bride. Yet Miss Satin is a "Miss" and stays that way: she is and is not married, wears and does not wear the gown. She stands between marriage and virginity, neither one nor the other, and yet both, and something in-between, just like Ix vis-à-vis the MS/SM couple and Mallarmé's translation vis-à-vis the literary section. As the fabric of the wedding gown, the *tissu* of the *hymen*, Miss Satin is literally the hymen par excellence in the Derridean sense.[27]

Miss Satin coincides simultaneously with the dress and the poet, as she is the fabric of the wedding dress (satin) turned into a name (Miss Satin), which, in turn, marks the name of the poet. *Satin*, in turn, names the fabric of a name, signature, and writing. The textile becomes textual. When Mallarmé weaves his own signature into "Miss Satin"'s texture, he disperses his poetic identity onto the mirrorlike surface. And this sheer reflective impenetrable surface veils and yet maintains the difference between the same and the other and between poetry and fashion. "Miss Satin" names the texture, the *tissu* and *milieu*, and thus the hymen of fashion and poetry.

When "Stéphane Mallarmé" (dis-)appears surreptitiously in the name of the m/other "Zizi" and "une Aïeule" in the sixth issue, the main fashion section opens with a fitting metaphor:

> Like two threads, one of silk or even of wool and the other of gold, that interrupt and connect with each other, mingled in their annual design, the evolution of fashion during the season and the festivities alternate here.
>
> *(Comme deux fils, l'un de soie ou même de laine et l'autre d'or, qui s'interrompent et se rattachent entre eux, mêlés dans leur dessin annuel, alternent ici et l'évolution de la mode durant la Saison, et les fêtes.)* [599]

When Mallarmé signs as Miss Satin, it could be said that "Stéphane Mallarmé" and "Miss Satin," SM and MS, and thus poetry and fashion weave themselves "like two threads . . . that interrupt and connect with each other" to unfold the seam of the Mallarméan *couture*.

On the satin surface, we begin to see the reflections of a number of familiar motifs of the Mallarméan poetics: virginity, hymen, jewels, whiteness, *blanc*, emptiness, *lieu*, absence, disappearance, the fetishism of the surface, and the material quality of language. And yet, how do we qualify this feeling of familiarity and déjà vu, since the satiny surface puts into question the notion of familiarity itself? Poetry and fashion seem familiar and yet foreign to each other.

La dernière mode functions like the term *satin*, a perfectly domesticated word that is, nonetheless, a "foreign name/word" blurring the line between familiar and foreign, inside and outside, inclusion and exclusion, and that, as a *mi-lieu* between *lieu* and *non-lieu*, resists all placement into one fixed category. To absorb it completely into Mallarmé's poetic writings would negate its foreignness, yet to exclude it as foreign would negate its familiarity:

As for a business venture, which doesn't count in literary terms—

Theirs—

To flaunt things all in the foreground, imperturbably, like street vendors, animated by the pressure of the moment: this is all very well—writing: in the event, why do it, unwarrantably, except to display banality upon your stall, rather than spread forth that thing of price, the cloud that floats upon the inward chasm of each thought, given that vulgarity resides in whatever is accorded, the character of immediacy, nothing more.[28]

(*Quant à une entreprise, qui ne compte pas littérairement—*

La leur—

D'exhiber les choses à un imperturbable premier plan, en camelots, activés par la pression de l'instant, d'accord—écrire, dans le cas, pourquoi, indûment, sauf pour étaler la banalité; plutôt que tendre le nuage, précieux, flottant sur l'intime gouffre de chaque pensée, vu que vulgaire l'est ce à quoi on décerne, pas plus, un caractère immédiat.) *["Le mystère dans les lettres" 2: 231]*

On this passage on mystery in literature, Mallarmé opposes journalistic writing ("flaunt things all in the foreground, imperturbably, like street vendors, animated by the pressure of the moment"; "display banality") to literary writing ("spread forth that thing of price, the cloud that floats upon the inward chasm of each thought"). If nonliterary journalistic writing seems all surface ("flaunt . . . in the foreground"; "display banality"), literary writing seems to be about depth ("the inward chasm of each thought"). Yet this surface-depth opposition is only an illusion. If journalistic writing writes as a surface ("flaunt"; "display"), literary writing, too, writes as and on the surface ("spread forth . . . the cloud" [tendre le nuage]). The uncovering ("flaunt"; "display") and covering ("spread forth . . . the cloud") both happen on and across the surface. Depth, if there is such a thing, can only be suggested in Mallarmé by a veiling, that is, by a highlighting of the surface itself.

"Miss Satin," as a text/texture of sheer surface, seems both to expose the brilliant surface in journalistic style and to veil, obscure, and cloud this surface in literary style. She performs an "obnubilation des tissus" (clouding of the fabric) that is also a "tissu d'obnubilation" (fabric of clouding).[29]

The "vast, iridescent clouds of fabric in which [the woman] envelops herself" (les vastes et chatoyantes nuées d'étoffes dont elle s'enveloppe) fascinated Charles Baudelaire, who, convinced that a woman and her dress form "an indivisible totality," wrote the following in *Le peintre de la vie moderne* in 1863: "What poet, in rendering the pleasure caused by the apparition of beauty, would dare separate the woman from her costume?" (Quel poète oserait, dans la peinture du plaisir causé par l'apparition d'une beauté, séparer la femme de son costume?) [2: 714]. The pen of Mallarmé the poet continues to envelop the woman in the "nuées d'étoffes" (clouds of fabric):

> All in all, never have there reigned so superbly opulent and even heavy fabrics—velvet and almost to brocades of silver or gold—but no less the light, soft, and bright new cashmere worn in the evening; but within this envelope, sumptuous or simple, more than in any other period the Woman is going to transappear, visible, outlined, herself, with the whole

grace of her contour or the principal lines of her person (while, in the back, the vast magnificence of the train attracts all the folds and the massive fullness of the fabric).

(Somme toute, jamais ne régnèrent plus superbement les tissus opulents et même lourds, le velours et presque les brocarts d'argent ou d'or, non moins que, léger, moelleux, clair, le nouveau cachemire qui se porte le soir; mais parmi cette enveloppe, somptueuse ou simple, plus qu'à aucune époque va transparaître la Femme, visible, dessinée, elle-même, avec la grâce entière de son contour ou les principales lignes de sa personne [alors que, par derrière, la magnificence vaste de la traîne attire tous les plis et l'ampleur massive de l'étoffe].) [640]

The Woman is about to transappear ("va transparaître la Femme") through the "cloud of suave fabrics, vast and elongated to the extreme" (nuage de suaves étoffes, vaste et allongé à l'extrême) [618]. With its "nuage . . . allongé à l'extrême" (cloud . . . elongated to the extreme)—or the "nuage tendu" (cloud spread forth)—fashion crosses over and tends/spreads toward poetry: "tendre le nuage" (to spread forth the cloud).[30] "What reader, in savoring the pleasure caused by Mallarmé's words, would dare separate Mallarmé and his poetry from the cloud of fabric, or 'tissu d'obnubilation'?" one could say, paraphrasing Baudelaire. In Mallarmé, poetry and fashion meet in the clouds in the most obscurely and yet dazzlingly high fashion.

Mallarmé loved to go on boating trips on the Seine, alone or with friends, when he was at Valvins. Buying "ruinous boats" is one reason why he had to do works of "concessions" (which includes the writing of *La dernière mode*), as mentioned in his letter to Verlaine. Mallarmé purchased his own boat in 1878 and named it *Vève* after his daughter Geneviève. When his friend Eugène Manet, the brother of the painter Edouard Manet, asked whether he planned to have something inscribed on the sail, Mallarmé answered, as Jean-Luc Steinmetz recounts in his biography of Mallarmé, "no, I shall leave this great page blank" (non, je laisse cette grande page blanche).[31] The unmarked white sail eventually bore Mallarmé's initials, SM.[32] Steinmetz writes that

Paul Valéry frequently spoke of Mallarmé as the "mariner" of that "ever so literary fluid skiff," "draw[ing] a white page on the water of the Seine."[33]

The sail (*la voile*) of the boat meets the veil (*le voile*) of the satin fabric, both surfaces of inscription for the name of the daughter—Vève and Miss Satin—and the poet's initials "SM" as well. The white surfaces of the satiny fabric, sailboat, and paper come together.

In his "ever so literary fluid skiff," Mallarmé's *fugues*—whether escapades to Valvins or into the world of Miss Satin—become acts of writing that "draw a white page on the water of the Seine" and movements of rhythm permeated by the pervasive "musicality of everything," from which Mallarmé's cosmic poem "Un coup de dés" will finally issue forth.

The little sailboat that was so much *in tune* with Mallarmé's life seems to have carried him away in his final *fugue*. Steinmetz writes that Mallarmé's coffin resting in the courtyard of the poet's house seemed like a bark, "not far away from the anchored boat," "the peaceful S.M. without its sailor," which friends and guests coming to the funeral passed by when crossing the bridge at Valvins:[34]

> Specifically, the dancer is *not a woman who dances* for these combined reasons: *she is not a woman*, but a metaphor summing up one of the elementary aspects of our form—sword, cup, flower, etc.; and *that she does not dance*, suggesting, through the miracle of shortcuts and bounds, with a corporal writing what it would take paragraphs of prose, in dialogue and description, to express: she is a poem set free of any scribe's apparatus.[35]
>
> (*À savoir que la danseuse* n'est pas une femme qui danse, *pour ces motifs juxtaposés qu'elle* n'est pas une femme, *mais une métaphore résumant un des aspects élémentaires de notre forme, glaive, coupe, fleur, etc., et* qu'elle ne danse pas, *suggérant, par le prodige de racourcis ou d'élan, avec une écriture corporelle ce qu'il faudrait des paragraphes en prose dialoguée autant que descriptive, pour exprimer, dans la rédaction: poème dégagé de tout appareil du scribe.*) [*"Ballets"* 2: 171, original emphasis]

Mallarmé the sailor on his SM is not a man and does not navigate but is "a corporal writing" on "a white page on the water of the Seine," a "poem set free," a *fugue*.

Mallarmé's *fugue* is the time and space of *difference*. Through his writing of *La dernière mode*—one of a kind, since no other writers who wrote about fashion then, among them Baudelaire, d'Aurevilly, and Balzac, did so as fashion journalists—Mallarmé experiences and experiments with a different way of writing, thinking, being, that is, of living. The fluidity of the magazine's status—whether it is a "besogne propre" written to earn a living during a time of financial difficulty or a "concession to pleasure"—is what opens it to life, to the possibility of life. For it bears witness to the different facets that compose life—from earning a living (the weight of life's imperative) to vacationing (the lightness of life's pleasure) and so many more —and to what makes life a "jeu suprême," a wondrous playing that embraces the full dimension of life.

La dernière mode, the odd enterprise within Mallarmé's corpus, with a different *style*, is part of the "jeu suprême." On its playground, foreign language unfolds and resonates within maternal language, enters into a rhythmic relation, and rhymes with maternal language. Deleuze, referring to Proust's words in *Contre Sainte-Beuve*—"Beautiful books are written in a kind of foreign language"—speaks of writing as "invent[ing] a new language within a language, a foreign language, as it were.... When another language is created within language, it is language in its entirety ... that communicates with its own outside." "The limit," Deleuze continues, "is not outside language, it is the outside *of* language."[36]

La dernière mode is one such instance of "invent[ion] [of] a new language within a language," where language "communicates with its own outside," creating a matrix in which new possibilities of syntax and grammar emerge. The meticulousness with which Mallarmé devoted himself to the layout and design of the fashion magazine led to his final experience/experiment with typography in the oddly designed poem "Un coup de dés" twenty-three years later, in 1897, a design that opened up meaning. The style of *La dernière mode* led to the style of "Un coup de dés," commonly thought of as Mallarmé's final poetic achievement: Bertrand Marchal, who edited the *Œuvres complètes* of 1998–2004, calls it the "ultimate work," which has become the "emblem of Mallarmean modernity" [1: 1315]. Considered a poem by many—Mallarmé himself called "Un coup de dés" a poem, but one that partakes of free

verse and prose poetry, the new writerly enterprise of his time [1: 392]—
"Un coup de dés" is also regarded as a prose piece by some: Henri Mondor
and G. Jean-Aubry, the editors of the *Œuvres complètes* of 1945, call it the "last
of [Malllarmé's] prose works" in their editorial notes.[37] Both Miss Satin
and the white page of "Un coup de dés," defying categories with their carefully (mis)placed words, open up the two-dimensional surface to infinite
dimensions. Valéry said it took Mallarmé "*to raise . . . a page to the power of the
star-filled sky*" (*d'élever enfin une page à la puissance du ciel étoilé*).[38]

Mallarmé's experimental texture reveals the potential of poetry within
language. Poetry turns language inside out. Mallarmé's writing, in its turn(ing), joins Orpheus in his turning to look at Eurydice. The "insouciant,
weightless gaze of Orpheus," Maurice Blanchot writes, is "all levity, unconcern, and innocence," and yet "everything is risked . . . in the decision to
look." "Everything is risked." "Tout se joue."[39] The French for "is risked,"
se joue, comes from the verb *jouer*, "to play." To Mallarmé, risk is poetry's
"supreme play" (jeu suprême). At once absolute and circumstantial, Mallarmé's writing risks opening the certainty and weight of meaning to contingency and lightness.

CHAPTER THREE

"Vise of Stone" and Open Air

"The Weight of Living" and
"The Search for Lightness"

ITALO CALVINO OPENS HIS *Six Memos for the Next Millennium*, on qualities indispensable to literature, with a memo on "lightness."[1] He "uphold[s] the values of lightness." He does not "consider the virtues of weight any less compelling" but has "more to say about lightness" [3]. In forty years of writing fiction, "exploring various roads and making diverse experiments," his "working method has more often than not involved the subtraction of weight." He has "tried to remove weight, sometimes from people, sometimes from heavenly bodies, sometimes from cities; above all [he has] tried to remove weight from the structure of stories and from language" [3].

Calvino refers to the "lightness of thoughtfulness" [10] and to "weightless gravity" [19]. In lightness is nothing "frivolous." Indeed, "thoughtful lightness can make frivolity seem dull and heavy" [10]. Light play with the gravity of thought bears the seriousness of thinking of literature as fulfilling "an existential function, the search for lightness as a reaction to the weight of living" [26].

There is a "gulf" between the "quick light touch" Calvino wants for his writing and "the facts of life"—"the weight, the inertia, the opacity of the world," the "raw materials" of his writing. In that opaque world, "the inexorable stare of Medusa" is slowly turning everything into stone and engulfing him, too, in a "vise of stone" [4]. Unless he can find a way of "evading them," writing suffers from weight and petrifaction: heaviness "sticks to writing from the start" [4]. Calvino's "working method" removes weight from people, stories, and language in direct response to this gulf and to the weight of life.

"The only hero" who can cut off Medusa's head, Calvino writes, is Perseus, he "who flies with winged sandals": "To cut off Medusa's head without being turned into stone, Perseus supports himself on the very lightest of things, the winds and the clouds, and fixes his gaze upon what can be revealed only by indirect vision, an image caught in a mirror. I am immediately tempted to see this myth as an allegory of the poet's relationship to the world, a lesson in the method one should follow when writing" [4, slightly revised translation].

Calvino finds in Ovid's *Metamorphoses* further details of Perseus as exemplar. Perseus has killed a sea monster to save Andromeda's life:

> After such an awful chore—[Perseus] wants to wash his hands. But another problem arises: where to put Medusa's head. And here Ovid has some lines (IV.740–52) that seem to me extraordinary in showing how much delicacy of spirit a man must have to be a Perseus, killer of monsters: "So that the rough sand should not harm the snake-haired head (*anguiferumque caput dura ne laedat harena*), he makes the ground soft with a bed of leaves, and on top of that he strews little branches of plants born under water, and on this he places Medusa's head, face down." I think that the lightness, of which Perseus is the hero, could not be better represented than by this gesture of refreshing courtesy toward a being so monstrous and terrifying yet at the same time somehow fragile and perishable. But the most unexpected thing is the miracle that follows: when they touch Medusa, the little marine plants turn

into coral and the nymphs, in order to have coral for adornments, rush to bring sprigs and seaweed to the terrible head.

This clash of images, in which the fine grace of the coral touches the savage horror of the Gorgon, is so suggestive that I would not like to spoil it by attempting glosses or interpretations. [5–6]

In Calvino's sentence, most extraordinarily suggestive is the move from "clash" to "touch" to describe the mode of encounter between two antithetical images. Fine grace does not clash with but touches horror. Calvino finds in the delicacy of Perseus's gesture of softening the hard ground for the head of Medusa the best representation of "lightness, of which Perseus is the hero." In consequence, Medusa's head—the symbol of stony hardness—does not clash with another hardness of massive stony ground but is permitted to touch the soft ground slightly and lightly. The massiveness of Medusa's head, its monstrous violence and weight, becomes "at the same time" light and soft, "somehow fragile and perishable." Softness and lightness emanate from hardness and heaviness.

But Calvino marvels most at the "miracle that follows" Perseus's act of courtesy—weed twigs turning into coral "when they touch Medusa." Thus Medusa's head, whose look is so horrendous that it literally kills, gives rise to "adornments," as Calvino terms them, that are beautiful to look at. The "savage horror of the Gorgon" that produces terrifying statues of death generates through Perseus the "fine grace of the coral."

In *Metamorphoses*, Ovid gives us further details of this "miracle." As Perseus "softens the ground with leaves, strews seaweed over these, and lays on this the head of Medusa" [4.742–43]:

> The fresh weed twigs, but now alive and porous to the core,
>   absorb the power of the monster and harden at its touch
>   and take a strange stiffness in their stems and leaves.
> And the sea-nymphs test the wonder on more twigs and
>   are delighted to find the same thing happening to them all;
> and, by scattering these twigs as seeds, propagate the wondrous thing
>   throughout their waters.

> *(virga recens bibulaque etiamnum viva medulla*
> *vim rapuit monstri tactuque induruit huius*
> *percepitque novum ramis et fronde rigorem.*
> *at pelagi nymphae factum mirabile temptant*
> *pluribus in virgis et idem contingere gaudent*
> *seminaque ex illis iterant iactata per undas.)*
>
> [4.744–49]

Twigs "harden" (*induruit*), leading to "stiffness" (*rigorem*). But this petrifaction comes from "absorb[ing] the power of the monster" (*vim rapuit monstri*). The verb *rapuit* means "to seize or snatch in order to keep." The weed twigs capture Medusa's power, making it their own; their hardening is not so much infliction—unwanted and resisted—as acquisition—sought and received. The "strange stiffness in their stems and leaves" comes more as transformative gain than as paralyzing loss. The verb *percepit* in "[the fresh twigs] *take* a strange stiffness" further marks the metamorphosis as enabling rather than disabling, since it means "to take possession, gather, take in, and gain."

The weed twigs' capacity to "absorb" Medusa's power is linked to youth and hence force of life. The twigs are "fresh" (*recens*, or "recent, new, young, vigorous") and thus "alive and porous to the core" (*bibulaque . . . viva medulla*). *Bibula*, rendered as "porous," from the verb *bibere*, "to drink," means "fond of drinking." The "freshness" of the twigs translates into their inherent open disposition ("porous to the core") and a corresponding vigor to drink/draw in (*bibula*). The livelier—the more porous, pliant, and tender—the twigs, the more vigorously they draw in Medusa's power, and the stiffer they become. *Novum*, the adjective qualifying *stiffness* ("novum . . . rigorem"), meaning "new, fresh, novel, unusual, extraordinary," echoes and extends *recens*, which denoted the liveliness of the twigs ("virga recens") two lines before. The correspondence between adjectives highlights the link between freshness and stiffness, life and death. The weed twigs "absorb" death into the "core" as if drinking for life ("viva medulla").

Death enters with an energy equal to life. There is no resistance, only "porous" osmosis between softness and hardness, mobility and stiffness, life and death that dissolves the rigid boundaries of opposition. The force of life is force both for life and for death. There is no clashing, but touching of states of intensities that support each other as in the body of the artist-child-convalescent (in Baudelaire's *Le peintre de la vie moderne*), where the vigor of youthful health opens up to sickness and trauma. Both *recens* and *novum* are linked further to *mirabile* (unusual, extraordinary, wonderful, marvelous) in "factum mirabile," the "wonder" of the coral that the sea nymphs "test" again and again. Coral as manifestation of life *touching* death, and beauty as contiguity between life and death—these are the "wonder" that rejoices the nymphs and the "miracle" at which Calvino marvels.

The nymphs, who "test the wonder on more twigs," "are delighted to find the same thing happening to them all" (idem contingere gaudent). The verb *contingere*, used here intransitively, means "to happen," "to befall." Used transitively, *contingere* means "to touch." What happens (*contingere*) over and over again is the miracle of touch (*contingere*). It is as if the original miracle —contact with a direct object—continued to happen even in the absence of direct object of contact. Ovid tells us:

> And even till this day the same nature has remained in coral
> so that they harden when exposed to air,
> and what was a pliant twig beneath the sea is turned to stone above.
>
> *(nunc quoque curaliis eadem natura remansit,*
> *duritiam tacto capiant ut ab aere quodque*
> *vimen in aequore erat, fiat super aequora saxum.)*
>
> [4.750–52]

Even without Medusa's head, coral hardens at *contact* with air ("duritiam *tacto* capiant ut ab aere") and eventually comes to harden above water on its own as if by its inherent nature ("*fiat* super aequora saxum"). The hardening-upon-full-frontal-contact-with-the-monster's-head transforms into hardening-at-the-contact-with-air and finally into just hardening. From the original touching ("vim rapuit monstri *tactu*que induruit huius" [absorb the power of the monster and harden at its *touch*]) to the final becoming (*"fiat super aequora saxum"* [*is turned* to stone above]), Medusa, the direct object (of contact), disappears literally into air, since air turns coral hard just as Medusa did. The verb *contingere* loses its direct object and goes from transitive (to touch) to intransitive (to happen), leaving us with pure happening, becoming. Ovid's poem is as much about original metamorphoses as it is about metamorphoses over time of these original metamorphoses.

The miracle of coral touches upon the core of Ovid's poetics. It forms a microcosm of Ovid's "encyclopedic poem" [9], showing the law of "universal contiguity," to borrow from the title, "Ovid and Universal Contiguity," of Calvino's preface to an edition of *Metamorphoses*.[2] Ovid's poetry brings to light the intimate proximity and "contiguity between all the figures and forms of existing things, anthropomorphic or otherwise." "We are thus given the impression of a . . . world," Calvino writes, "in which there is an interaction between events that are usually considered in isolation."[3] It reveals the transitive nature—transitional and passing over to affect (a person or thing, hence taking a direct object, as is said of verbs)—of the intransitive *contingere* of all happenings. Contingencies are contiguities. They touch each other, and they touch us. Ovid's poetry revives the memory of the *first touch*. It "re-*im-presses*" it on events and on us.

The shift from transitive touching to intransitive happening records grammatically the passage from contiguity to contingency. The loss of direct object corresponds to the disappearance of Medusa's head, which is abstracted into thin air, becoming intangible, invisible, and forgotten. Ovid's words and worlds lift the amnesia and blindness. The object returns. In Ovid, it is as if the object were allowed back to hover in the intimate vicinity of the verb, as Medusa's head stayed within reach of Perseus. Perseus is the hero of lightness not out of "refusal of the reality in which he is fated to live," but because "he carries the reality with him and accepts it as his particular burden" [5].

Perseus's lightness comes not from eliminating, but from accepting and bearing the weight of Medusa. "Perseus does not abandon [the severed head] but carries it concealed in a bag," Calvino writes. Accepting a burden is lighter than refusing a burden. Heaviness is the weight of refusal of reality more than the weight of reality itself. Fear weighs, and so, too, do the concomitant denial, resistance, and forgetting. When life weighs, and air feels heavy, and we feel "caught in a vise of stone" [4], it may be Medusa, invisible and forgotten, yet ineluctably present in the air, who exerts all the more her power on us, making us unable to perceive (her), killing our capacity to see, and thus continuing to give death through/in looking. To clash with Medusa face-on or to relegate her into invisibility is each an act of fear that blinds and denies universal contiguity and its generative power.

What is the difference between coral and statues of stone created by Medusa? In Ovid's account, coral results from petrifaction, as the statues do. The word *saxum* (stone) [4.752], which Ovid uses for coral, belongs to the repertoire of other terms including *silex* [4.781] and *lapis* [4.660], both meaning "stone," and *signum de marmore* (marble statue) [5.183]. But coral comes as "wonder" that delights, others as disaster that horrifies.

Those who are seized by terror and adopt an oppositional stance contract and harden on their own. According to the law of action and reaction, as universal as the law of contiguity, Medusa strikes with an offensive force that is proportionate to their own defensive hardening. In petrifaction are suffocating paralysis and deadly constriction. The weight of fear, refusal, deadlock, and dead end crushes them. But when there is no fear or resistance, and when weight is accepted openly, as with the fresh weed twigs, the violent conflict of defense/offense need not take place. To the contrary, the power of Medusa is absorbed as enabling and generative "drink." Hardening, here, occurs as proof of fluid movement and open reception. Coral's petrifaction is wondrous transformation and fearless acceptance. For the sea nymphs it is a beautiful thing to rejoice about, make more of, adorn themselves with.

Thus it is less the weight of the monster per se than our reaction to and fear of it that produce heaviness. Petrified statues are the form that refusal takes; coral is the form that acceptance takes. Life pushing death away collapses into stone; life opening to death blossoms into coral. Clashing is rigid separation and violent striking that produce stone. Touching is mutual meeting and fluid sharing that yield coral.

The young twigs touching Medusa's head and absorbing its stiffness continue the "gesture of refreshing courtesy" that Perseus has extended to Medusa, allowing him to appropriate as his own the monster's power. Perseus uses Medusa's head as a weapon against his enemies. The law of action and reaction applies here, too. Medusa, the "being so monstrous and terrifying," responds—not reacts—to Perseus's courtesy and becomes "at the same time somehow fragile and perishable" [6]. Calvino admires Ovid's account of Perseus's exploit for "showing how much delicacy of spirit a man must have to be a Perseus, killer of monsters" [5]. It takes "delicacy of spirit" to make the monstrous body "fragile" and "perishable," and thus vulnerable. "Delicacy of spirit" constitutes the true conquering power of the hero. In the face of it, stony hardness becomes perishable flesh. In Perseus's hands, Medusa meets her match, her own "Medusa" that turns her soft.

When young twigs touch Medusa's head, Medusa absorbs freshness and tenderness from the twigs. As twigs touch Medusa, so, too, Medusa touches. She becomes even touchingly beautiful in her vulnerability. In a metamorphosis of reciprocal contiguity, receiving youthfulness from the twigs, Medusa becomes the mortal and beautiful maiden of her younger days.[4] Perseus says that Medusa was "once most beautiful in form" (clarissima forma) and "the jealous hope of many suitors. Of all her beauties, her hair was the most beautiful—for so [Perseus] learned from one who said he had seen her" [4.794–97]. Medusa was so beautiful that Neptune, the god of the ocean, fell in love with and "ravished" her in the temple of Minerva. Minerva, offended, "punished" Medusa by turning her "locks to ugly snakes" [4.794–801].

Perseus's delicacy lifts for a moment the violence inflicted upon Medusa by the goddess of reason, who negated her beauty and erased it forever from vision and memory. Perseus allows us to see Medusa as she first appeared in the eyes of the "one who said he had seen her" and those who fell in love with her in the beginning. Ovid's poetics, through Perseus as its hero, brings us the first touch and the first sight in all their "fragility" and "perishability." "How can we hope to save ourselves in that which is most fragile?" Calvino asks [6]. Life suffers inevitably from separation, isolation, and petrifaction that destroy the delicate fragility of the contiguity and fluidity of the world. Coral, whose solidity is at the same time fragile and delicate, like Medusa's, comes as a rare instance of beauty blossoming in celebration of that which is "most fragile"—the "wonder" (factum mirabile) [4.747] of the "new" and "novel" (recens [4.744]; novum [4.746]), of the first time, reaching far back to the forgotten past and yet hovering around us now, invisible in its presence.

The clash between weight and lightness is the core of "Spleen et Idéal," the first and longest section of Baudelaire's *Les fleurs du mal*. Pitting a dark and oppressive weight of "Spleen" against a luminous and expansive lightness of "Idéal," Baudelaire's verse collection, at its opening, is deeply marked by the abyssal weight of life. Under the title "Spleen," four poems describe a desolate and constricting world from which life slowly drains out, all "living matter" in that world hardened to a "block of granite" ["Spleen" II 1: 73], "a vise of stone," as if pressed down by the "inexorable stare of Medusa."[5] Numbing paralysis seizes the speaker of these poems, who becomes like a "skeleton," a "cadaver" ["Spleen" III 1: 74], even a "graveyard" and a "pyramid" ["Spleen" II 1: 73]. Air is so damp and heavy that it condenses into liquid—it rains a lot in the Baudelairean universe—and also into solid: "the low and heavy sky weighs like a lid" (le ciel bas et lourd pèse comme un couvercle) ["Spleen" IV 1: 74]. Instead of releasing breathing space, the thickened air suffocates, traps, and crushes down body and soul. At the end of the last "Spleen" poem, "Hope, / Defeated, weeps, and Anguish, atrocious and despotic, / In [the speaker's] bowed skull plants its black flag" (l'Espoir, / Vaincu, pleure, et l'Angoisse atroce, despotique, / Sur mon crâne incliné plante son drapeau noir) [1: 75].

Other poems of Baudelaire convey the weight, pain, and despair of life. Only a handful are on the side of "Idéal," such as "Parfum exotique" [1: 25–26], "L'invitation au voyage" [1: 53–54], and "Élévation" [1: 10], which trace the movement of flight into a realm of expansive sensuality or into the pure open air of a higher plane—the "ethereal regions of true Poetry" (les régions éthérées de la véritable Poésie) where "Evil is not, nor Good" (le Mal n'est pas, non plus que le Bien) [1: 187], as Baudelaire wrote in the first draft of the dedication of *Les fleurs du mal*, to Théophile Gautier.

In *Les fleurs du mal*, "Spleen" outweighs "Idéal." Gloomy depression becomes the hallmark of Baudelaire's poetry, as Ross Chambers reminisces about his "earliest attempt to teach *Les fleurs du mal*," when an "earnest delegation of students" came to ask him, "Why do we have to read this morbid stuff?"[6] But in the very weight it gives to "Spleen," *Les fleurs du mal* fulfills a profoundly "existential function, the search for lightness as a reaction to the weight of living." Baudelaire upholds "the values of lightness" not as a mere negation of weight, but as stemming, on the contrary, from full appreciation and bearing of weight. Perseus is the hero of lightness because he carries, and does not abandon, the heaviest of weights. Baudelaire, too, bears the crushing weight of "Spleen" "as his particular burden."[7]

According to the ancient theory of humors, "Spleen" is the organ that secretes the black bile that causes melancholy, a disease believed to result from "an invasion of the brain by mists or vapors rising from the spleen," "an attack . . . endanger[ing] the seat of reason and order, causing dizziness and nausea, fainting spells and weakness," and "in more serious cases, produc[ing] a state of 'madness' that we would now call angst or depression, but that 19th-century doctors diagnosed as 'melancholia.'"[8] In early nineteenth-century France, melancholy was the disease of the century—*le mal du siècle*. It pervaded the atmosphere as repressive political regimes succeeded each other after the demise of the "great" Napoleon. The *mal* of *Les fleurs du mal* anchors itself thoroughly in the evil/pain/disease of the century that corrupts body and soul and spreads to physical and mental/moral spheres, causing loss of willpower, boredom (ennui), and paralysis.

The *mal* as evil has its full expression in Baudelaire's opening poem, "Au lecteur" ("To the Reader"). Satan—the active agent, the "chemist" of evil—appears in the third stanza, vaporizing our will and manipulating the strings that control us:

> On the pillow of evil, it is Satan Trismegistus
> Who cradles for a long time our bewitched spirit,

And the rich metal of our will
Is all vaporized by this cunning chemist.

It's the Devil who holds the strings that move us!

*(Sur l'oreiller du mal, c'est Satan Trismégiste
Qui berce longuement notre esprit enchanté,
Et le riche métal de notre volonté
Est tout vaporisé par ce savant chimiste.*

C'est le Diable qui tient les fils qui nous remuent!)

[1: 5]

The Devil's dominion is complete: we are irremediably damned ("Each day we descend toward Hell a step further" [Chaque jour vers l'Enfer nous descendons d'un pas]) as the entire world becomes Satan's playground, laboratory, and theater. As the master alchemist and puppeteer, he dissolves into air the "metal of our will" and toys with our body and soul, now his puppets. Subjugated to Satan's power, we have neither the lucidity to perceive and discern, nor the resolve to revolt against, our horrifying predicament. What vanishes with our vaporized will is awareness of evil and the ability to detect its workings. We thus come to accept the vilest of sins "without horror," rather with complacency, complicity, and even pleasure ("We find charm in disgusting things" [Aux objets répugnants nous trouvons des appas]). We do not see or feel evil as it works its way inside us in an "invisible" and "mute" fashion ("When we breathe, Death, within our lungs / Descends, an invisible river, with muted complaints" [Et, quand nous respirons, la Mort dans nos poumons / Descend, fleuve invisible, avec de sourdes plaintes]). As Jonathan Culler has said, "what is most diabolical about the Devil . . . is that we can never be sure when he is at work."[9]

At the end of the poem, "Ennui," or "Boredom," the ugliest, meanest, and most disgusting of the noisy monsters in the "infamous menagerie of our vices," appears, just like the Devil, as most undetectable at the height of its omnipotence and omnipresence:

But among the jackals, panthers, hound bitches,
Monkeys, scorpions, vultures, snakes,
The yapping, howling, growling, crawling monsters
In the infamous menagerie of our vices,

There is one more ugly, more nasty, more foul than all!
Although he does not make big moves nor give out big cries,
He would willingly reduce the earth to rubble
And swallow the world in a yawn.

It is Boredom!—an involuntary tear welling in his eye,
He dreams of scaffolds smoking his hookah.
You know him, reader, that delicate monster
—Hypocritical reader,—my fellow-man,—my brother!

*(Mais parmi les chacals, les panthères, les lices,
Les singes, les scorpions, les vautours, les serpents,
Les monstres glapissants, hurlants, grognants, rampants,
Dans la ménagerie infâme de nos vices,*

*Il en est un plus laid, plus méchant, plus immonde!
Quoiqu'il ne pousse ni grands gestes ni grands cris,
Il ferait volontiers de la terre un débris
Et dans un bâillement avalerait le monde;*

*C'est l'Ennui!—l'œil chargé d'un pleur involontaire,
Il rêve d'échafauds en fumant son houka.
Tu le connais, lecteur, ce monstre délicat,
—Hypocrite lecteur,—mon semblable,—mon frère!)*

[1: 6]

Chambers has shown that the reader's hypocrisy, which the poem denounces at its closing, stems from loss of will, as vaporization's clouding of the brain and blurring of boundaries bring about the reader's "failure to acknowledge his acquaintance with 'Ennui.'"[10] According to Chambers, the poem, a denunciation of such hypocrisy, points out this unacknowledged knowledge, brings to awareness what has been allowed to remain below the threshold of awareness, and in doing so attempts to shake readers out of debilitating torpor and forcefully make visible the very principle of invisibility: satanic vaporization and the state of "Ennui."

For Baudelaire, "Ennui"—"spleen" manifesting as moral paralysis—weighs heaviest of all. Just as Medusa, who kills with her stare, obliterates our vision and hence our capacity to see her, so "Ennui," in dissipation of will, in complacency and boredom, induces moral numbness that robs us of our ability to perceive it. Medusa, the monster of ancient mythology, returns as "Ennui," the most redoubtable "delicate monster" of modernity. The same weight of fear and denial weighs in modernity as in antiquity. Like his sister monster of antiquity, "Ennui" engulfs the world in numbing "weight," "inertia," and "opacity."[11] It is poetry's task, then and now again, to bring this denial to awareness. Baudelaire's direct address to the reader and his explicit targeting of the reader's hypocrisy compel whoever continues beyond the liminal poem and enters the space of "Spleen et Idéal" to acknowledge denial; face the monster, "spleen"; and become aware of the "weight," "inertia," and "opacity" of the world.

"Spleen," secreting the black bile of melancholia, "is always," in Baudelaire, as Arden Reed has observed, "the world of the weather," rainy and depressive.[12] Three out of four "Spleen" poems begin with rain, both literally and metaphorically. Everything resembles rain and pours down upon us. The first word of the first "Spleen" poem, "pluviôse," designates the fifth month in the Revolutionary calendar, corresponding to the period from mid-January to mid-February; it comes from *pluvieux*, meaning "rainy": "Pluviôse, irritated with the whole city, / From its urn pours down in great flood the cold darkness / Upon the pale inhabitants of the nearby cemetery / And mortality upon the foggy suburbs" (Pluviôse, irrité contre la ville entière, / De son urne à grand flots verse un froid ténébreux / Aux pâles habitants du voisin cimetière / Et la mortalité sur les faubourgs brumeux) [1: 72]. The third poem picks up on *pluvieux*, opening with these words: "I am like the king of a *rainy* country, / Rich but powerless, young and yet very old" (Je suis comme le roi d'un pays *pluvieux*, / Riche mais impuissant, jeune et pourtant très vieux) [1: 74, my emphasis]. And in the last poem, the "horizon" "pours down on us a black day more sad than nights" (Il [horizon] nous verse un jour noir plus triste que les nuits) [1: 74]. It is as if the celestial body itself were infected by melancholy, secreting and emitting fog and rain. Cosmic humor penetrates the body. There is osmosis between celestial and corporeal humors. In "Spleen," the site of both physiological and meteorological secretions, "correspondance" exists between "corporeal mechanism" and "celestial mechanism." Physical organ maps onto moral/mental space and out to the endless expanse of rainy universe. It is a microcosm of a macrocosm. Not just "Idéal" but "Spleen," too, is the site of Baudelairean "Correspondances." The "transports of the spirit and senses" (les transports de l'esprit et des sens) [1: 11] that the sonnet "Correspondances" celebrates occur here, too, as bodily senses, mental and spiritual faculties, and the cosmos all bathe in the same black humor. There is correspondence between "Spleen" and "Idéal."

Walter Benjamin writes that "cosmic forces have only a narcotic effect on empty and fragile man; this is proven by the relations he entertains with one of the highest and most suave manifestations of these forces: the weather. Nothing is more characteristic than that the profoundly intimate and mysterious influence weather exerts on men should have become the theme of their emptiest of conversations. Nothing bores the ordinary man more than the cosmos. Thus, for him, the very intimate link between weather and ennui."[13] Benjamin's "empty and fragile" "ordinary" man bored by the weather is Baudelaire's "hypocritical" reader, who, deeply infected by ennui, fails to acknowledge his state. Ennui is this failure to acknowledge; it is hypocrisy.[14]

The "very intimate link" that "hypocritical" and bored readers establish between "weather and ennui" is of a frivolous kind. But that "frivolity" is, in fact, "dull and heavy."[15] In considering weather a light topic of conversation, these readers deny "cosmic forces" and the profound weight and effects of those forces upon them. They are blind both to their own consequent weighty state and to the penetrating weight of the cosmos. Benjamin justly points out that "cosmic forces have only a narcotic effect" on "empty," "ordinary" persons. Those who find the cosmos boring and weather a soporific subject are like hashish eaters who feel high and light, failing to recognize that they are, in reality, weighed down and trapped by the bonds of addiction. Their frivolity has the heaviness of stupidity and denial. The physiology of hypocrisy and ennui resembles that of hashish: each yields a state in which the intimate link, and awareness of the link, between corporeal and celestial mechanisms have been obliterated and forgotten. Indeed, "Ennui" appears in the poem "Au lecteur," "smoking his hookah" (en fumant son houka). Baudelaire's condemnation of hashish in *Les paradis artificiels* and his denunciation of hypocrisy in *Les fleurs du mal* have the same intent: to resist and fight the narcotic relation of stupidity and numbness we tend to hold with the universe and to sustain lucidity.

Baudelaire presents poetic intimacy against frivolous intimacy, between weather and spleen: a relation of "critical intelligence" against a narcotic one, as Chambers has said. Weather is not a light topic in Baudelaire. It weighs heavy. The poet, intimately tuning into cosmic forces, perceives lucidly the weight of splenetic weather and makes it the mighty poetic subject par excellence. "Pluviôse," the rainy month of spleen, and the first word inaugurating the series of "Spleen" poems, is not only the topic but also the personified corporeal and celestial subject that "pours down in great flood the cold darkness" on us [1: 72]. Baudelaire's weather produces poetic effect against "narcotic effect." His poetry aims at making us see that the weight of refusal and denial, which our hypocritical indulgence has helped to conceal, is the heaviest and most insidious of burdens, more than the weight of life itself. Poetry's task is to make us recognize that denial and its weight separate us from life. It seeks to unburden us of this weight—so that we may bear the *sheer* weight of life.[16]

The "Spleen" poems, in their clear-sighted and even painfully sharp awareness of weight, give proof of poetic consciousness and its weightless lucidity. So it is with Orpheus's gaze: it rises lucid, carefree, and weightless amid the gravest of losses.[17]

The splenetic body of the poet-artist-genius that opens to the cosmic spleen is in a state of sheer corporeal intensity—spleen within a spleen as sun within a sun. It is a receptive and inspired state that relates to weather not as boring but as the "highest and most suave manifestations," to borrow Benjamin's words, of celestial measures.[18] Weight in its "highest and most suave" intensity—this is Baudelaire's Spleen. "How much delicacy and suavity of spirit one must have to be a Baudelaire, poet of Spleen"—Calvino's assessment of Perseus holds true for Baudelaire, too.

Perseus's "delicate courtesy" brings forth "fragile and perishable" beauty within Medusa's horrendous terror. Baudelaire's delicate suavity detects in suffocating air the poetic marvelous. He writes in the last section of *Salon de 1846*, "De l'héroïsme de la vie moderne": "Parisian life is fecund in subjects that are poetic and marvelous. The marvelous envelops us and soaks us like atmosphere; but we do not see it" (La vie parisienne est féconde en sujets poétiques et merveilleux. Le merveilleux nous enveloppe et nous abreuve comme l'atmosphère; mais nous ne le voyons pas) [2: 496]. Saturated air, oozing out black rain, simultaneously "soaks us" with the "marvelous." But as we did not acknowledge "ennui," so "we do not see" what is marvelous. Blocking one blocks the other.

The violence of denial and hypocrisy takes the form of clashing that severs us both from "ennui" and from the "marvelous." But it is violence that hides its own harshness by numbing us and muting the impact of the clash—a "hypocritical" violence. Poetry uncovers hypocrisy so that violence and its weight can be truly perceived and experienced. Poetic relation to the world, in contrast to narcotic relation, is "delicacy and suavity of spirit," in intimate correspondence with both "Spleen" and "Idéal," the horrible and the wondrous, "the savage horror of the Gorgon" and "the fine grace of the coral," Evil and Beauty. Poetry's delicate move from clash to touch allows a new mode of encounter in which each element of these opposing pairs *bears* the other in all senses of the term—to carry, to possess as a part, to give birth to, to bring forth, to sustain the burden of, to endure—in a relation of synergetic intensities, in which we readers, too, take part.

Baudelairean "correspondance" is not only weightless expansion of airy perfumes, sounds, colors; it is also weighty bearing. "Idéal" bears "Spleen," and "Spleen" "Idéal"; the success of correspondence bears failure, and failure success. Poetry puts us in touch with the *awfulness* of life, invites us to see the profoundly "intimate link" between apparently opposing elements and hence to recognize the genitive and generative relation of *Les fleurs du mal*. Flowers blossom out of Evil just as the "fine grace of the coral" did out of the "savage horror of the Gorgon," by passing through again and again into the other.

Air "presses" upon and "suffocates" us, yet this same air "soaks us" (nous abreuve) with the "marvelous." The French *abreuver*, from the Latin *bibere*, "to drink"—the same word that denoted the "porousness" (bibula) of the weed twigs in Ovid—means to supply amply with drink. Baudelaire writes, in *Salon de 1845*, that "the heroism *of modern life* surrounds us and presses us.—Our true senses suffocate us enough to let us know" (l'héroïsme *de la vie moderne* nous entoure et nous presse.—Nos sentiments vrais nous étouffent assez pour que nous les connaissions) [2: 407, original emphasis]. Heroism is in the air. Baudelaire's "hero of modern life" is he who delicately perceives the imperceptible pressure that air exerts (which "we do not see") and receives from it both salutary liquid and suffocating weight, drinking and constricting at the contact with air, just like Ovid's fresh weed twigs "drinking in" Medusa's power and hardening into coral at the touch of air. Perseus's heroism is the model for ancient and for modern life. Ovid's antiquity proposes universal contiguity; Baudelaire's modernity proposes cosmic correspondence.[19] A poetic relation to the world—this means contingencies that touch and soak.

The thick and heavy air of Baudelaire's first section, "Spleen et Idéal," seeps through the second, "Tableaux parisiens." We are now in the streets of Paris, "invariably overpopulated" in Baudelaire, as Benjamin writes in his essay "On Some Motifs in Baudelaire."[20] The poet enters the crowd of the streets as if entering "an immense reservoir of electricity" (un immense réservoir d'électricité) [*Le peintre de la vie moderne* 2: 692]: "Crowd is his domain, just as air is that of birds, and water, of fish" (La foule est son domaine, comme l'air est celui de l'oiseau, comme l'eau celui du poisson) [*Le peintre de la vie moderne* 2: 691].[21] Crowd is the poet's milieu. The cosmic atmosphere descends, condenses, and morphs into an "amorphous crowd of passersby."[22] The crowd continues to strike the poet with lightning jolts, drenching him with water yet providing air. In the prose poem "Les foules" ("Crowds"), the poet "takes a bath of multitude," "takes pleasure in the crowd," "at the expense of the human race binges on vitality," "draws a singular excitement/intoxication from this universal communion" (prend[re] un bain de multitude; jouir de la foule; faire, au dépens du genre humain, une ribote de vitalité; tire[r] une singulière ivresse de cette universelle communion) [1: 291]. Benjamin sees a "close connection in Baudelaire between the figure of shock and contact with the metropolitan masses": "This crowd, of whose existence Baudelaire is always aware, has not served as the model for any of his works, but it is imprinted on his creativity as a hidden figure. . . . We may discern the image of the fencer in it; the blows he deals are designed to open a path through the crowd for him" [165].[23] For Baudelaire, Benjamin writes, "the mass was the agitated veil; through it Baudelaire saw Paris" [168].

The mass is like fog and rain—the heavy and yet marvelous atmosphere through which Baudelaire experiences Paris, an invisible saturating air, a hidden object against which the poet, encountering it, stiffens and against which he fences.[24] Just as Medusa, concealed in a bag, accompanies Perseus, so, too, the mass accompanies Baudelaire. The modern poet bears a weight similar to that of the ancient hero, if in modern form—"mass" as weight morphing into crowd.

"Tableaux parisiens" unfolds against a thick and dense crowd that is never explicitly described. "In the sonnet 'A une passante,'" Benjamin writes, "the crowd is nowhere named in either word or phrase. And yet the whole happening hinges on it, just as the progress of a sailboat depends on the wind" [168]:

> The deafening street was howling all around me.
> Tall, slender, in deep mourning, majestic grief,
> A woman passed by, with fastidious hand
> Raising and swinging festoon and hem;
>
> Agile and noble, with a leg like that of a statue.
> And I drank, contorted like a madman,

From her eye, livid sky where hurricane germinates,
Softness that fascinates and pleasure that kills.

A flash . . . then night!—Fugitive beauty
Whose glance suddenly made me reborn,
Shall I not see you again till eternity?

Elsewhere, very far from here! too late! *never* perhaps!
For I do not know where you flee, you do not know where I go,
O you whom I would have loved, o you who knew it!

(La rue assourdissante autour de moi hurlait.
Longue, mince, en grand deuil, douleur majestueuse,
Une femme passa, d'une main fastueuse
Soulevant, balançant le feston et l'ourlet;

Agile et noble, avec sa jambe de statue.
Moi, je buvais, crispé comme un extravagant,
Dans son œil, ciel livid où germe l'ouragan,
La douceur qui fascine et le plaisir qui tue.

Un éclair . . . puis la nuit!—Fugitive beauté
Dont le regard m'a fait soudainement renaître,
Ne te verrai-je plus que dans l'éternité?

Ailleurs, bien loin d'ici! trop tard! jamais peut-être!
Car j'ignore où tu fuis, tu ne sais où je vais,
Ô toi que j'eusse aimée, ô toi qui le savais!)

[1: 92–93, original emphasis]

From the amorphous crowd of the "howling" street, a form emerges in the vision field of the speaker of the poem. A woman passes by—in "mourning," hence carrying death, elegant in allure, fluid in movement, and yet also like a "statue," a "Fugitive beauty" with a "hurricane" in her eye. The speaker of the poem contracts and "drinks" from her both life (he is "reborn") and death ("pleasure that kills").²⁵ The figure, simultaneously, of death and rebirth, beauty and terror, mobility and stiffness, is Ovid's Medusa, emerging in her "clarissima forma" [Ovid 4.794], "fragile and perishable,"²⁶ in an awesome beauty that both fascinates and kills. Quoting Benjamin, with a slight modification, "the delight of the urban poet," in this fleeting encounter, is love "at last sight" *and* "at first sight."²⁷

Beautiful Medusa in her original form, yet also horrendous Medusa embodying the power of fascination and death, returns dressed in modern fashion, as the figure of the "modern beautiful" that Baudelaire defines in *Le peintre de la vie moderne:*

> The beautiful is made of an eternal and invariable element whose quantity is excessively difficult to determine and of a relative and circumstantial element, which are, if you will, one after another or all together, epoch, fashion, moral, passion. Without this second element, which is like an amusing, titillating, and appetizing envelope of the divine cake, the first element would be indigestible, unappreciable, not adapted to and not appropriated by human nature.

> *(Le beau est fait d'un élément éternel, invariable, dont la quantité est excessivement difficile à déterminer, et d'un élément relatif, circonstanciel, qui sera, si l'on veut, tour à tour ou tout ensemble, l'époque, la mode, la morale, la passion. Sans ce second élément, qui est comme l'enveloppe amusante, titillante, apéritive du divin gâteau, le premier élément serait indigestible, inappréciable, non adapté et non approprié à la nature humaine.)* [2: 685]

Ancient and immutable Medusa appears enveloped in the latest Parisian fashion, but Medusa of Antiquity already is double, perishable flesh encased in stony immobility. Soft and perishable core/hard and immovable envelope —"eternal and invariable" core/"relative and circumstantial" envelope. Modern beautiful is ancient monster turned inside out, or rather, the modern envelope reveals the originary softness and transitoriness within the antique immutable core. The enveloping both layers and lifts the layer. To highlight surface and present is to touch the core and the past. Medusa appears in her "memory of the present" (la mémoire du présent) [2: 696] in the streets of Paris.

Chambers sees the woman as "a figure of death, albeit of death in its most beautiful aspect." The woman, the figure of "rhythmic grace," "statuesque nobility," and "order," carries within herself the source of disorder: in her eye, "hurricane germinates." To "read correctly the meaning of beauty," Chambers writes, "is to receive the fulgurant shock of the chaos against which it works but of which it is also the vehicle." If the hurricane "represents death and disorder in the world, it is perhaps, in a cosmic sense, a source of life that 'I' has been granted the privilege of briefly, but directly, glimpsing. Disorder, in this latter case, would then be not an accidental and secondary manifestation but something primary and essential, and the manifestations of order we perceive as beauty . . . but passing phenomena against this eternal background."[28] Chaos and death hitting us with a force that is life-giving—that is beauty. "Hurricane," in the eye of the woman, is cosmic order in its "highest and most suave manifestations." Poetic relation is to receive the full impact of a "fulgurant shock," like a flash of lightning, that throws off balance human measure and control and opens human order to cosmic order—as in the myths of Icarus and Orpheus.

"A une passante" ("To a Woman Passing By") shows poetic encounter with cosmic forces and death, in direct opposition to narcotic encounter in the poem "Au lecteur." "Hypocritical" readers bored with weather and life breathe in death, but without sign of reception or recognition: "And when we breathe, Death, within our lungs / Descends, an invisible river, with muted complaints (Et, quand nous respirons, la Mort dans nos poumons/ Descend, fleuve invisible, avec de sourdes plaintes) [1: 5]. Death enters unnoticed— "invisible" and "muted"—into our complacent, self-indulgent, flaccid bodies, which remain numb, in contrast to the "delicate" body of the poet, which contracts and drinks in death.

"Fugitive beauty" in "A une passante" accentuates the brevity of the encounter, the convergence and concentration into an instant of all the dimensions of time: antiquity and modernity, first sight and last sight, transitoriness and eternity.[29] It is almost like a chemical precipitation, occurring when all the substances that are present react with each other, coalescing into a new solid entity. In the streets of Paris, air, heavy with the marvelous and the mass, precipitates under atmospheric pressure into a beautiful woman who emerges suddenly, crossing the path of the "I." The "I" precipitates, in turn, as if in a chain reaction—he receives the shock of encounter and *falls* in love. It is love as concentration into one single point of the vast expanse of time and space, the vector of extreme intensity that befalls and traverses us. And it is also love as receptivity, where no clash of denial or refusal deflects or mutes the force that comes to touch, befall, and stun us.

Of this lightning strike/stroke of love, Benjamin uses the word "catastrophe" [169]. *Catastrophe*, from the Greek *kata* (down) and *strephein* (to turn), literally a turning down, an overturning, means the conclusion, especially in drama, of a tragedy, hence a great misfortune, a ruin. *Strephein* yields *strophe*, a stanza of a poem, but it is a turning, too, in the sense of *strobos*, spinning, whirling. A woman, shock of beauty, storm in the eye, cosmic order befalling human order, upsetting and opening it to whirling chaos of celestial measure, shaking and touching us to our deepest core—contingency hitting us full force as contiguity—love, "un frisson nouveau" (a new shiver)—this is poetry.[30]

Orpheus's turning back to see Eurydice opens to the whirling disorder of entropy, which is transformed into order of cosmic measure. In the mythic love between Orpheus and Eurydice, and in the modern love between the "I" and the woman passing in the street, two humans come together, but the intensity of their binding breaks the ties of human measure into the gift of freedom. Poetry, whirling, turns things around in ways that are absolute. It generates catastrophe, but catastrophe in its "highest and most suave manifestations"—the marvelous, the miraculous, the wondrous—the "factum mirabile" that the sea nymphs in Ovid "scatter and propagate throughout their waters," the gift that Orpheus lets go of in the deep open space of the starry immensity, and the rise and fall of Icarus between the waters and the sky.

CHAPTER FOUR

Beyond Hell and Paradise

The Poet and the Critic

ITALO CALVINO SEES THE MYTH of Perseus, the hero of lightness, as an "allegory of the poet's relationship to the world, a lesson in the method one should follow when writing."[1] Perseus's "lesson" holds not only for poets but also for readers and critics of poetry. For poetry, as acute perception, as "delicacy of spirit," and "gesture of refreshing courtesy,"[2] demands of its readers and critics equal refinement and precision of perception through the practice of purification, concentration, and intensification of language. John Dewey sees as fundamental in art a responsibility to avoid establishing criticism as "something 'judicial,'" a responsibility particularly urgent in poetic criticism. Judicial criticism "obstruct[s]" and "cut[s] short" perception by "an influential rule" and by "the substitution of precedent and prestige for direct experience."[3] It leads to an "inability to cope with the emergence of new modes of life—of experiences that demand new modes of expression."[4] Gilles Deleuze, in effect, concurs: "Judgment prevents the emergence of any new mode of existence." Deleuze asks, "What expert judgment, in art, could ever bear on the work to come?"[5]

Baudelaire's trial of 1857 brought into sharp focus the difficult and intricate relationship among criticism, perception, and judgment. Baudelaire's *Les fleurs du mal* was published at the end of June 1857, about two months before he went on trial for "outrage to public morality."[6] He was convicted, fined, and ordered to excise six poems from his book. It would take ninety-two years before the book could be legally published as he wrote it.[7]

Les fleurs du mal's first public review appeared soon after publication, in the July 5 issue of the newspaper *Le figaro*:

> Never has such brilliant quality been so insanely spoiled. There are moments when one has doubts about Mr. Baudelaire's mental state; there are others when one no longer does: most of the time, it is a monotonous and premeditated repetition of the same words, the same ideas. The hateful is alongside the base; the repulsive mingles with the foul. Never have so many breasts been bitten and even chewed in so few pages; never have we attended to such a survey of demons, fetuses, devils, chloroses, cats, and vermin. This book is a hospital open to all the dementia of the mind, to all the putridities of the heart; if only it were to cure them, but they are incurable. We might understand that at age twenty, the imagination of a poet could let itself be carried away to treat such subjects, but nothing can justify a man past thirty having given the publicity of a book to such monstrosities.[8]

This short review written by Gustave Bourdin, the son-in-law of *Le figaro*'s director, was enough to draw the attention of the French government's Board of Public Safety (La Direction générale de la sûreté publique).[9] Two days later, the board issued a report that filed charges against the book on grounds of obscenity and religious immorality: "The book of Mr. Charles Baudelaire entitled *Les fleurs du mal* challenges the laws that protect religion and morality," the report began. Numerous poems were labeled blasphemous, among them "Le reniement de saint Pierre" ("Saint Peter's Denial"), "Abel et Caïn," "Les litanies de Satan," and "Le vin de l'assassin" ("The Murderer's Wine"). They "reduce to nothing" "the immortality of the soul and the most valued beliefs of Christianity," said the severe board. Others, such as "Femmes damnées," "Les métamorphoses du vampire," and "Les bijoux" ("The Jewels"), were stigmatized as "the expression of the most revolting lubricity," "present[ing] at each moment the most licentious images with all brutality of expression." "In short," the board concluded, "the book of Mr. Baudelaire is one of those pernicious and profoundly immoral publications that are destined for a success caused by scandal. Recommendation to hand it over to the court."[10]

On July 17 the general prosecutor agreed, and on August 20, 1857, *Les fleurs du mal* was attacked at a public trial with Baudelaire and his publisher and printer, Auguste Poulet-Malassis and Eugène de Broise, as defendants. The inquisition occurred before the Sixth Chamber of the Correctional Tribunal of the Seine (La sixième Chambre correctionnelle du Tribunal de la Seine). The poet, the publisher, and the printer were all found guilty of "outrage to public morality and to good morals" in printing and circulating a work that contained "obscene and immoral passages or expressions." The charge of religious immorality was dropped as having insufficient grounds. The prosecutor himself did not insist on the religious charge, detecting in Baudelaire's verses profound marks of Christian faith, but he did press hard for the obscenity charge. The "error of the poet," the verdict read, "in the aim he pursued and the way he followed," was that "no amount of stylistic effort he might have made, no amount of blame that precedes or follows his depictions, would undo the baneful effects of the tableaux he presents to the reader, and which, in the incriminated pieces, lead necessarily to excitation of the senses through a crude realism that is offensive to the public sense of decency" [1: 1181–82].[11] Six poems out of the one hundred original *Les fleurs du mal* were ordered to be excised from the volume, and Baudelaire and his publisher/printer were fined three hundred and one hundred francs respectively.[12]

Dominick LaCapra tells us that, during the Second Empire, "those accused no longer had the right to a jury trial but went before a magistrate presiding over a *tribunal correctionnel,* where common criminals such as pimps and prostitutes were the customary delinquents." Writers indicted for obscenity were judged as having committed "ordinary deviance or crime."[13]

Each trial followed a highly stylized ritual: "no direct questioning of witnesses or cross-examination," only a speech for the prosecution, a speech for the defense, and then the judgment of the court.[14] Claude Pichois' editorial notes report that the speeches for the prosecution and defense in Baudelaire's trial were first published in 1885 in the *Revue des grands procès contemporains* (Journal of Great Contemporary Trials), but with no indication of sources and hence no guarantee of authenticity. The law at the time prohibited written accounts of trials, and Baudelaire himself did not collect or set down notes, nor did the newspapers.[15]

Almost ninety years later, on September 25, 1946, a new law granted members of the Society of Men of Letters the right of appeal, after twenty years had elapsed, to lift a ban from a book previously condemned for outrage to public morality. Thus, on May 31, 1949, after ninety-two years, the 1857 condemnation of *Les fleurs du mal* was annulled by the Criminal Chamber of the Supreme Court of Appeal (La chambre criminelle de la Cour de cassation). Articulating three criteria that must be met for a book to constitute an outrage to public morality—the "fact of publication," the "book's obscenity," and the "intent of the author"—the new judgment asserted that the latter two lacked sufficient grounds. The "fact of publication" of Baudelaire's poems was undeniable, but the condemned poems "[did] not have any obscene terms or even crude ones, and [did] not cross the limit of freedom accorded to artists in their expressive form." The new judgment criticized the old one for having dwelled exclusively at the level of "realist interpretation" while neglecting "symbolic meaning," hence revealing judgment as "arbitrary." The 1857 judgment "[had] been ratified neither by public opinion nor by scholarly assessment." As for the author's intent, the court of appeal said that it "recognize[d] the poet's effort to attenuate the effect of his descriptions" and noted that the condemned poems, "containing no obscene expression, as [had] been advanced," were "manifestly of honest inspiration."[16]

In January 1857, seven months before Baudelaire's trial, Flaubert had been tried for his novel *Madame Bovary* by the same prosecutor, Ernest Pinard, who put Baudelaire in the courtroom, but Flaubert was acquitted. Yet charges brought against the poet and the novelist were similar. Both concerned primarily the "realism" of the works, which painted with "lascivious" colors morally "degrading" and "despicable" conduct and situations.[17] Pinard claimed that in *Madame Bovary*, "all the wonders" of Flaubert's "style" were employed to advance the "glorification of adultery" and the "undermining of marriage."[18] Pointing to the absence of a "stable, secure, or reliable" vantage point "within the novel from which to condemn Emma"—the result of Flaubert's famous free, indirect style of narration—Pinard asserted that readers, unable to rely on an authoritative moral guide and hence vulnerable and without anchor, would inevitably fall prey to the temptations and vices to which Emma Bovary herself had readily succumbed.[19] As for Baudelaire's *Les fleurs du mal*, its excess and explicitness would shock a sense of propriety. "[Baudelaire's] principle, his theory," Pinard claimed, "is to paint everything, to strip everything bare. He digs into the innermost recesses of human nature," "exaggerat[ing] especially its hideous aspects," "magnify[ing] it out of bounds" to "create impressions, sensations" [1: 1206].

It happened that Baudelaire had read Flaubert's *Madame Bovary* and followed its trial. He sent to Flaubert a copy of *Les fleurs du mal* soon after its publication. The poet and the novelist each became interested and sympathetic toward the other and toward the other's work and its public prosecution.[20] Baudelaire had begun an article on Flaubert, but his own trial kept him from finishing it on time: "And the article on *Madame Bovary* delayed again for several days!" (Et l'article sur *Madame Bovary* reculé encore de quelques jours!) Baudelaire wrote to Flaubert on August, 25, 1857, five days after his own trial, to inform his friend of the negative outcome and to thank him for his sympathy [*Corr* 1: 424]. Baudelaire's article "M. Gustave Flaubert. *Madame Bovary.—La tentation de saint Antoine*," finally completed, appeared in the October 17, 1857, issue of the journal *L'artiste*. It said in part:

> Several critics have said: this work [*Madame Bovary*], truly beautiful for the meticulousness and vivacity of its descriptions, contains not a single character who represents morality, who speaks for the consciousness of the author. Where is the proverbial and legendary character en-

trusted to explain the fable and direct the intelligence of the reader? In other words, where is the indictment?

Absurdity! Eternal and incorrigible confusion of functions and genres!—A true work of art needs no indictment. Its logic satisfies all postulations of morality, and it is up to the reader to draw conclusions about its conclusion.

(Plusieurs critiques avaient dit: cette œuvre, vraiment belle par la minutie et la vivacité des descriptions, ne contient pas un seul personnage qui représente la morale, qui parle la conscience de l'auteur. Où est-il, le personnage proverbial et légendaire, chargé d'expliquer la fable et de diriger l'intelligence du lecteur? En d'autres termes, où est le réquisitoire?

Absurdité! Eternelle et incorrigible confusion des fonctions et des genres!—Une véritable œuvre d'art n'a pas besoin de réquisitoire. La logique de l'œuvre suffit à toutes les postulations de la morale, et c'est au lecteur à tirer les conclusions de la conclusion.) [2: 81–82][21]

Baudelaire's essay on *Madame Bovary*, written after both trials were concluded, reveals Baudelaire's stance on morality in arts and literature: "You know that I have always considered arts and literature only as pursuing a goal foreign to morality, and that, for me, the beauty of conception and of style suffices" (Vous savez que je n'ai jamais considéré la littérature et les arts que comme poursuivant un but étranger à la morale, et que la beauté de conception et de style me suffit) [*Corr* 1: 410]. So Baudelaire wrote to his mother on July 9, 1857, just after the publication of *Les fleurs du mal* and in the midst of the ensuing accusations of its immorality, which were increasingly pointed to the possibility of juridical sanction. Several works of Baudelaire had set poetry, literature, and the arts as distanced from morality. Before his trial, and as early as November 1851, Baudelaire, in an article in *Semaine théâtrale*, "Les drames et les romans honnêtes" ("Of Virtuous Plays and Novels") [2: 38–43], had denounced the contemporary trend of moralization in literature, "preached" with the "fervor/fever of missionaries" (une fièvre de missonnaires) that turns art into mere "propaganda" [2: 41]. In his pieces on Poe, especially in the "Notes nouvelles sur Edgar Poe" ("Further Notes on Edgar Poe") of January 1857, appearing just five months before *Les fleurs du mal*'s publication, Baudelaire ranged poetry directly against morality: "I say that if the poet has pursued a moral goal he has diminished his poetic power; and it is not imprudent to bet that his work will be bad. Poetry cannot, on pain of death or extinction, become assimilated to science or the moral; nor is truth its object, it has only Itself" (Je dis que si le poète a poursuivi un but moral, il a diminué sa force poétique; et il n'est pas imprudent de parier que son œuvre sera mauvaise. La poésie ne peut pas, sous peine de mort ou de défaillance, s'assimiler à la science ou à la morale; elle n'a pas la vérité pour objet, elle n'a qu'Elle-même) [2: 333].[22]

For both Flaubert and Baudelaire, the trials of their works were incomprehensible. In a letter written before the trial, Flaubert asked: "Why? There begins the mystery.... It's all so stupid that I have come to enjoy it greatly."[23] And Baudelaire wrote in the introductory note to the dossier he prepared for his defense: "No one, no more than I, could have imagined that a book imprinted with such ardent and glaring/dazzling spirituality as *les fleurs du mal* was to become the object of prosecution, or rather, the occasion of misunderstanding" (Personne, non plus que moi, ne pouvait supposer qu'un livre empreint d'une spiritualité aussi ardente, aussi éclatante que les *Fleurs du mal*, dût être l'objet d'une poursuite, ou plutôt l'occasion d'un malentendu) [1: 193].[24] Baudelaire was truly surprised at his indictment. Pichois tells us that, just before the hearing, Baudelaire met with prosecutor Pinard and "expressed with complete sincerity his stupefaction, explaining candidly his theory of art" [1: 1182]. After the trial and outside the courtroom, when his friend Asselineau asked if he thought he would have been acquitted, Baudelaire responded: "Acquitted!—I expected that I would receive a full apology!" (Aquitté!—j'attendais qu'on me ferait réparation d'honneur!) [1: 1182].

The judgment of 1949 seems to agree with Baudelaire's own assessment almost a century earlier. It calls the 1857 judgment a "misreading" based on a "misunderstanding." That early judgment had been too nearsighted, attaching itself exclusively to the "realist interpretation" while blinded to the "symbolic meaning," hence incomplete and "arbitrary." Yet the "new" reasoning that dismissed the "old" "realist interpretation" was itself "literal" and much like the judgment it overturned. It reasoned that the condemned poems contain no obscene or crude words and therefore that the poems are not obscene nor crude. As LaCapra has pointed out, pragmatic reasons—the embarrassment caused by the fact that six poems by one of France's most celebrated authors were still banned—motivated the overturning of the former condemnation more than any change in the judiciary system's claimed capacity to "read" and "understand" the poems "correctly."[25]

It was an occasion not only of "misunderstanding" but also of "hypocrisy." In notes to his attorney at the trial, Baudelaire pointed to the rhetoric of censorship of the pervading "prudish morals" of his time. It would, he said, "go so far as to say: FROM NOW ON ONE WILL ONLY MAKE BOOKS THAT CONSOLE AND SERVE TO PROVE THAT MAN IS BORN GOOD, AND THAT ALL MEN ARE HAPPY,—abominable hypocrisy!" (Cette morale-là irait jusqu'à dire: DESORMAIS ON NE FERA QUE DES LIVRES CONSOLANTS ET SERVANT A DEMONTRER QUE L'HOMME EST NEW BON, ET QUE TOUS LES HOMMES SONT HEUREUX,—abominable hypocrisie!) [1: 196]. Hypocritical readers who misunderstand were Baudelaire's readers, "the least rewarding type of audience," as Walter Benjamin noted.

Baudelaire himself had anticipated all this. "Baudelaire envisaged"—by inference in his introductory poem—"readers to whom the reading of lyric poetry would present difficulties." Thus begins Benjamin's seminal essay "On Some Motifs in Baudelaire":

> The introductory poem of the *Fleurs du mal* is addressed to these readers. Will power and the ability to concentrate are not their strong points; what they prefer is sensual pleasures; they are familiar with the "spleen" which kills interest and receptiveness. It is strange to come across a lyric poet who addresses himself to this, the least rewarding type of audience. There is of course a ready explanation for it. Baudelaire was anxious to be understood; he dedicated his book to kindred spirits. The poem addressed to the reader ends with the salutation: "*Hypocrite lecteur,—mon semblable,—mon frère!*" It might be more fruitful to put it another way and say: Baudelaire wrote a book which from the very beginning had little prospect of becoming an immediate popular success.

The kind of reader he envisaged is described in the introductory poem, and this turned out to have been a far-sighted judgment. He was eventually to find the reader at whom his work was aimed.[26]

In Baudelaire, the act and consequence of reading seem to hinge deeply upon hypocrisy—of both the readers and the poet (Baudelaire does not dissociate himself from hypocritical readers but calls them "mon semblable, mon frère"): upon the degree of one's awareness of one's own and of others' hypocrisy, the call to acknowledge it, and the willingness and capacity to make this call and respond to it. Understanding/misunderstanding, interpretation/misinterpretation, reading/misreading pivot around hypocrisy.

"The judge is not a literary critic," Pinard says early in his prosecution speech against Baudelaire, "called upon to express his opinion on opposing modes of appreciating art and of rendering it." Rather, he is someone who has been granted the "discretionary authority to discern if morality has been offended, if the limit has been transgressed. The judge is a sentry who must not let the border be crossed. That is his mission" [1: 1206]. Strategically unhinging the issue of the public reception of a work of literature from the domain of literary criticism, Pinard shifts terrains and sets the trial on military grounds. The trial henceforth becomes a military operation, a "mission" fueled with the "fervor/fever of missionaries," as Baudelaire notes in "Les drames et les romans honnêtes."

On the battlefield of offense and defense, the prosecutor is a "sentry" —a soldier posted to guard against, and warn of, danger—patrolling the borders to protect the people. The term *sentry*, from the Latin *sentire*, "to feel, sense," makes the "mission" into one of "sensing," of serving as a "sense detector," like a lie detector that goes off when "the limit has been transgressed." And it is indeed of "sensory overload" that Pinard accuses Baudelaire. Baudelaire's poems "exaggerate" and "magnify" "out of bounds" to "create impressions, sensations," as if "waging to provide senses to those who no longer feel." Combining excerpts of poems and his own paraphrasing, Pinard argues that Baudelaire's poetry pushes far beyond the limits of decency and privacy and, if not condemned, will become a "permanent danger," whose obscenity will "corrupt those who don't yet know anything of life"; it will "excite ill-minded curiosities" and serve as "spice to dulled senses." The poet's undue sensationalism that sets off the "sensitive" alarm system will necessarily and forcefully, so goes Pinard's logic, impinge upon the reader's mind and body, which, defenseless, will become forever marked by "pernicious impression[s]" [1: 1206–09].

The military metaphor soon becomes medical. What is "sensed," feared, and hence in need of containment, is the spread of an infectious disease, threatening the health of the general public: "Do we think it good to breathe in the vertiginous fragrance of certain flowers? The poison they bear does not keep us away; it goes to the head, intoxicates the nerves, and causes agitation and dizziness, and it can kill, as well" [1: 1207]. "Those many readers, of all rank, of all age, of all conditions, will they take the antidote you speak of with so much complacency?" [1: 1208]. Pinard's speech joins the longstanding tradition in France of fearing "dangerous" and "bad" writers who "demoralize" the people as "public poisoner[s]" (empoisonneur public). To read *Les fleurs du mal* is to inhale literally the poisonous fragrance of evil flowers. Prosecutor, soldier, and doctor merge in their common role and goal, monitoring the infiltration and circulation of dangerous substances and infections that might corrupt the health of the people, ready to eradicate them when necessary.

Above all, Pinard speaks from the side of, and with the voice of, reason that has been threatened by the insurgent senses. This is reason as "sentry" —which means that reason's "mission" consists in controlling and keeping the senses within "proper" boundaries:

> Even in your learned readers, in mature men, do you believe there are cold reckoners who weigh the pros and cons, put counterweight next to weight, are level-headed and in possession of soundly balanced imagination and senses! Man won't admit it, he is too proud for that. But the truth is that man is always more or less crippled, more or less feeble, more or less sick, carrying all the more the weight of his Fall, however much he may doubt or deny it. If such is his innate nature, unless it is

set upright anew by virile efforts and strong discipline, who knows how easily he will acquire the taste of lascivious frivolity. [1: 1208]

In his speech indicting Flaubert, Pinard constructed his argument on a strict binary opposition between reason and the senses:

> Who reads the novel of Mr. Flaubert? Is it men who deal with political and social economy? No! The light pages of *Madame Bovary* fall into hands that are even lighter, the hands of young women, sometimes of married women. Well! Once the heart has been seduced, once this seduction has reached down to the heart, once the heart has spoken to the senses, do you think cold reasoning will be strong enough to counter this seduction of senses and of emotion? A man must not drape himself too much in his power and virtue; man carries instincts from below and ideas from above, and in all men virtue is the consequence of effort alone, laborious more often than not. Lascivious depictions generally have more influence than cold reasonings do.[27]

The founding antithesis between reason and the senses generates a cascade of oppositions between head-cold-discipline-effort-health-antidote-virtue-gravity-high-good, on the one hand, and heart-hot-indulgence-seduction-infection-poison-pleasure-frivolity-low-evil, on the other. "Les bijoux," the first poem of Baudelaire that Pinard quotes in his speech to make his case, portrays such "disturbance" of reason/mind by the arousal of senses:

> And her arm and her leg, and her thigh and her hips,
> Sleek as oil, undulating like a swan,
> Passed before my eyes, clear-sighted and serene;
> And her belly and her breasts, those clusters of my vine,
>
> Moved forward, more caressing than the Angels of evil,
> To trouble the tranquility in which my soul was resting,
> And disturb it from the crystal rock
> Where, calm and solitary, it had settled itself.

I thought I was seeing united by a new design
The haunches of Antiope to the torso of a beardless boy,
So strongly did her waist set off her pelvis.
On that wild, brown complexion the make-up was superb!

(*Et son bras et sa jambe, et sa cuisse et ses reins,*
Polis comme de l'huile, onduleux comme un cygne,
Passaient devant mes yeux clairvoyants et sereins;
Et son ventre et ses seins, ces grappes de ma vigne,

S'avançaient, plus câlins que les Anges du mal,
Pour troubler le repos où mon âme était mise,
Et pour la déranger du rocher de crystal
Où calme et solitaire, elle s'était assise.

Je croyais voir unis par un nouveau dessin
Les hanches de l'Antiope au buste d'un imberbe,
Tant sa taille faisait ressortir son bassin.
Sur ce teint fauve et brun le fard était superbe!)

[1: 158]

More seductive than "the Angels of evil," the woman's body, the "poisonous" "flower of evil," dislodges the speaker's soul from the "crystal rock" seat of reason and perturbs his "clear-sighted and serene," his "tranquil" vision and mind. What happens to the speaker of the poem is what Pinard fears will happen to its readers. Both the poem and Pinard's speech are about the "influence" of the senses on reason—what happens, what goes on, what is. The poet and the prosecutor have two divergent ways of facing *what is*. Baudelaire's way is to *observe and say* what is. Pinard's way is *not* to see or say, because what is, in fact, *ought not* to be. It ought not to be, but it *is*—"man won't admit it, he is too proud for that. But the truth is that man is always more or less crippled, . . . feeble, . . . sick, carrying all the more the weight of his Fall, however much he may doubt or deny it"; "a man must not drape himself too much in his power and virtue; man carries instincts from below and ideas from above." Yet we do not want to see what is and the discrepancy and antagonism between "what is" and "what we think should be," and so we deny and refuse to see any of this in whatever way we can.

Pinard's discourse is the moralistic discourse par excellence, a voice speaking from a position of division where one side (the idea of what should and should not be) conflicts with and takes as its "mission" the suppression of the other (the fact of what is), eliminating all occasions that might bring out, and hence force us to admit, our own duplicitous way of being, which must, at all costs, be kept below the threshold of awareness. As the "sentry" guarding the border between awareness and denial, as the mechanism that protects and perpetuates its own duplicitous functioning, morality is necessarily both censorship and hypocrisy. Morality, a violent suppression that mutes itself so as not to disturb or exceed the limit, avoiding triggering the alarm of consciousness, is twin to "Ennui"—boredom—the monster that engulfs the world in "weight," "opacity," "inertia"[28] without making itself, and the state it induces, known. To be moralistic is to deny what is and hence to hold a narcotic relation to the world: "Ennui," in the poem "Au lecteur," is "smoking his hookah" (fumant son houka) [1: 6]. To see lucidly what is—that is poetic relation to the world. "Each man who does not accept the conditions of life, sells his soul" (tout homme qui n'accepte pas les conditions de la vie, vend son âme) [1: 438], Baudelaire writes in "Le poème du hachisch." Morality, as embodied by Pinard and the political and social regime of the Second Empire, turns out to be moral numbness—a state of infection by ennui—and thus itself hypocritical and immoral. It is itself the *mal*, both physical and moral.

In preparation for the trial, Baudelaire wrote to his attorney, "*my only fault was to have counted on universal intelligence and not to have written a preface in which I establish my literary principles and bring forth the question, so important, of Morality*" (*mon unique tort a été de compter sur l'intelligence universelle, et ne pas faire une préface où j'aurais posé mes principes littéraires et dégagé la question si importante de la Morale*) [1: 194, original emphasis]. As if to make up for this initial "fault," Baudelaire wrote several drafts of a preface (which he never published) for the second edition of *Les fleurs du mal*, which he was assembling in the aftermath of the trial, the first edition having been sold out in about a year and out of print by August 1858.[29]

On the manuscript page of one of these "plans for prefaces" appears a short "canvas of dedication" used for *Les paradis artificiels*,[30] on which Baudelaire was also working during this period.[31] Reflections on the moral, prompted by the obscenity trial of *Les fleurs du mal*, on the one hand, and the completion of *Les paradis artificiels*, on the other, coincided in the writing and *on the page*.[32] *Les paradis artificiels*, with the "moral" content of its first part, "Le poème du hachisch," seems to have come as a direct response to the trial and hence as a kind of "postface" to the first and "preface" to the second edition of *Les fleurs du mal*.

LaCapra, in his study of Flaubert's trial for *Madame Bovary*, writes that "a trial is a locus of social reading that brings out conventions of interpretation in a key institution—the judicial system—and the way a text is read at a trial has decisive significance for the 'literary' and 'ordinary' life of the writer." LaCapra's analysis follows a double movement: to see how the trial judged *Madame Bovary* but also to "elucidate how the novel confronted the trial," for "while the trial was 'reading' the novel in one way, the novel may be argued to have read the trial in a rather different way."[33]

"Le poème du hachisch" shows the "decisive significance" and repercussions of the trial for Baudelaire's "literary" and "ordinary" life. And if Flaubert's novel "read" its trial, so, too, did Baudelaire's poetry read its own. Baudelaire took the case to the "higher" court—of poetry—where the poet, now the judge, hears and delivers the final sentence against immorality from the side of poetry.[34] "Le poème du hachisch" comes as "poetry's appeal,"[35] where the poet-philosopher–Apollo figure, in the final section, "Morale," pronounces a severe judgment on the immorality of hashish and addiction.[36]

Baudelaire turns the tables. Now, poetry accuses hashish of the very thing it was itself accused of in the trial. Pinard's description of the effect and danger of reading Baudelaire's verse—"Do we think it good to breathe in the vertiginous fragrance of certain flowers? The poison they bear does not keep us away; it goes to the head, intoxicates the nerves, and causes agitation and dizziness, and it can kill, as well"—sounds close to the poet's account of the effect of ingesting the "green jam": hashish, a kind of "vertiginous spirit," "ascends maliciously" to the brain, creating "whirlwinds" and "a great languor" that "spreads through [the] faculties" "like fog," weakening the limbs, taking away willpower, making us incapable of action and work that require energy and concentration [1: 388, 426]. Hashish, several times called "poison," is "suicide." The poet-judge condemns hashish as evil—it is referred to as "a perfect satanic instrument" [1: 434] of "the Spirit of Evil" [1: 403]—and pronounces it guilty of immorality in tempting us into dissipation of the senses.

It is as if Baudelaire, charged with seducing and poisoning the public with his poems of evil flowers, were saying: My poems are poison? Let me show you what real poison is, the poison you ingest every day without knowing it, the poison that is already inside you all: ennui. Baudelaire, Benjamin writes, expresses ennui in "both the oldest and the most recent foreign word in his language"—spleen.[37] He materializes ennui, too, in "both the oldest and the most recent foreign *substance* of his time"—hashish. Baudelaire's choice is apropos.

Hashish was newly in vogue in mid-nineteenth-century Paris. Intoxicants, not yet subjected to regulation, were freely available in pharmacies.[38] In both England and France, intoxicants, hard and soft, were being revived and discovered.[39] Opium, imported earlier and in use as medicine, gained new converts after 1821, with the publication of De Quincey's *Confessions of an English Opium Eater* and with the first opium war of 1839–42 between China and England. In France, writers and doctors both experimented and documented their experiments/experiences in writing. Théophile Gautier, to whom Baudelaire dedicated *Les fleurs du mal*, wrote three short stories on the subject ("La pipe d'opium" [1838], "Le hachisch" [1843], and "Le club des hachischins" [1846]); Balzac published a "Traîté des excitants modernes" (1838) on softer drugs like coffee and tea; Maupassant, Dumas, and Nerval were "into" drugs, and so were Daumier and Delacroix, whom Baudelaire studied in his art criticism. In medical circles, Dorvault issued *L'officine ou répertoire général de pharmacie pratique* (The Dispensary or General Repertory of Practical Pharmacy) in 1844, and Moreau de Tours his seminal *Du hachisch et de l'aliénation mentale. Etudes psychologiques* (*Hashish and Mental Illness*) in 1845. Baudelaire consulted both of these for "Le poème du hachisch."[40]

The literary and medical circles—the two active loci of hashish experimentation—collaborated in exploring hashish in sessions of "fantasias." A physician would administer a dose of "green jam" to a group of writers in a salon. Pharmacology and "in-toxicology" came together under the guidance of Dr. Moreau de Tours under the roof of the Hôtel Pimodan on the Ile Saint-Louis, in the apartment of the painter Boissard de Boisdenier. There, Baudelaire, Gautier, Balzac, Nerval, Daumier, Delacroix, and other artists and intellectuals "got high."

Hashish, which, Baudelaire informs us in "Le poème du hachisch," "comes to us from the Orient" (Le hachisch . . . nous vient de l'Orient) [1: 405], was part of the vogue of "Orientalism" that permeated the political, social, and cultural milieu of nineteenth-century France. It was the new high fashion, with the added cachet of the Orient.[41] To take up hashish and to pitch poetry against it was a bold move, simultaneously going along with and going against the *air du temps.*

The public reception of Baudelaire's *Les paradis artificiels,* in 1860, repeated to a lesser degree the reception of *Les fleurs du mal.* It replayed the trial from within and from without. To the public who had witnessed the sentencing of his poetry three years before, the new book on the two "hot" and mysterious stimulants, opium and hashish, seemed another "scandalous" and "immoral" work. It was as though Baudelaire, who had corrupted readers with "evil flowers," were now in the business of growing and feeding readers with hemp and poppy plants. Public criticisms stemmed from the same logic: one cannot display "jouissances" and at the same time condemn. The 1857 judgment asserted that "no amount of stylistic effort," "no amount of blame that precedes or follows" the depictions, "would undo the baneful effects of the tableaux present[ed] to the reader." By the poet's own account, the "severe and minute *study*" of "jouissances" and "dangers" of stimulants committed the same "crime" as his condemned first book.[42] Yet no trial ensued.

The coexistence of "jouissances" and "dangers" generated diverging interpretations of the moral content of *Les paradis artificiels.* Barbey d'Aurevilly, the author who had fervently defended the morality of *Les fleurs du mal* during the time of the trial,[43] cast doubt on the new volume, pointing out that Baudelaire was "the poet of twisted irony" who "give[s] the desire to touch the apple of delight and perdition" in order to give us "the fear of having touched it." And even "if his conclusions against those drugs, alienating human freedom and intelligence, but whose story is written a little too poetically, are ones Christianity could acknowledge, it is not, let us admit it!" d'Aurevilly says, "the moralist who is in *Les paradis artificiels*."[44] This interpretation has prevailed into the twentieth century, as Claude Pichois notes: "The stimulant is an adjuvant. That is what Baudelaire intimates to his reader. Otherwise, what good is it to write a book of three hundred pages? And even if the moral intention is acknowledged—especially in the first part ["Le poème du hachisch"] and it corresponds to failure—the book would belie this point; one does not give such grandiose or moving visions in order to dismiss them" [1: 1365].

Even if *Les paradis artificiels* itself was never sanctioned, the content of its dubious morality brought it certain forms of censorship. Not only did the editors of the journal *Le moniteur*, to whom Baudelaire initially submitted the manuscript, refuse to publish it,[45] but the Department of the Interior (the Commission du colportage of the Ministère de l'intérieure) refused to accord it the official stamp, which meant it could not be sold at newspaper stands in train stations, guaranteed outlets for sales [editorial notes, *Corr 2*: 682]. To the authorities, Baudelaire's book on drugs was itself a drug, a dangerous "opiated substance" (substance opiacée), whose accessibility and distribution must be controlled and banned *especially* from train stations, the public space par excellence of circulation and crossing of boundaries. The judiciary sentry—the prosecutor-soldier-doctor—continued to patrol the borders undercover.

Immoral according to many, *Les paradis artificiels* was equally, and paradoxically, judged too moralistic by others. Flaubert, to whom Baudelaire sent his new book, wrote to the poet in June 25, 1860:

> I like everything, the intention, the style, down even to the paper. I read it very carefully.
>
> Here is . . . my only objection. It seems to me that in a subject treated from such a high point of view, in a work that is the beginning of a science, in a work of natural observation and of induction, you

have (and several times) insisted too much (?) on *the Spirit of Evil*. It is like a leaven of Catholicism here and there. I would have preferred that you did *not blame* hashish, opium, and excess. Do you know what will come out of that later?[46]

Flaubert was puzzled, and justifiably so, to see the poet of *Les fleurs du mal* so hostile to *mal*, launching such a severe attack against it.

Despite its clear and austere ending, and numerous other moralistic passages of "Le poème du hachisch," the moral status of *Les paradis artificiels* has constantly been questioned, remaining uncertain. For those who never took the moralizing gesture seriously, dismissing it as mere rhetoric, as did d'Aurevilly, there was simply no moral at all even to begin with. For those who did take it seriously, as did Flaubert, it was considered something that ought precisely *not* to be. Questioned—and thus undermined—from both sides, the moral of *Les paradis artificiels* appeared, despite its explicitness, or because of it, as a double im-posture: if not a lie, at best it had no place, no stance.

Baudelaire expressed his distress at such criticisms of im-posture coming from both ends in two letters of June 26, 1860. The first is the famous and oft-quoted answer to Flaubert's letter referred to above:

> I was struck by your observation, and having sincerely gone deep into the memory of my reveries, I have realized that, all of the time, I have been obsessed with the impossibility of explaining to myself certain actions or sudden thoughts of a man without the hypothesis of intervention of a wicked force external to him.—Here is a big avowal of which the whole of the nineteenth century conjured up/conspiring together will not make me blush.
>
> (*J'ai été frappé de votre observation, et étant descendu très sincèrement dans le souvenir de mes rêveries, je me suis aperçu que de tout temps j'ai été obsédé par l'impossibilité de me rendre compte de certaines actions ou pensées soudaines de l'homme sans l'hypothèse de l'intervention d'une force méchante extérieure à lui.—Voilà un gros aveu dont tout le 19ᵉ siècle conjuré ne me fera pas rougir.*) [Corr 2: 53]

In the second letter, to the editor of *Le moniteur*, Dalloz, who had refused to publish the opium piece, Baudelaire defended himself against accusations of lying:

> I think I can guess that you ... consider the author of *Les fleurs du mal* as always bringing you bad luck. Know that what can bring bad fortune to the *Paradis* in question, is the severity of moral and religious principles, which has already brought upon me, from many people, the disgracious word: *ah! there you are now, hypocrite!*—It seems as though one does not want to suppose that I could be naturally virtuous.

> (*Je crois deviner que vous et Turgan vous considérez l'auteur des* Fleurs du mal *comme devant toujours vous porter malheur. Sachez que ce qui peut porter malheur aux* Paradis *en question, c'est la sévérité des principes moraux et religieux, qui m'a attiré d'une foule de gens déjà ce mot disgracieux:* ah! vous voilà, hypocrite!—*Il paraît qu'on ne veut pas supposer que je sois naturellement vertueux.*) [Corr 2: 53, original emphasis]

The paradox is clear. On the one hand, there was the immoral Baudelaire, easily recognizable as such as the scandalous poet of *Les fleurs du mal*; on the other, there was, in a rather unbecoming way and unrecognizable as such, the highly moral Baudelaire. The latter, the moralizing Baudelaire, troubled people. If his immorality caused a scandal at the obscenity trial, now his morality was taken to be scandalous. It was immoral, it seemed, for Baudelaire to be moral.

In *Les fleurs du mal*, the poet denounces the readers as hypocrites, and the trial judges the poet and his poetry as immoral. In *Les paradis artificiels*, the poet exposes and appeals against the immorality and hypocrisy that hide beneath the veneer of morality of the judging public. The readers accuse the poet of immorality and hypocrisy disguised as the moral and virtuous. Poet and readers find in each other the same faults: hypocrisy and immorality.

"Those who lead disorderly lives tell those of orderly lives that it is they who stray from nature, and think they follow nature themselves; just as those who are on board ship think that those who are on shore are moving. The language is the same from all sides. We must have a fixed point to judge it. The harbor judges those aboard ship, but where shall we find a harbor in morality?" Pascal's reflections alone from the seventeenth century could scarcely be more pertinent to the nineteenth century's concern about morality. "When everything is moving at once," Pascal writes, "nothing appears to be moving; as on board ship, when everyone is tending toward dissoluteness, no one seems to be doing so. The one who stops makes noticeable the others' being carried away, as if a fixed point."[47]

When "the language is the same from all sides"—immoral and hypocritical—how are we to read the words and to judge? "Where shall we find a harbor in morality?"—where can we find the "fixed point"? Pascal reveals the necessity and yet the ambiguity, the difficulty, and the impossibility of finding that "fixed point"—the almost geometrically precise and immutable metaposition and metadiscourse that are capable of discerning all and hence make the principle of judgment possible. We work instead with approximation, aware of our relative position and movement. The "fixed point," in Pascal, shifts positions from a theoretical and abstract standpoint, to the harbor, then aboard the moving ship, and then to the people moving about on the moving ship, and finally to one among the jostling people aboard ship, who stops moving. One's (own) slowing down and stopping function "*as if* a fixed point," making others' movement apparent. The "fixed point" is not so much "fixed" as "moving" in a *different* direction. Baudelaire's moral stance, accused of double "im-posture," occurs within the larger (im)possibility of identifying, stabilizing, and occupying the "fixed point" in matters of morality and judgment. Baudelaire, however, insists on his moral position; he claims his "fixed point" in "Le poème du hachisch" in a glaringly strong voice of indictment.

If the absence of a central moralistic voice in Flaubert's *Madame Bovary* and Baudelaire's *Les fleurs du mal* is the hallmark of modern literary writing, how are we to read the moral voice in "Le poème du hachisch," which coincides with the poet's voice? What is poetry's moral? Among the readers reacting to "Le poème du hachisch"'s strong moralistic voice, most of them dismissing it as mere rhetoric or as a faux pas, one person stops—"as if a fixed point." It is Flaubert. Flaubert's letter to Baudelaire, where he wrote, "I would have preferred that you did *not blame* hashish," continues: "But take note that this is a *personal* opinion, one in which I am not invested. I do not give the criticism the right to substitute its idea for the other."[48] Flaubert "admires" in particular certain passages of "Le théâtre de Séraphin" and "L'homme-dieu."[49] "Those drugs," he says, "have always caused a great desire in me. I even have some excellent hashish mix concocted by the pharmacist Gastinel. But *it scares me.*—for which I blame myself."[50]

Flaubert reads—and lives—the full extent of the "jouissances" and "dangers" of "Le poème du hachisch." He hears the voice that tempts and the voice that judges. He acknowledges where and how the book touches him, what it stirs and arouses: desire, fear, blame. In turning inward to contemplative awareness, Flaubert slows down, pauses, now able to discern the state of affairs within himself, and from self-reflective observation, makes his choice. Tempted but "scared," he chooses not to take drugs, all the while aware that this choice of prudence that lets fear have its way creates self-blame. He "personally prefers" to see no condemning of hashish in the text, so as to leave open, for other readers, the experience of tension and attraction between desire and fear. Recognizing his "preference" as "personal," he does not claim a judgment of right or wrong and hence unhinges the act/right of expressing from the act/right of imposing. He does not say to the other what "ought to be," does not "substitute" his own ideas for the other's. For to impose/substitute would undermine the very thing he wishes for—not to blame, not to impose a point of view.

Flaubert acknowledges where Baudelaire stands and where he himself stands, neither identifying nor opposing the two, not measuring one against the other or establishing a hierarchy. "And what I blame in your book is, perhaps," Flaubert continues his letter, "what constitutes its originality, and the mark even of your talent? Not to resemble the neighbor, that is the key."[51] Difference is not a faulty excess to be eradicated, but a "mark of talent," of "originality," hence outside comparison, incomparable. In another letter, of July 13, 1857, written just after he had received and read *Les fleurs du mal*, Flaubert noted Baudelaire's "originality": "You have found a way to rejuvenate romanticism. You do not resemble anyone (which is the first of all qualities). The originality of style flows directly from conception."[52]

Flaubert "moves" in a direction different from the others who "misread" Baudelaire's moral stance. He is *like* a "fixed point," first for himself, discerning desire and the impulse (energy and movement) it generates to propel him to act *and* then the fear to act upon desire. At this point of vortex, where desire, excitement, fear, and blame seek immediate realization and prompt resolution—acting out/on or censoring in a rush—Flaubert stands still, pauses, and becomes present. He holds still at the point of precarious discomfort from diverging forces, neither agreeing nor disagreeing, in the manner of his fluid, free, indirect style of writing.

This still point is neither a "point"—a concrete and identifiable unit at a specific location—nor "fixed," but like the "point mass" in physics and mathematics of zero volume/extension and zero mass, it is the principle of focus, of gathering and awareness, moving simultaneously as if into infinite minuteness and into infinite expanse, boundless and weightless, in its move almost motionless. Here is stillness that is, to borrow Kristin Ross's articulation concerning poetic work in Rimbaud, a "kind of weightlessness affiliated with pure speed," "moving fast, too fast," "a kind of absolute motion, absolute speed that escapes from the pull of gravity"—like the fatal and yet "insouciant, weightless" gaze of Orpheus that unbinds Eurydice and causes her to fall.[53]

The "fixed point" is, for Baudelaire, the "exclusive point of view" of the critical stance as he defines it in his *Salon de 1846*, an account of the art exhibit of 1846 published as a brochure. The *Salon de 1846* opens with a dedication "To the Bourgeois," which is a pastiche of Pascal's fragments on "Justice, Force." Baudelaire asks, "What good is criticism?" (A quoi bon la critique?), and writes: "To be just, that is to say, to have a raison-d'être, criticism should be partial, passionate, and political, that is to say, written from an exclusive point of view, but a point of view that opens up the widest horizons" (Pour être juste, c'est-à-dire pour avoir sa raison d'être, la critique doit être partiale, passionnée, politique, c'est-à-dire faite à un point de vue exclusif, mais au point de vue qui ouvre le plus d'horizons) [2: 418]. Flaubert responds to Baudelaire's challenge. He speaks from his exclusive point of view, his "personal preference," which opens up to Baudelaire's originality.[54] The exclusive point is (all-)inclusive.

Flaubert, in fact, was so inspired by Baudelaire's "Le poème du hachisch" that he considered writing a novel, "La spirale," the story of a painter addicted to hashish.[55] "Just" criticism brings together reading, inspiration, and writing. It inspires Flaubert to go from reading to writing. There is passage —an "absolute motion"—into the vast open space of originality and difference, as Gilles Deleuze articulates in *Difference and Repetition*. We "do not think difference in itself," Deleuze says. Rather, we "tend to subordinate" it to "identity," to "resemblance," to "opposition," and to "analogy."[56] He proposes unhinging difference from "forms of representation which reduce it to the Same," on the one hand, and from "forms which make it pass through the negative," on the other. He elaborates "a concept of difference without negation, precisely because unless it is subordinated to the identical, difference would not extend or 'would not have to extend' as far as opposition and contradiction."[57] Inspiration's "absolute speed" "escapes from the pull of gravity"[58] that "identity," "resemblance," and "opposition" exert. It enables one to read, write, and live differently and hence *freely*.

Deleuze speaks of "a swarm of differences, a pluralism of free, wild or untamed differences; a properly differential and original space and time; all of which persist alongside the simplifications of limitation and opposition":

> Oppositions are roughly cut from a delicate milieu of overlapping perspectives, of communicating distances, divergences and disparities, of heterogeneous potentials and intensities. . . . Limitations correspond to a simple first-order power—in a space with a single dimension and a single direction. . . . As for opposition, it represents in turn the second-order power, where it is as though things were spread out upon a flat surface, polarized in a single plane. . . . In any case what is missing is the original, intensive depth which is the matrix of the entire space and the first affirmation of difference: here, that which only afterwards appears as linear limitation and flat opposition lives and simmers in the form of free differences. . . . Space and time display oppositions (and

limitations) only on the surface, but they presuppose in their real depth far more voluminous, affirmed and distributed differences which cannot be reduced to the banality of the negative. It is as though we were in Lewis Carroll's mirror where everything is contrary and inverted on the surface, but "different" in depth. We shall see that it is the same with every space: geometrical, physical, biophysical, social and linguistic. . . . There is a false profundity in conflict, but underneath conflict, the space of the play of differences. The negative is the image of difference, but a flattened and inverted image, like the candle in the eye of the ox—the eye of the dialectician dreaming of a futile combat?[59]

Baudelaire's "just" criticism and Flaubert's inspired reading entail the Deleuzian project of entering the "*original* time and space," the "intensive depth which is the matrix of the entire space and the first affirmation of difference." Poetry, in the song of Orpheus, becomes the "invitation des profondeurs" that "open[s] an abyss in every utterance."[60] Poetry is the passage from unidimensional constraints (the one-liner or banality/platitude) to "depth far more voluminous" in which "heterogeneous potentials and intensities"—intense potentials and potent intensities of a sun within a sun, a spleen within a spleen—"live and simmer." To think, to read, to write, and to live with absolute intensity, absolute potential, and "absolute motion"—that is poetic and critical relation to the world.

The true "expérience" of poetry and criticism is risk and freedom. *Experience* and *experiment*, both etymologically related to *expertise*, derive from the Latin *experiri* (*ex* + *peritus* [peril]), meaning "to try out, to test." True poetic "expérience" contains peril at its heart. Poetry is about facing, *going through*, and emerging from perils and dangers. It is to take the risks of entering a state where the known and the familiar have no root and no simple binary mold into which to fit comfortably. Ungrounded themselves, the known and the familiar provide no ground. Poetic enterprise is extreme risk for thinking based on knowledge, because poetry, and the reading and writing it inspires, is the passage to what is *different* from knowledge, whose difference cannot be conceived from the point of view of already existing knowledge. It is the extreme risk of *not* knowing.[61]

But poetry tells us that at that perilous point where knowing touches not-knowing, where there is freeing from the bonds of the known, there and only there do thinking, reading, writing, and living truly emerge. "How else can one write but of those things which one doesn't know, or knows badly?" Deleuze asks. "It is precisely there that we imagine having something to say. We write only at the tip of our knowledge, at the extreme point which separates our knowledge from our ignorance *and makes the first pass through/into the other.* Only in this manner are we resolved to write. To fill in ignorance is to put off writing until tomorrow—or rather to make it impossible."[62] To pass not from unknown to known, but the reverse, from known to unknown, from the ease and comfort of safety lines and flat solid ground to dangerous depth—that is poetry's way. *Les fleurs du mal* calls for such a passage: "To plunge into the depths of the abyss, Hell or Heaven, what does it matter? / To the depths of the Unknown to find something *new!*" (Plonger au fond du gouffre, Enfer ou Ciel, qu'importe? / Au fond de l'Inconnu pour trouver du *nouveau!*) ["Le voyage" 1: 134, original emphasis].[63] The same logic of the genitive and generative *of* is constitutive of both *Les fleurs du mal* and "Le poème du hachisch."

With the end and the beginning of *Les fleurs du mal* ("To the depths of the Unknown to find something *new!*"; "Hypocritical reader"), Baudelaire asks us to be experts who experience and experiment—hold a relationship of *difference*—with peril, neither recklessly throwing ourselves into it in easy indulgence nor rejecting it through denial or suppression: a relation of difference, as Deleuze writes in *Difference and Repetition*, that is freedom from subordination to identity (indulgence) or to opposition (denial) and opening of new depths in the world of platitude and commonplace where "all roads lead to Rome." He demands that we, who are literary critics, be aware of the "pull of gravity" that knowledge exerts on us, its promise of security, comfort, and established hierarchy. He demands that we not fall into the trap of expertise that negates the peril that exists at its own heart, hence in denial of its true nature. He demands that we not be false experts who grab tight onto knowledge, bringing it in close and manageable range, indulging in and settling on acquisition. He demands finally that we not become benumbed and bored, thinking everything is either identical (hence already known and with no need for further experience/experiment) or opposite (hence negated and suppressed below the threshold of awareness, out of the field of vision and experience/experiment). Expertise as commitment to live in a *poetic* relation to the world, *not* in a narcotic one, means taking risks, the risks of difference, uncertainty, and ultimately of freedom. Expertise as commitment also to explore the unknown rather than to hoard and guard the known, to create and open many *possibilities* rather than to narrow possibilities down to a few *probabilities* or *certainties*—such expertise and experimentation are, as Deleuze writes in *Spinoza: Practical Philosophy*, "the contrary of a Judgment."[64]

False experts are like the hashish eater and the cowardly Ulysses who avoid risks—*hypocritical experts*—unwilling to explore what is outside their small view. They perceive the cosmos in its "flattened and inverted image" with "the eye of the dialectician dreaming of a futile combat"—or, the eye of "Ennui," an "involuntary tear welling in his eye," "dream[ing] of scaffolds smoking his hookah" (l'œil chargé d'un pleur involontaire, / Il rêve d'échafauds en fumant son houka) [1: 6]. How much do we, readers and critics, read, think, write, and live with the small and narcotized eye/I, dreaming, as Deleuze says, of the "false profundity of combat" and debate, unaware that we have already flattened out difference onto a plane, "forced [it] into a previously established identity," "placed [it] on the slope of the identical which makes it reflect or desire identity, and necessarily takes it where identity wants it to go—namely, into the negative"?[65] The gravity of thought presses the universe down to flatness. On that carefully and yet recklessly bulldozed terrain, "the eye of the dialectician" and of "Ennui" and perhaps our own eye, too, "dream" of "combats" and "scaffolds," that is, of opposition, negation, and condemnation. But thought's gravity is, as Deleuze says, a "false profundity," flat and banal. It is the mirror image of what Italo Calvino describes as the false lightness of frivolity, "dull and heavy."[66]

"To think difference in itself"—to entertain a poetic relation of difference with the cosmos, others, and ourselves—means in Deleuze and in Baudelaire to put into question the "traditional image of thought." Deleuze states that "we suppose that thought possesses a good nature, and the thinker a good will (naturally to 'want' the true)":

> We take as a model the process of recognition—in other words, a common sense or employment of all the faculties on a supposed same object; we designate error, nothing but error, as the enemy to be fought; and we suppose that the true concerns solutions—in other words, propositions capable of serving as answers. This is the classic image of thought, and as long as the critique has not been carried to the heart of that image it is difficult to conceive of thought as encompassing those problems which point beyond the propositional mode; or as involving encounters which escape all recognition; or as confronting its true enemies, which are quite different from thought; or as attaining that which tears thought from its natural torpor and notorious bad will, and forces us to think.[67]

The "natural torpor and notorious bad will," the "true enemy" at the heart of thought, is "Ennui." Baudelaire's address to the reader ends with getting to the heart of our thought and making the monster visible. "Ennui," tear-eyed from yawning, is the monster in the labyrinth of our thinking. We do not want to go there. Our "natural torpor and notorious bad will" refuse to acknowledge the monster we harbor in us. As long as we do not face the monster, our thinking is duplicitous, hence hypocritical. Our own slumber nurtures the monster, but it is not certain, as Deleuze writes, that "it is only the sleep of reason that gives rise to monsters: it is also the vigil, the insomnia of thought, since thought is that moment in which determination makes itself one, by virtue of maintaining a unilateral and precise relation to the indeterminate. Thought 'makes' difference, but difference is [the monster]. We should not be surprised that difference should appear accursed, that it should be error, sin or the figure of Evil for which there must be expiation. There is no sin other than raising the ground and dissolving the form."[68]

And "raising the ground" Baudelaire did, and so, too, did he expose the hidden monster, the "image of our own thought," and "force us to think."

Victor Hugo wrote of Baudelaire's writing, in his letter to the poet of October 6, 1859, as "one of those pages that powerfully provoke thinking/the thought. Rare merit, to make [us] think; gift of the elected few."[69] The "sleep of reason" and the "vigil/insomnia of thought" both make the monster, "Ennui." For if "the sleeping reason" cannot/does not/refuses to see the monster, the "unilateral and precise," "insomniac" thought curses the monster as "error, sin or the figure of Evil for which there must be expiation." The monster, whether seen or not seen, is *not*, ought *not* be. Reason cannot think difference. Deleuze says: "It is as though Difference were Evil." *The Flowers of Evil* exposes this deeply ingrained "image of thought," which thinks of "Difference" as "Evil." Poetry's imperative is to raise the monster of difference up from its deep labyrinthine center—"Difference must [come out of] its cave," as Deleuze affirms—and, in so doing, to let difference blossom into *Flowers of Difference*, as the "mark not of original sin but of original difference," to borrow Octavio Paz's words.[70] How can difference be a flower and not a monster (of evil)? Or rather, how can flower blossom out of monster? Can flower and monster exist in a relation not of opposition and clash, but of difference, of contiguity, and of touch?

Perseus, the hero of lightness in Calvino's reading of Ovid's *Metamorphoses*, transforms the relation between the "fine grace of the coral" and the "savage horror of the Gorgon" from "clash" to "touch" with his "gesture of refreshing courtesy toward a being so monstrous and terrifying yet at the same time somehow fragile and perishable."[71] Perseus, who vanquishes the monster Medusa and carries the severed head in a bag "as his particular burden," is one who has "seen" and "touched" the monster that no one else could bear to see.[72] He uses his bronze shield as a mirror to avoid Medusa's direct stare, which would turn him into stone. Perseus's indirect gaze does not clash with the Gorgon's but entertains a *different* relationship with it. The reflection Perseus sees on his shield-mirror is the monster's, but he recognizes it as his own, too, as his intimate company and self. Light and lucid, he does not negate or deny but sees and acknowledges the monster we carry inside us. Perseus's gaze does not see difference as *representation* of the other but lives it as *experience* of the self.[73] Perseus's indirect vision is less cunning avoidance than it is true facing from within—it is *not* hypocritical. Perseus succeeds in beheading Medusa, because he has already made her his own (self) in his gaze. It is thus only normal that he carries the severed head with him, "as his particular burden." The bag in which he hides the head of Medusa is less separation than a means to keep her near him, at his side.

In Perseus's hands, the shield functions differently. It is not so much an impenetrable and defensive wall as it is a reflective surface opening a passageway—like Alice's mirror. It is as though Perseus has passed through the shield and stands at the side of the monster, in the "voluminous" space of difference. In so doing, he undoes Medusa's "flattened and inverted image," which Minerva imposed upon her, restores the first, original, and undistorted sight of Medusa, who, before she became the horrifying monster, was a beautiful maiden. Ovid recounts that Neptune, the god of the sea, fell in love with her and "ravished" her in the temple of Minerva. Minerva, the goddess of reason, was offended by the impure and obscene act of sexual copulation, which she saw as desecrating her temple [4.797–78]. Minerva judged it an offense; it was obscene; hence it had to be punished. She identified as the culprit not Neptune but Medusa and punished her. Minerva's way is reason's way. Ovid's account offers us the "image of thought or reason" in its (mythic) origin. Reason *is* binary opposition, establishment of hierarchy: its mode, negation and clashing; its action, punishment and combat; its power, violence.

It is no accident that Minerva is also the goddess of war. Minerva shows the intrinsic affinity and necessary convergence among the acts of reasoning, dividing, judging, and making war. Ovid writes, "And, that the deed might be punished as was due, [Minerva] changed the Gorgon's locks to ugly snakes" [4.800–01]. For why punish only Medusa? Is it because Neptune, as god, stands outside judgment? Or perhaps because Medusa felt ravishing pleasure and seemed to love it, and in truth, Minerva was jealous of her beauty and envied her *jouissances*? Whatever "obscenity" the eyes of Minerva saw—but she saw nothing, because Ovid tells us that she "turned away and hid her chaste eyes behind her aegis" [4.798–99]—Minerva's punishment of Medusa is blind and misplaced. Minerva embodies the monstrous copulation of reason and violence, justice and force, and hence the injustice of reason and its judgment.[74]

Minerva is the monster, but we do not see her, for she hides on the other side of her shield, upon which she has placed Medusa's head, which Perseus offered her. Ovid tells us that "now to frighten her fear-numbed foes, she still wears upon her breast the snakes which she has made" [4.802–03]. She is the monster behind the monster, the real, unsuspected monster, who puts forth a decoy monster she has fabricated to avert the eyes from the "traditional," indeed ancient, "image of thought." Minerva uses her shield of Medusa in several ways. She puts it between herself and her enemies to secure victory in all battles; between the two terms of "opposing" pairs so that each term cannot bear the other and is locked and petrified in the position of binary antagonism; between herself and the monster, which means she never faces the monster. Minerva, the goddess of reason, with "natural torpor and notorious bad will," is hypocritical. Minerva, in all her glory, is fearful and in denial of the monster she cannot face. Her unfailing reason serves as self-protection. But just like hashish, reason's infallibility denotes immorality.

Perseus's gaze operates otherwise. Poetry, with the gaze of Perseus and also of Orpheus and Icarus, escapes the "pull of gravity" of self-protection, prudence, and knowledge; takes the risk of losing the self; and moves into the depth of difference, the space of freedom and of "universal contiguity" that reason flattens, prohibits, and divides. Reason looks with the gaze of Minerva and of Narcissus, of opposition and identity, which both produce irremediable disconnection. Narcissus, with "slender form" and "pride so cold that no youth, no maiden touched his heart" [3.354–55], is arrested and paralyzed by his own image on the other side of the reflecting pool. Seeing the self as representation of the other, incapable of reaching, touching, and passing to the other's side, separated only by a "thin barrier of water," Narcissus withers away. Even when he finally recognizes the image as his own —the moment of identity—he does not meet/join himself. The moment of identity merely confirms the law of disconnection (of the self from the self) and opposition (of the self to the self).[75] Perseus's gaze functions the other way. It is not stasis that separates but passage that joins. Recognizing the other as self, in a moment not of identity/opposition but of difference, he joins the other across the thick barrier of solid and stands next to it.

The trial of obscenity and the ensuing censorship in the ancient world continue in modern nineteenth-century Paris. In Baudelaire's trial, similar issues resurface. The defense lawyer subordinates difference to identity, arguing that *Les fleurs du mal* conforms to the moral; the prosecutor subordinates it to opposition, insisting that it goes against the moral. Both sides dwell on the same plane, limited in their scope, unable to "think difference in itself" and unable to think differently of the relation between "flowers" and "evil." Pinard's speech during the trial of Flaubert, according to LaCapra, indicates that he "felt poisoned or contaminated by the novel's portrayal of passion and, when faced with his own temptation, set out in a kind of quest for self-preservation to find a legal antidote to Flaubert's writing."[76] Pinard feels desire, fear, and blame (as did Flaubert in reading Baudelaire's "Le poème du hachisch"), but he feels threatened and resists and suppresses these feelings. He experiences no inward awareness, only denial and blockage. What he has denied to himself, he seeks to do to others by projecting his own desire, fear, and blame into a compulsion to censor them in others. His move is a great rush and energy—a "mission." The prosecutor in the courtroom is a soldier ("sentry") on a battlefield. He manifests an outward busyness that distracts him from facing what is within *himself*—this is the Pascalian "divertissement." Pinard indicts with Minerva's voice of reason and war. Pinard's setting the trial on military ground is an act that is overdetermined—it is a move that is not out of place but puts things in their "right" place.

In "Le poème du hachisch," the poet asserts that the trial had it wrong. Baudelaire sets poetry's court of appeal not on military grounds, but on the center stage of "Le théâtre de Séraphin." Intoxicated voices speak as actors/puppets. "Ennui," of the poem "Au lecteur," appears on stage—"an involuntary tear welling in his eye," "dream[ing] of scaffolds smoking his hookah" (l'œil chargé d'un pleur involontaire, / Il rêve d'échafauds en fumant son houka) [1: 6]. Ross Chambers writes that the "involuntary tear" that "fills (literally *loads* or even *weighs upon* ['*chargé*']) the eye of the hookah-smoker" is the poem's "most important self-referential figure": "This tear is *involuntary*, the very sign of the Devil's vaporization of the will" and "appears also as a kind of condensation of the vapors, a secretion of Ennui. As such, it manifests the possibility of a poetic production—however involuntary—that responds" to the mode of existence under "the tyranny of the Devil."[77]

The production of the poetic monograph by melding (*fondre*) anecdotes of intoxication in "Le poème du hachisch" takes up and extends the "possibility of poetic production"—the tear welling up involuntarily—in the poem "Au lecteur." In "Le poème du hachisch," the process of condensation/concentration from gas (the vapor of our will) to liquid (tear) is *willfully* pushed further to solidify into metal. The monograph results from the activity of *fondre*—"to melt, meld, smelt, and cast"—which designates the process of working the metal: liquefying, amalgamating, purifying, and solidifying through giving form. Poetic work gives solid substance and form to our will. It works "the rich metal of our will" that Satan vaporizes and gives it a *perfect* form, a circle. The shape of a tear is a circle deformed by the pull of gravity. Poetry's *formed metal*—its mono*graph*—counters the demonic powers of both vaporization and weight. Baudelaire, Chambers writes, is "remarkable" for "the classic facture of his verse, the firmness of its poetic structure": "Baudelaire seems to use the firm grid of the Alexandrine and the quatrain as something of a defense against the invasive fog of vaporized discourse."[78]

The metal of will may be neither "gold" nor "rich," as the poem "Alchimie de la douleur" [1: 77] warns us—where gold changes to iron—but, rather, a will of "iron," perfectly shaped. As *matter*, "iron" may be mere "mud," but as *form* it has the value of "gold." Transformation of matter from gold to iron and to mud corresponds, at the formal level, to a reverse transmutation from mud to gold. "Every form created, even by men, is immortal. For form is independent of matter," Baudelaire affirms (Toute forme créée, même par l'homme, est immortelle. Car la forme est indépendante de la matière) [*Mon cœur mis à nu* 1: 705]. Baudelaire's project "to extract *beauty* from Evil/Pain (d'extraire la *beauté* du Mal) [1: 181, original emphasis] consists, as Suzanne Guerlac sees, of "develop[ing] a *form* powerful enough to neutralize the deformity it carries, a harmony beyond the reach of any dissonance."[79]

In the poem "Une charogne" ("Carrion") [1: 31–32], flesh, matter, and forms all dissolve to generate, at the end, "*the* form and divine essence" (*la* forme et l'essence divine) [my emphasis]. "Essence" and "form" are the "quintessence" the poet extracts in the projected "Epilogue" for the second edition of *Les fleurs du mal* ("I have extracted the quintessence from every single thing, / You have given me your mud and I have turned it into gold" [j'ai de chaque chose extrait la quintessence, / Tu m'as donné ta boue et j'en ai fait de l'or] [1: 192]). The law of poetry reigns over *both* matter and form, hence conquering the law of nature, limited to governing only matter. Poetic creation harnesses the energy released by decomposing matter and channels it into composing form; it turns (material) disorder into (formal) order, hence following a different and higher law of entropy.

In the laboratory of "Le poème du hachisch," a meticulous study in vivo/vitro of the satanic substance takes place. Baudelaire observes the "workings" of the evil "mechanism" of intoxication as if through a "transparent glass" [1: 435]. He describes attentively the process of isolating hashish's active ingredient in its purest, concentrated resinous extract. Through a series of mixing, separating, boiling, vaporizing, and condensing—a kind of (al)chemical "melding," or *fondre*—the hidden substance, diluted and mixed with other matter, is made visible.[80] The essence of hashish, or Evil, precipitates. Satan falls. Since Satan is himself *the* Fall, falling makes Satan *be*: it exposes him. Baudelaire uses Satan's own nature as the weapon that causes Satan's own demise. He engages in poetry's battle against Evil, undertaking his most ambitious "phantasmagoria." Baudelaire often refers to the artistic process of extracting and capturing the essence of the world as "phantasmagoria." Of the works of M.G., "the painter of modern life," Baudelaire writes that "phantasmagoria has been extracted from nature" [2: 694]. In extracting Satan out of concealment, Baudelaire achieves the highest poetic phantasmagoria.

The poet-philosopher–Apollo figure in "Le poème du hachisch," observing the phenomenon of intoxication in the laboratory, hearing the contorted mimicry of addicts in the theater, and working the metal to a perfect form, is the all-mighty rival to the thrice-mighty Satan, the puppeteer and chemist vaporizing the "rich metal of our will" in the poem "Au lecteur."[81] He is also the all-mighty rival to "Pinard" (as the figure of censorship), the "sentry" in his triple role of prosecutor-soldier-doctor. It is "Poet, Trismegistus" against both "Satan, Trismegistus" and "Pinard, Trismegistus."

Baudelaire's phantasmagoria and re*staging* of the trial go straight to the root of hypocrisy and expose it. *Hypocrisy*, or pretending to be what one is not, comes from the Greek *hupokrisis*, "play-acting, mimicry," and hence "simulation." A *hupokritês* is one who responds; it is the actor in the Greek play who responds to the chorus—a person, therefore, who does not speak his/her own feelings and thoughts. *Hupokrisis* comes from *hupokrinein*, with the verb *krinein*, meaning "to sift, to divide," hence "to decide, to judge." *Krinein* yields *krisis* (*crisis*: a decisive moment in the course of illness), *kritêrion* (*criterion*: what allows distinction), and *kritikê* (the art of judgment, especially of literary works). On the stage of "Le théâtre de Séraphin," hypocrisy unfolds in diverse and original ways. The verb *krinein*, which from "to sift, to divide" becomes "to decide, to judge," reveals the "slope" of binary opposition Deleuze speaks of. Binary opposition confuses the differences among the four related but distinct movements. The slide from "sift" to "divide" to "decide" to "judge" indicates an increasing degree of solidification, closure, unilateral settlement, hence less and less freedom, space, and movement. We go from the "voluminous" space of difference, to borrow Deleuze's word, a space in which separate entities may coexist in infinite ways, to narrowing the relation of difference to division, then to decision (which chooses one side), and finally to a judgment that imposes hierarchy. Dewey, too, points out and cautions against the strong pull, or the "disposition to erect criticism into something 'judicial.'"[82]

Can there be discernment of difference that is unhinged from condemnation of difference? Can we bring critical awareness to the act and concept of criticism and see the difference between discernment (refinement and acuity of perception) and judgment (condemnation or approval in the legal or moral sense) so that we do not slide down automatically, and unknowingly, the slope of binary opposition that prevents true perception? To see and hear but not to condemn as if going back up the slope of *krinein* from judgment to decision to division to separation to discernment—that would be the task of criticism in Baudelaire, Deleuze, and Dewey.

The 1857 trial of *Les fleurs du mal* followed the solid and linear division-decision-judgment course of *krinein*. It was a trial where difference—the other and the monster—was punished to reestablish safety and comfort. Poetry's appeal in "Le poème du hachisch" exposes the reductive and dangerous slope of *krinein* and the complexity of hypocrisy in all its forms. This is a trial in the sense of trying out experiments and experiences and hence of facing perils as a true expert. To uncover the world of difference that our own simplification and reduction hide, to see the harsh division that our binary thinking imposes on the fluidity and "universal contiguity" of the world—that is poetry's trial, a trial in which "knowledge of the world tends to dissolve the solidity of the world" and invites us to take a voyage to the "depths of the Unknown," the different, and the *new*.[83] An expert who *responds* to this "invitation to the voyage"—this may be the "*hypocrite* lecteur" Baudelaire calls for.

In the twentieth century, an American writer would confront the same ordeal. Henry Miller, whose first book, *The Tropic of Cancer*, caused scandal when it was published in Paris in 1934, was accused of obscenity, his work banned in the United States until 1960. Miller speaks in his piece "Obscenity in Literature" of "cosmic insensitivity" that turns people into "unthinking, unfeeling monster[s]."[84] Monstrous ennui and the lack of "universal intelligence" to which Baudelaire attributed the public "misunderstanding" of *Les fleurs du mal*—the stiffness and inertia of human thinking from Minerva's time pervade centuries and cultures. "Cosmic insensitivity" reduces to platitudes the "highest and most suave manifestations" of cosmic forces, weather—Benjamin's "empty and fragile man" is of all time and space.[85]

"Deceit and hypocrisy, such as are prevalent in our time," Miller writes, "have a way of provoking honest men to explosive language, to shocking language."[86] "Freedom of expression is always interpreted as license," Miller says in another piece, "Obscenity and the Law of Reflection": "The artist must conform to the current, and usually hypocritical, attitude of the majority. He must be original, courageous, inspiring and all that—but never too disturbing. He must say Yes while saying No." If beauty is in the eye of the beholder, so, too, is obscenity for Miller: "What man dreads most is to be faced with the manifestation, in word or deed, of that which he has refused to live out, that which he has throttled or stifled," and the "sordid qualities imputed to the enemy are always those which we recognize as our own and therefore rise to slay, because only through projection do we realize the enormity and horror of them."[87] Miller's analysis echoes closely LaCapra's reading of the inner motivations of Pinard at Flaubert's and Baudelaire's trials. Miller goes further: "If there is anything which deserves to be called 'obscene' it is this oblique, glancing confrontation with the mysteries, this walking up to the edge of the abyss, enjoying all the ecstasies of vertigo and yet refusing to yield to the spell of the unknown. . . . Acknowledged by all, it is nevertheless despised and rejected. . . . When it is recognized and accepted, whether as a figment of the imagination or as an integral part of human reality, it inspires no more dread or revulsion than could be ascribed to the flowering lotus which sends its roots down into the mud of the stream on which it is borne."[88]

In listening to the song of the Sirens without paying the price, in turning inner repression into outer censorship, both Ulysses and Pinard, not Flaubert or Baudelaire, commit obscene acts. As the cowardly denial and perversion of the fundamental spirit of trial—to test, to experiment, and to risk—judgment is violent deflowering of budding differences. *Judgment* is the ultimate obscenity.

CHAPTER FIVE

Quantum Elegance

Content and Form in Science, Fashion, Poetry

"As for long poems, we know what to think of them; it is the resource of those who are incapable of making short ones" (Quant aux longs poèmes, nous savons ce qu'il faut en penser; c'est la ressource de ceux qui sont incapables d'en faire de courts). So Baudelaire writes in a letter of February 18, 1860, to Armand Fraisse, a critic of Lyon who faithfully defended *Les fleurs du mal* throughout Baudelaire's life and after his death. "All that exceeds the span of attention a human being can pay to the poetic form is not *a* poem" (Tout ce qui dépasse la longueur de l'attention que l'être humain peut prêter à la forme poétique n'est pas *un* poème) [*Corr* 1:676, original emphasis]. Baudelaire got the idea/ideal of a short poem directly from Edgar Allan Poe, whose work marked Baudelaire in a profound way. In that same letter, Baudelaire speaks of his first encounter with Poe's work in 1846 or 1847. He mentions "a peculiar/remarkable commotion," "something . . . almost unbelievable" (une commotion singulière; quelque chose de . . . presque incroyable). It was the beginning of Baudelaire's faithful "enthusiasm and long patience" (mon enthousiasme et de ma longue patience) for the work of Poe. He wrote essays on and translated the American poet's work from as early as 1848, nine years before the publication of *Les fleurs du mal*.[1]

In his "Notes nouvelles sur Edgar Poe" ("Further Notes on Edgar Poe") [2: 319–37], a preface to the second volume of his translation of Poe's work, *Nouvelles histoires extraordinaires*, which appeared in March 1857, three months before *Les fleurs du mal* came out, Baudelaire writes: "I refer naturally to the article entitled: *The Poetic Principle*, and find there, from the beginning, a vigorous protest against what one could call, in matters of poetry, the heresy of length or of dimension,—the absurd value attributed to bulky poems. 'A long poem does not exist; what one means by a long poem is a perfect contradiction in terms'" (Je recours naturellement à l'article intitulé: *The Poetic Principle*, et j'y trouve, dès le commencement, une vigoureuse protestation contre ce qu'on pourrait appeler, en matière de la poésie, l'hérésie de la longueur ou de la dimension,—la valeur absurde attribuée aux gros poèmes. "Un poème long n'existe pas; ce qu'on entend par un long poème est une parfaite contradiction de termes") [2: 332].[2]

Poe's actual sentence reads: "I hold that a long poem does not exist. I maintain that the phrase, 'a long poem,' is simply a flat contradiction in terms."[3] In "The Poetic Principle" of 1850 and "The Philosophy of Composition" of 1846, both of which Baudelaire read (citing, commenting upon, and incorporating them into his own poetics), Poe states that "Beauty is the sole legitimate province of the poem" [553].[4] That is, a poem has a single authentic purpose: to produce in the reader the experience of "Beauty" in the most effective way possible.

Poe's "principle" and "philosophy" of poetry are an exposition, as Poe puts it, of "an obvious rule of Art that effects should be made to spring from direct causes—that the objects should be attained through means best adapted for their attainment" [554]. Poe establishes "Unity" as "the vital requisite in all works of Art" [569] and hence essential to the creation of Beauty. A poem's content and its form must align themselves as a "Unity," a maximizing of the "totality of effects or impressions" [569], in order to create in the reader the greatest "Poetic Sentiment" [575]. "Unity" is organization, correspondence, concentration, coherence, the principle of simplicity that heightens poetic power and maximizes the possibility of an impact on the reader that is complex, profound, intense, and everlasting. Poe relates the poetic law of "Unity" directly to the "extent," or length, of the work: "If any literary work is too long to be read at one sitting, we must be content to dispense with the immensely important effect derivable from unity of impression. . . . It appears evident, then, that there is a distinct limit, as regards length, to all works of literary art—the limit of a single sitting" [552]. Poe's equation is simple: a poem is "to read at one sitting." The equation constitutes, at the same time, the definition of poetry itself: "a long poem does not exist"; it "is simply a flat contradiction in terms" [568]. A short poem *is*; a long poem is *not*.

Yet the poem's brevity has a lower limit. Poe declares: "It is clear that a poem may be improperly brief. Undue brevity degenerates into mere epigrammatism. A *very* short poem, while now and then producing a brilliant or vivid, never produces a profound or enduring, effect. There must be the steady pressing down of the stamp upon wax" [570, original emphasis]. Baudelaire heeds Poe's warning about "undue brevity," writing in his February 18, 1960, letter to Fraisse of "a poem that is too short" (un poème trop court): "one that does not provide enough *pabulum* [pasture] to the excitement that has been created, one that is not equal to the reader's natural appetite, is also defective" (celui qui ne fournit pas un *pabulum* suffisant à l'excitation créée, celui qui n'est pas égal à l'appétit naturel du lecteur, est aussi défectueux) [2: 332, original emphasis]. Not too long, not too short, the poem is framed in "a single sitting" in time and space, distilling and optimizing the condition of the poem's reception and communication.

Through that notion of "a single sitting," Poe transposes poetics to mathematics: "Within this limit [of a single sitting], the extent of a poem may be made to bear mathematical relation" to the "true poetic effect": "the excitement or elevation" of "the soul." "Brevity," Poe writes, "must be in direct ratio of the intensity of the intended effect" [553]. The "extent," or "brevity," of a poem is a mathematical ratio. *Exact* brevity intends to create response in "direct" "mathematical" "ratio," hence *precise* in "intended effect" and "intensity," each a necessary and sufficient condition of "poetic effect." With Poe, and Baudelaire (through Poe), poetry comes to acquire and require *exact* measure; it is elevated to its *absolute* dimension. Poetry is an art of exactitude.

The aesthetic issue of form and content in poetry, in Poe's formulation, corresponds to the law of cause and effect (means and ends) in science and mathematics. Poe wrote his essay "Philosophy of Composition" with a "design to render it manifest" that the composition of "The Raven" had "proceeded, step by step, to its completion with the precision and rigid consequence of a mathematical problem" [551–52]. "Philosophy of Composition" exposes, through demonstrative style, the mathematics of the writerly process; it must advance with impeccable logic to its "completion," or "*dénouement*" (ending, outcome, result, solution) [562, original emphasis], as in an equation. The poet is to position and order words, phrases, sentences with the same meticulousness that a mathematician adopts in demonstrating a proposition or solving an equation. Thus, the poetics of exactitude in poetry joins the elegance of mathematical proof and reasoning.

In mathematics itself, the shortest of competing proofs that demonstrate a theorem is considered superior and, hence, "elegant." Its elegance requires brevity and is modeled on yet another mathematical truth, that there can be only one shortest path between two points in space: a straight line (in Euclidean geometry). An elegant proof goes straight to the point, literally and figuratively, or "mathematically." From the Latin *eligere*, "to select," elegance is the principle of distinction, a criterion of discrimination. Of all roads that may lead to Rome, only one can be called elegant. An elegant proof takes the smallest number of steps in reducing the distance from ignorance to knowledge, a minimalism best adapted to fulfillment of purpose. "The minimum could be defined," the architect John Pawson writes, "as the perfection that an artifact achieves when it is no longer possible to improve it by subtraction. [It] is the quality that an object has when every component, every detail, and every junction has been reduced or condensed to the essentials. It is the result of the omission of the inessentials."[5] Every link among and between the parts and the whole, every transition, is absolutely necessary and sufficient.

Elegance, the internal structure of the proof and the singular way in which means corresponds to end, and form (*how* a proof demonstrates) to content (*what* it demonstrates), requires precision, conciseness, simplicity, and coherence. The more complicated the theorem and simpler the demonstration, the more elegant the proof. When we marvel at the elegance of a simple proof to a complex theorem, we are seized simultaneously by its appropriateness (its necessity and sufficiency are such that it cannot be otherwise) and also with surprise (how can such a complex thing be so simple?). "Yes, it can only be this way!" and "No, how can it be?" Elegance creates and sustains surprise within logic. Explanation becomes inexplicably surprising and satisfying. In the end, what surprises and pleases in an elegant proof is its ability to explain so that we understand. Einstein once said: "The most incomprehensible thing about the universe is that it is comprehensible."[6]

Brian Greene, a theoretical physicist, chose *The Elegant Universe* as the title of his book positing string theory as a comprehensive way to explain the universe.[7] Physicists' dream of a Final Grand Theory stems from the desire to contain within a single equation—in a single view or "a single sitting"—the vast and complex workings of the universe, the desire to write one sentence that tells the whole story. The search for elegance brings us closer to the enigma of truth. Elegance in mathematics and physics is efficiency and optimization of knowledge; it models and performs ideal and perfect knowing. Through the masterful process of pure economy, our mind reaches the complex through the simple, or the simple through the complex, the whole through the parts, the infinite through small steps—*maximum via minimum.*

When Poe writes that "brevity must be in direct ratio of the intensity of the intended effect" [553], his poetics of brevity is a calculation that puts "in direct ratio" a minimum ("brevity") and a maximum ("intensity"): it is a poetics of elegance in precise proportion to the enigma of beauty. Baudelaire's "pythagoric beauty" (la beauté pythagorique), a notion he discusses in his letter to Fraisse, corresponds to Poe's "direct ratio." Baudelaire writes:

"Because form is constraining, idea springs forth all the more intense" (Parce que la forme est contraignante, l'idée jaillit plus intense). "Have you noted," he asks, "that a partial view of the sky, glimpsed through a basement window, or between two chimneys, two rocks, or through an arcade, etc., gives an idea of the infinite that is more profound than the grand panoramic view from the top of a mountain?" (Avez-vous observé qu'un morceau de ciel, aperçu par un soupirail, ou entre deux cheminées, deux rochers, ou par une arcade, etc., donnait une idée plus profonde de l'infini que le grand panorama vu du haut d'une montagne?) [*Corr* 1: 676]. Formal constraint, discipline, closure, lead, paradoxically yet surely and directly, to intensive and extensive openness; the finite leads to the infinite, as if from cause to effect or effect to cause.

In "Le poème du hachisch," Baudelaire denounces hashish's circle—vague and hypocritical because it hides behind vapors of dissipation—which keeps us spinning forever unconscious in habit's orbit. We are not in "direct ratio" to life when we are high. Narcotic life is inelegant and in dissonance with "the universal rhythm and prosody" (le rythme et la prosodie universels) [2: 334]. Poetry's elegant and precise circle counters hashish's imprecise and blurred circle. In "Le poème du hachisch," the production of the poetic monograph is compared to the process of working metal (*fondre*). Baudelaire tells Fraisse that he favors sonnets (numerous poems in *Les fleurs du mal* are sonnets) because they have the "beauty of well-crafted metal and mineral" (Il y a là la beauté du métal et du minéral bien tavaillés). But poetry traces the firm and definite contour of a circle so that its measure can finally break open to infinite expanse. It seeks elegance of form as the most effective way to communicate the experience of Beauty to the reader. Poetry shocks us with briskly "*astringent effects,*" to borrow from Stengers,[8] so that, through intense contraction and extreme solidification pushed to the limit in a split second, we may be jolted out of habit's circle, awakened, and able to relate directly and elegantly to life.[9]

Baudelaire's poetics of high elegance in "Le poème du hachisch" and *Les fleurs du mal* achieves explicit formal articulation in his prose poetry, *Le spleen de Paris*. In this experimental genre, (new) form equals breaking up (old) form:

My dear friend, I send you this little work of which it cannot be said, without injustice, that it has neither head nor tail, since, on the contrary, everything in it is both tail and head, alternatively and reciprocally. Consider, I beg you, what admirable convenience that combination offers us all, you, me, and the reader. We can cut wherever we want, I my reverie, you the manuscript, the reader his reading; for I do not bind the latter's recalcitrant will to the endless thread of a superfluous plot. Remove one vertebra, and the two pieces of that tortuous fantasy will reunite without difficulty. Chop it up into many fragments, and you will find that each one can exist separately. In the hope that some of those segments will be lively enough to please and divert you, I dare dedicate to you the entire serpent.[10]

(Mon cher ami, je vous envoie un petit ouvrage dont on ne pourrait pas dire, sans injustice, qu'il n'a ni queue ni tête, puisque tout, au contraire, y est à la fois tête et queue, alternativement et réciproquement. Considérez, je vous prie, quelles admirables commodités cette combinaison nous offre à tous, à vous, à moi et au lecteur. Nous pouvons couper où nous voulons, moi ma rêverie, vous le manuscrit, le lecteur sa lecture; car je ne suspends pas la volonté rétive de celui-ci au fil interminable d'une intrigue superflue. Enlevez une vertèbre, et les deux morceaux de cette tortueuse fantaisie se rejoindront sans peine. Hachez-la en nombreux fragments, et vous verrez que chacun peut exister à part. Dans l'espérance que quelques-uns de ces tronçons seront assez vivants pour vous plaire et vous amuser, j'ose vous dédier le serpent tout entier.) [1: 275]

In this dedication of his prose poems to Arsène Houssaye, the director of the journal *La presse*, Baudelaire refers to the collection of his prose poems as a "serpent," fragmented and yet whole, ambiguously head and tail at every point. The head might bite the tail and trace a circle. That would be the serpent's circle, the figure of eternity and the evil seducer who causes the fall of humankind in the Garden of Eden. That circle permeates Baudelaire's work.[11] The poetics of prose poetry correlates directly with the poetics of *Les fleurs du mal*, giving it formal treatment. For Baudelaire, to experiment with new form means, fundamentally, to cut open the circle of the serpent of habit, denial, hypocrisy, and inertia. Writing and reading are acts that break, in content and in form, systematically and methodically, that eternal and evil spell of the serpent that encircles and suffocates us; they are acts that cut up/out the "endless" and the "superfluous," allowing each segment to be "lively enough" and to "exist separately." They are practices of brevity, concentration, and intensification, as in Poe, that lead to awareness and awakening. Baudelaire's poetics is an ethics of lucidity and elegance.[12]

To Paul Valéry, Stéphane Mallarmé pushes to its "perfection and poetic purity" the experimental poetics of elegant form of Poe, Baudelaire, and Baudelaire's Poe.[13] Valéry writes that, for Mallarmé, syntax was "an algebra that he cultivated for itself" (La syntaxe était à ce poète une algèbre qu'il cultivait pour elle-même) ["Sorte de préface" 1: 685]: "Ordinary literature seemed comparable to arithmetic, that is, the search for particular results, in which it is difficult to distinguish the precept from the example; the one [Mallarmé] was conceiving seemed analogous to algebra, because it presupposed the willingness to make evident, to conserve through thoughts, and to develop for themselves, the *forms of language*" (La littérature ordinaire me semblait comparable à une arithmétique, c'est-à-dire à la recherche de résultats particuliers, dans lequel on distingue mal le précepte de l'exemple; celle qu'il concevait me paraissait analogue à une algèbre, car elle supposait la volonté de mettre en évidence, de conserver à travers les pensées et de développer pour elles-mêmes, les *formes du langage*) ["Dernière visite à Mallarmé" 1: 631, my emphasis]. Mallarmé's intense meditation on syntax, his painstaking shaping of language, is an act of awareness and awakening that counters the "automatism" of daily life,[14] forcing not only language but also its users "out of [their] customary furrows."[15]

Mallarmé's "algebraic" lucidity resides in his faithful and honest facing and acceptance of the constraint and difficulty of form as "his particular burden."[16] Just as Perseus is the "hero of lightness" because he is willing to carry about the head of Medusa as "his particular burden," so Mallarmé becomes the poet of weightless lucidity because he chooses to write with heightened consciousness of form's gravity. Mallarmé bears that oppressive constriction of form as "his particular burden," just as Baudelaire bears that of spleen. Form is Mallarmé's spleen. As spleen takes form in Baudelaire, the difficulty of form takes form in Mallarmé.

Mallarmé meets the dread of writing poetry, the terror of formal exactitude that poetry demands, with courage and precision. He turns the terror of exactitude into exactitude of terror, that is, into an exactitude of facing and bearing witness to the task of writing poetry. He observes with clarity the blockage, the paralysis, and the sterility that invade him in that demanding and relentless process. His "Hérodiade" [1: 17–22], with her untouchable beauty of cold reptile and mineral, is the *form* of poetic consciousness of blockage, paralysis, sterility. He turns to form—his hell, his spleen—and makes this turning his business. "I am profoundly and scrupulously a syntaxer/maker of syntax" (Je suis profondément et scrupuleusement syntaxier), Mallarmé confesses in his letter to Maurice Guillemot.[17] The term *syntaxier*, a neologism in French, invents poetry as the profession of making syntax; like a mathematician who discovers new equations and solves and refines them, the poet creates new orders and arrangements of words, images, sounds, and thoughts, by bringing focus and attention to the spatial disposition of language.

Disposition, a key term in Mallarmé's poetics, appears at the beginning of his "Observation relative" to "Un coup de dés" ("A Throw of Dice"): words, "disposed as they are" (disposés comme ils sont), create "spacing of reading" (espacement de la lecture). The "blank/white" space (les blancs) of the page "strike[s] at first/once" (frappent d'abord) and "lead[s]" (amènent) the reader from beginning to end [1: 391]. "Disposition" is the strategic placement of words that guides the reader, almost making him/her glide from the first to the last words, as if moved by forces of gravity inherent in the poem's space. Poetic "disposition" taps into the matrix of space and activates the latent potential energy of all positions. Exact placement allows each word full access to, and harnessing of, the maximum propensity of its own position and thereby allows it to reach maximum openness, inclination, and movement toward dis-position. It imparts momentum to words, ungrounding them from the flat page. Words move in space, on/into/out of the page, floating, rising, spreading, moving apart then close, clashing and touching, solidifying and liquefying. Words are set free to follow their own *inclinaison*, a term that appears on the third page of the poem. Words fall, like dice, as if rolling down an inclined plane. Poetry is form and body—a corpus—in free fall: it is language that awakens and in awakening becomes sensitive to the gravity of form.

In "Un coup de dés," Mallarmé creates precise ratios among brevity, mobility, speed, acceleration and deceleration, weight and lightness, expansion and gathering, dispersion and concentration, position and disposition. He attains "exact spiritual staging" (quelque mise en scène spirituelle exacte) [1: 391], a scenic view, "to open the eyes" (pour ouvrir des yeux) [1: 392]. Eyes open because "Un coup de dés" "strikes at first/once" with the "spacing of reading," the "blanks," and "a simultaneous vision of the Page" (une vision simultanée de la Page), delivering as a "single unit" (unité) [1: 391], as "*the* Page," the two leaves of the open book of poetry. The brevity of poetic elegance expands to double dimension. Not words alone but the entire page, not one page but two enter our eyes simultaneously, opening them wide, as wide as the boundless starry sky. "Un coup de dés," "*rais[ing] . . . a page to the power of the star-filled sky!*" as Valéry puts it (*d'élever . . . une page à la puissance du ciel étoilé!*) [*"Le coup de dés.* Lettre au directeur des *Marges* 1: 626, original emphasis], is cosmic poem giving birth to the vast poetic universe.

Mallarmé scrutinizes the relationship between content and form and subjects it to radical experimentation. It is as if he were a particle physicist of language, spinning, accelerating, and colliding words, applying extreme pressure in order to create maximum ex-pression. He pressures form, seeking maximum precision (overdetermination of syntax), to create maximum semantic multiplicity (underdetermination of content).[18] He forces poetry to the limits of expressivity. He makes form transform: crafted meticulously as if in metal or crystal ("Hérodiade"), a poem becomes like a "prism," a source of pure visibility that focuses, refracts, and disperses light.[19] It passes from solid materiality (metal, crystal) to transparency (prism) and to pure lucidity that breaks the solid form from which it sprang. Intense focus and formalization make language explode from within. Julia Kristeva calls such "dis-position" and "dispersion" "pulverization." "The whole mystery resides in this," she writes: "there is a sentence, . . . but the sentence is pulverized."[20] Syntax, the fundamental baseline of our language, is "pulverized" in "Un coup de dés."

Gilles Deleuze, referring to Proust's words, says that writers "invent a new language within language, a foreign language, as it were. They bring to light new grammatical or syntactic powers. They force language outside its customary furrows. . . . When another language is created within language, it is language in its entirety that tends toward an 'asyntactic,' 'agrammatical' limit."[21] Deleuze's observation pertains to Mallarmé's poetics, too. Mallarmé brings "new grammatical or syntactic powers" to French language; he renders it *étranger*—strange and foreign—to the native ear. Not just for speakers of French but for everyone, and especially for poets, "Un coup de dés" appears, in Valéry' words, *"prodigiously strange/foreign"* (*prodigieusement étrangers*) ["Lettre sur Mallarmé" 1: 635, original emphasis]. Mallarmé's language, perhaps *the* purest of French, is also the most foreign. Intense purification does not eliminate but leads directly to the foreign and the other. His poetry brings out—discovers and uncovers—the inherent foreignness of language in its original purity.

Poetic elegance and mathematical (or scientific) elegance, both exact relationships between minimum and maximum, differ fundamentally in spirit and syntax. *Syntax*, from the Greek *suntaxis*, means "to order together." The syntax of equation and the syntax of verse have different premises, ways of resolution, and solutions. The "coordination of facts," the main goal of "all true science," as August Comte affirms, concerns only quantities.[22] To "order" things together scientifically is, first, to quantify, measure magnitudes, and relate these measurements via equations. Once established, equations demand resolution. The initial equation must be transformed step by step into new and yet equivalent equations until the solution is reached and the unknown articulated in terms of the known. Equation, equivalence, equality: to equate—to "acquiesce to equality," in Isabelle Stengers' words—is to equalize.[23]

Mathematics' task is to bring and subordinate the unknown to the known so that it becomes measurable by the known, so that it acquires the *same measure* as the known. In the mathematical universe, the law of gravity pulls all forms of the unknown—ambiguity, uncertainty, difficulty, difference, that is, any disturbance or newness—toward the known as if toward its center. Newton's law of inertia, that a body "perseveres in its states either of resting or of moving uniformly in a straight line," defines the force field of an equation that imparts tremendous momentum to reason, propelling it to seek resolution and to come finally to rest only by reaching a single solution.[24] By ensuring what Michel Serres calls "single propagation and final solution," the equal and equivalent signs are the very syntax of mathematical elegance.[25] They allow passage with zero resistance and total recuperation from the left side of the equation to the right side.

In physics, this translates, among other things, into "the whole effect is always equivalent to its full cause"—the principle of sufficient reason, as Leibniz elaborated it.[26] Stengers writes that "sufficient reason constituted the ideal of perfection because it was the ideal of a complete definition, which lets nothing escape."[27] A "complete definition" holds firmly what it defines with a clear, indubitable, and immutable boundary: it assures the certainty of the object and of its possession. A "complete definition" solidifies the entity, sets it in stone, as it were. Solid state means grounded, firm, and unchanging. It is not a coincidence that classical mechanics and its concomitant determinism of the Newtonian universe, for example, work only with/on solids and relations between solids.[28]

Truth is a matter of maximum solidity in the deterministic universe of classical thinking: it wants bedrocks, building blocks, cornerstones, not "sand" or "mud." Descartes often uses images of architecture to pitch mathematics—the true and only science, according to him, standing on "foundations that are so firm and solid"—against all other faulty systems that might appear to be "superb and magnificent palaces" but that are, in fact, "built merely on *sand* and *mud*," and hence lacking properly solid ground.[29]

The Cartesian "I" represents a victory of solid entity and its permanence over dissolution and impermanence. "The existence of 'I,' 'I am,' 'I exist,' is clearly uncovered by a minimum-maximum move," Michel Serres writes of Descartes' cogito: "it is the minimal remainder of a maximized strategy or ruse. At the end of which, as soon as *everything* that can be in *any way* disputed has been dismissed, I [Descartes] obtain 'a *more* certain and *more* evident knowledge than *all* the knowledge I had earlier.'"[30] The strategy of minimum-maximum zooms into a single focus, "cogito ergo sum," the only point from which, in a reverse move again of minimum-maximum, the entire space of human knowledge becomes accessible. Descartes' "I" constitutes the *summum* of theoretical elegance. The "I" is "no longer possible to improve by subtraction"; it has attained the perfection of minimalism, as Pawson defines it. "I," the elegant subject, omnipotent and omnipresent, presides over the "elegant universe" in its universal panopticon.[31]

Descartes' elegance dispels the indubitable. The Latin *dubitare* (from *dubare*, or *duo-habere*, "to have two," "to be in two minds") means "to hesitate," "to be indecisive," "to be/oscillate between two." Dubiousness—with its fluid, hesitant, oscillating, and unknown *quality*—is reduced to duality, which delimits, measures (that is, quantifies), solidifies, and determines exactly the terms of the relationship. Duality is dubiousness that is "mastered and possessed," to use Descartes' words.[32] *Dubitare* in Latin means also "to fear." The term *redoubtable*, "fearsome or awesome," derives from *dubitare*: it is "to doubt back," "to dread." It is ultimately fear Descartes dispels in the name of error.

Poetry's purpose is not to make objects, or the world itself, exact and indubitable by eliminating fear; but to produce exactitude in our relationship to the universe *including* fear. To live poetically and thus elegantly is to meet the world with Keats's "*Negative Capability,* that is when man is capable of being in uncertainties, Mysteries, doubts, without any irritable reaching after fact and reason."[33] It is to engage in an *exact* relationship with mystery and uncertainty that is not a unilateral relationship of reason and fact. It is what Jean-Luc Marion defines as a "negative phenomenology," which "culminates in clearing away of the obstacles "that would "encircle . . . and . . . hide" "lived experiences." It is a "counter-method" to Cartesian metaphysics:

> The method should not . . . secure indubitability in the mode of a possession of objects that are certain because produced according to the a priori conditions for knowledge. It should provoke the indubitability of the apparition of things, without producing the certainty of objects. In contrast to the Cartesian or Kantian method, the phenome-

nological method, even when it constitutes phenomena, is limited to letting them manifest *themselves*. Constituting does not equal constructing or synthesizing, but rather giving-a-meaning, or more exactly, recognizing the meaning that the phenomenon itself gives from itself and to itself. The method does not run ahead of the phenomenon, by *fore*-seeing it, *pre*-dicting it, and *pro*-ducing it, in order to await it from the outset at the end of the path (*meta-hodos*) onto which it has just barely set forth. From now on it travels in tandem with the phenomenon, as if protecting it and clearing a path for it by eliminating roadblocks.[34]

Exactitude in poetry means that words "travel in tandem with the phenomenon," intimately, "as if protecting it." It is the exactitude of Perseus, carrying Medusa's head—*the* symbol reason dispels in horror—and offering it a "gesture of refreshing courtesy," allowing Medusa's original "fragile and perishable" beauty to manifest itself in all its "exuberant splendor."[35] Perseus's exactitude is intimacy and protection that see, acknowledge, and accompany *all* of Medusa with *precision*. Her stiffness and fluidity, beauty and terror, immutability and fragility/perishability, life and death—all of what she has been and is now—emerge in extravagance and abundance. Nothing is cast out as error or horror. The "fine grace of coral" runs through the "savage horror of the Gorgon," and vice versa.[36]

Minerva, the Cartesian goddess of reason and war, turned Medusa into her antithesis and placed her on the other side of her shield in a relationship violently flat, simple, and poor: opposition or identity and nothing else. Perseus lives in a field of relationship larger than Minerva's: he can use Medusa as his weapon as Minerva does, but he can also carry her with him in his bag and, from time to time, put her down, let her loose, and let go of her. Minerva lives in a flattened plane of identity and opposition, Perseus in the rich and voluminous space of difference, to use Deleuze's distinction.[37] Poetry calls us to engage in a relationship with the lightness, exactitude, courtesy, and courage of Perseus, with respect to all that comes our way.

Poetry asks us to live in contiguity to our contingencies. From the scattered words of "Un coup de dés," the sentence, "A THROW OF DICE WILL NEVER ABOLISH CHANCE" (UN COUP DE DÉS JAMAIS N'ABOLIRA LE HASARD), rolls out to end in "Every Thought emits a Throw of Dice" (Toute Pensée émet un Coup de Dés) [1: 367–87]. We touch chance exactly, leaving it intact, allowing it to occur exactly. Exactitude and elegance are states of *our* being, when, awakened and attentive, we live in precise ratio with ourselves and the world. With how much precision can we meet the world in all its manifestations, good or evil, knowable or unknowable, certain or doubtful? Poetry's knowledge does *not* dispel but moves toward the experience of the unknown and the new. At the closing of Baudelaire's *Les fleurs du mal*, *the* terrifying unknown—the final inertia—becomes the beginning of a journey into an open sea:

> O Death, old captain, it is time! let us lift anchor!
> This country wearies us, o Death! let us prepare to leave!
> If the sky and the sea are as black as ink,
> Our hearts, which you know, are filled with rays of light!
>
> *(O Mort, vieux capitaine, il est temps! levons l'ancre!*
> *Ce pays nous ennuie, ô Mort! Appareillons!*
> *Si le ciel et la mer sont noirs comme de l'encre,*
> *Nos cœurs que tu connais sont remplis de rayons!)*
>
> ["Le voyage" 1: 134]

Poetry proposes not to harden, shut down, or run away from the unknown, the ultimate terror that is death, not even to conquer or dispel, but to go right into the face of terror. Only then do we open the possibility of radical transformation, comprehending that death, our enemy, is in fact an ally who stands by our side on our journey. "O Death, old captain!"—the apostrophe to death turns us toward it. Death shows itself as "old captain," giving its self to us as a human guide of longtime company. Together we start to move into the experience of final (dis)solution of life.

Baudelaire's use of homonymy between *ancre* (anchor) and *encre* (ink) emphasizes the passage from solid ground[ing] to ungrounding ("let us lift anchor" [levons l'ancre]) into the ocean of ink ("the sea [is] as black as ink" [la mer [est] noir[e] comme de l'encre]). Writing begins as passage from solid to fluid. Flowing into poetic writing coincides with raising the anchor, and hence raising the question of the solidity/stability of the world and our desire to have solidity/stability in life. Italo Calvino refers to Lucretius and Ovid as poets for whom "the knowledge of the world tends to dissolve the solidity of the world."[38] At what point does the solidity of the concepts and methods that have helped us navigate through life become an inexact solution and start to hinder us? At what point, for example, do we start to use concepts to sum up and simplify objects and phenomena "so that we can handle them easily" and "so as to mask their exuberant splendor," as Marion points out?[39] In passing from *ancre* to *encre*, poetry takes science's conceptual solution, hard and solid, and dissolves it *as genuine solution* into the creative and open flow of life's rhythm. There is solution, poetry says, when our theory, concepts, and ideas pass into life and become living knowledge. It says, do not look for equations and formulas but ask *relevant* questions. Resolution consists not in finding solid answers and thereby dissolving questions but in learning what questions to ask. Exact resolution, like the resolution of a lens, concerns the precision with which *we* discern appropriate questions.

To have the sharpness, presence of mind, and courage to ask true questions is like "lifting the anchor." Do we know our "anchors"? Do we know what stabilizes us? Do we know when stability becomes solidity, rigidity, immobility, and paralysis? Poetry asks us to live in exact relationship with our anchor, that is, with the forces of gravity that weigh upon us. It does not say to get rid of the anchor. It says to lift it up and bring it on board. Just as Perseus bears the head of Medusa as his "particular burden," poetry asks us to carry our anchors with *full awareness and exactitude.* And just this act alone, of looking into the deep sea of our being, seeing ourselves fully in that ink on the shores of which we are foundered, and accepting into our hearts the "particular burden" *given* to us, just this act alone, loosens our lives. The anchor lifts its self, and we are headed in a different and new direction.

To lift the anchor is to give our hearts a chance to take risks. "All that the human heart wants is its chance," William James writes. "It will willingly forego certainty in universal matters if only it can be allowed to feel that in them it has that same inalienable right to run risks."[40] Writing, reading, and receiving poetry into our hearts is tantamount to facing our fears, taking our chances at breaking out of our own secure ground and circle, and taking a leap of faith when no equation traces a clear path ahead of us, guaranteeing smooth passage and uncontested success.

Poetry begins where solutions truly dissolve in the passage from *ancre* to *encre*: it emerges as deep immersion, dipping its pen into an ocean of ink and flowing through us, like the blood of our veins, into our lives. A poem, ungrounded from the book that contains it, comes to us and moves us into the vast expanse of sky and sea, dark and fluid as ink, into (the writing of) poetry, so that we may receive it into our being and be "filled with rays of light" of "a sun within a sun."

Calvino devotes the third section of his *Six Memos for the Next Millennium* to "exactitude." In it he speaks of "a plague afflicting language, revealing itself as a loss of cognition and immediacy, an automatism that tends to level out all expression into the most generic, anonymous, and abstract formulas, to dilute meanings, to blunt the edge of expressiveness, extinguishing the spark that shoots out from the collision of words and new circumstances." Calvino sees literature as "the possibilities of health": "Literature, and perhaps literature alone, can create the antibodies to fight this plague in language."[41]

Poetry is exact and elegant *use* of language. It strikes us with formed language so that we may become aware of *how* we say what we say, *how* we read what we read, and *how* we live. It raises the question of style and of lifestyle. Style, as Deleuze writes in *Pourparlers* (*Negotiations*), is both aesthetics and ethics: "Style, in a great writer, is always a style of life, too, not anything at all personal, but inventing a new possibility of life, a way of existing." Michel Foucault, he says, "is a great stylist. Concepts take on with him a rhythmic quality, or . . . a contrapuntal one. His syntax accumulates the mirrorings and scintillations of the visible but also twists like a whip, folding up and unfolding, or cracking to the rhythm of its utterances. And then, in his last books, the style tends toward a kind of calm, seeking an ever more sober, an ever purer line . . ."[42]

To live in "ever more sober," "ever purer" style—this is elegance. Henri Focillon writes in his book *La vie des formes* that "the experimental state is one in which style seeks to define itself."[43] In Mallarmé, elegant style, in violent and "astringent" "pulverization" and "radiant dispersion," opens high poetry to high fashion.[44] Mallarmé, the high priest of French poetry in his ivory tower, is Miss Satin, the English fashion journalist in the streets and boutiques of Paris, and the ever contemplative sailor floating on the Seine. Mallarmé, the poet and the person, lives in rhythmic and stylistic relationship to life.[45] Mallarmé's corpus, in its entirety, is "rhythmic creation of elegance," to paraphrase Poe, who defines the "Poetry of words" as "*The Rhythmic Creation of Beauty.*"[46] Poetic elegance is Mallarmé's lifestyle.

And Baudelaire, the accursed poet of modernity, lived in "exact response" to his period, environment, and inner aspirations/nature, as Valéry writes in his essay "Situation de Baudelaire." He was, as Valéry points out, an exact reader of other poets (like Poe and the Romantics) and an exact critic of other arts (painting, music). His poetic creation springs forth as an exact response to all that is around and inside him. The poet of exactitude is also the dandy of elegance in an impeccable black suit, devoting meticulous attention to appearance. In a letter to his mother of December 26, 1853, Baudelaire writes: "As for your fearing *the degrading* of my person in misery, know that all my life, whether ragged or living decently,—I have always devoted two hours to my toilette" (Quant à tes craintes sur *l'avilissement* de ma personne dans la misère, sache que toute ma vie, déguenillé ou vivant convenablement,—j'ai toujours consacré deux heures à ma toilette) [*Corr* 1: 241, original emphasis]. Michel Butor, in his *Histoire extraordinaire: Essai sur un rêve de Baudelaire*, sees the elegantly dressed and carefully groomed body of Baudelaire itself as a body of work, a work of art.[47] The Baudelairean corpus, in all senses of the term/phenomenon, is a poetics of exactitude and elegance.

In both Baudelaire and Mallarmé, the relationship between writing and body/life, the corpus, undergoes constant metamorphoses, inventing, experiencing, and experimenting to become "ever more sober" and "purer," that is, ever more *exact*, thus opening, as Calvino states, new "possibilities of health" that revitalize us. Form is not only a shape chosen by the poet to match idea with writing but also, beyond that, a relationship of the poet with his/her own self and the world, through which he/she seeks to engage the reader's awareness. It is a poem's clarity, disposition, and courtesy toward the reader that activate and elicit clarity, disposition, and courtesy toward the poem. Through form, the poem addresses and unites itself with its reader. A balance between brevity and length, containment and openness, firmness and suppleness, stillness and dynamism, self-awareness and awareness of the other, autonomy and union, enables the most *precise* encounter between the poem and the reader, and the reader and the world. Form is the measure of (mutual) attention that versifies us into the world. Poetry fashions us. It gives us form, body, and meaning.

For Mallarmé, poetry—the "unique source" ["Observation relative" 1: 392]—is "the expression, through human language brought back to its essential rhythm, of the mysterious sense of the aspects of existence: as such, it endows our days with authenticity and constitutes the sole spiritual task" (La Poésie est l'expression, par le langage humain ramené à son rythme essentiel, du sens mystérieux des aspects de l'existence: elle doue ainsi d'authenticité notre séjour et constitue la seule tâche spirituelle) ["Sur la poésie" 2: 657]. Through poetry we open to our "essential rhythm" and "unique source"; we experience and live our true nature, as "authentic," "spiritual" beings.

Poe writes that "'a long poem,' is simply a flat contradiction in terms" [568]. Baudelaire, who translates "flat contradiction" as "perfect contradiction," asserts: "Among the rights that have been talked about in the recent past there is one that has been forgotten and in whose demonstration *everyone* is interested—the right to contradict oneself" (Parmi les droits dont on a parlé dans ces derniers temps, il y en a un qu'on a oublié, à la démonstration duquel *tout le monde* est intéréssé,—le droit de se contredire) [1: 708, original emphasis]. Exact diction in poetry does not mean absence of contradiction. It means absence of "flat" contradiction, which is, to use Calvino's words, "generic," "anonymous," "abstract," "diluted," " blunted," "extinguished."[48]

Rilke gives new form to the poetics of exactitude and contradiction of Poe and Baudelaire:

> Rose, O pure contradiction, delight
> in being no one's sleep under so many
> lids.
>
> *(Rose, oh reiner Widerspruch, Lust,*
> *Niemandes Schlaf zu sein unter soviel*
> *Lidern.)*[49]

Baudelaire's poetry asks us to live in exact response to life's "exuberant splendor," as flowers of evil, as a rose of "perfect" and "pure contradiction."[50]

For Mallarmé, like Rilke and Baudelaire, poetry means "pure" and exact perception of contradiction, that is, contradiction experienced and expressed, in Calvino's words, in all of the "spark[s] that [shoot] out from the collision of words and new circumstances."[51] In "Un coup de dés," Mallarmé, inventing a new style-syntax that explodes and scatters syntax and grammar, activates all the potential play of meaning so that language, with heightened, free, and new energy, may "[shoot] out" and impact the reader with full kinetic force. Mallarmé's style, a corpus of pure power and elegance, exploding like a bomb, scintillating like stars, stuns us with the pure shock of beauty.

CHAPTER SIX

The Eternal Enigma of Beauty

IN BAUDELAIRE'S POEM "Hymne à la Beauté" ("Hymn to Beauty"), the poet turns toward Beauty as to a goddess.[1] Faced with Beauty, the unknown and the "exuberant splendor" par excellence,[2] the poet does what any of us would do: asks two questions, one in the first stanza, the second in the third.

> Do you come from the depths of the sky or out of the abyss,
> O Beauty? your gaze, infernal and divine,
> Pours confusedly blessing and crime,
> And one can for that compare you to wine.
>
> You contain in your eye sunset and dawn;
> You diffuse perfumes like a stormy evening;
> Your kisses are a philter and your mouth an amphora
> That make the hero cowardly and the child courageous.

Do you come out of the black gulf or descend from the stars?
Destiny, charmed, follows your petticoats like a dog;
You sow at random joy and disaster,
And you rule everything and answer for nothing.

You walk over the dead, Beauty, for whom you do not care;
Of your jewels Horror is not the least charming,
And Murder, among your dearest trinkets,
On your proud belly dances amorously.

The dazzled dayfly flies toward you, candle,
Crackles, flares, and says: Let us bless this torch!
The lover panting bent over his beautiful one
Seems like a dying man caressing his tomb.

That you may come from heaven or hell, what does it matter,
O Beauty! enormous, frightening, ingenuous monster!
If your eye, your smile, your foot, open for me the door
To an Infinite that I love and have never known?

From Satan or from God, what does it matter? Angel or Siren,
What does it matter, if you make,—fairy with velvet eyes,
Rhythm, perfume, gleam, o my only queen!—
The universe less hideous and the instants less heavy?

(Viens-tu du ciel profond ou sors-tu de l'abîme,
O Beauté? ton regard, infernal et divin,
Verse confusément le bienfait et le crime,
Et l'on peut pour cela te comparer au vin.

Tu contiens dans ton œil le couchant et l'aurore;
Tu répands des parfums comme un soir orageux;
Tes baisers sont un philtre et ta bouche une amphore
Qui font le héros lâche et l'enfant courageux.

Sors-tu du gouffre noir ou descends-tu des astres?
Le Destin charmé suit tes jupons comme un chien;

> *Tu sèmes au hasard la joie et les désastres,*
> *Et tu gouvernes tout et ne réponds de rien.*
>
> *Tu marches sur des morts, Beauté, dont tu te moques;*
> *De tes bijoux l'Horreur n'est pas le moins charmant,*
> *Et le Meurtre, parmi tes plus chères breloques,*
> *Sur ton ventre orgueilleux danse amoureusement.*
>
> *L'éphémère ébloui vole vers toi, chandelle,*
> *Crépite, flambe et dit: Bénissons ce flambeau!*
> *L'amoureux pantelant incliné sur sa belle*
> *A l'air d'un moribond caressant son tombeau.*
>
> *Que tu viennes du ciel ou de l'enfer, qu'importe,*
> *O Beauté! monstre énorme, effrayant, ingénu!*
> *Si ton œil, ton souris, ton pied, m'ouvrent la porte*
> *D'un Infini que j'aime et n'ai jamais connu?*
>
> *De Satan ou de Dieu, qu'importe? Ange ou Sirène,*
> *Qu'importe, si tu rends,—fée aux yeux de velours,*
> *Rythme, parfum, lueur, ô mon unique reine!—*
> *L'univers moins hideux et les instants moins lourds?)*
>
> [1: 24–25]

As if to answer his two questions himself, the poet elaborates on Beauty's actions and effects on people and context.

But by the end, the poet has stopped questioning all together. The shift occurs in the last two stanzas, where something emerges that takes over the poet's attention. An insight moves the poet so deeply that he lets go, in a moment's time, of his questions and the attending urge to find immediate answers: "That you may come from heaven or hell, what does it matter, / O Beauty!" (Que tu viennes du ciel ou de l'enfer, qu'importe, / O Beauté!); "From Satan or from God, what does it matter? Angel or Siren, / What does it matter" (De Satan ou de Dieu, qu'importe? Ange ou Sirène, / Qu'importe). Matters have changed. There is a sudden breakthrough; the poet finds himself in a state of intense experience that brings him to here and now—to the universe as here and time as now: "What does it matter, if you make . . . / The universe less hideous and the instants less heavy?" (Qu'importe, si tu rends . . . / L'univers moins hideux et les instants moins lourds?)

If we could parse the energy of the poem, we would see a gradual change in its energy field, especially toward the end. Buildup toward critical mass would be seen as the poem flares up and, by its own momentum, tips over to a new state. The poem shows this through punctuation marks—like energy bundles it emits as signals to be detected. The "question-and-answer" stage of the first four stanzas contains two question marks that go with the two questions, which is logical and (ac)countable. In the last two stanzas (the sixth and seventh), there are three question marks and three exclamation marks, or four even, if one counts the first exclamation mark in the fifth stanza. The two initial questions are outnumbered and/or augmented not only by their own kind (the number of question marks goes up from two to three) but also by another—by three/four exclamation marks. At the end the reader of the poem is left with more questions and many feelings. There is much affective activity. The poem becomes animated—as if somewhere it has received some *"astringent effects"*;[3] now things feel wide awake.

What can we say about the fate of the first two questions based on a sheer energy scan? The poem's energetics, or, as one would say, its statistics or dynamics, tell us that the final state of insight/illumination is a movement of release of energy as both implosion and explosion, coming *not* in solving questions, or eliminating them, but in finding a way to rest *with* them. For in the last two stanzas, questions are still present, more so than ever. Resolution, here, is not about "single propagation and final solution,"[4] as in an equation, closing off questions, but rather about putting a brake on the linear drive toward answers, staying with and dropping into deep feeling and experience of questions *as they are*—in their wide *openness.* Insight concerns questions more than answers.

The shift in the poem's energy is parallel to a passage that moves from *conceptual thinking* of question to answer in a straight line to achieve "acquiescence to equality"[5] to an *experiencing* that moves not away from but closer to the question in front of us, freeing it from the burden of answer—from the compulsion and busyness with which we insist on one—in order to see what it is like to be with questions without answers. We explore ways of relating to the unknown that are new and different from our ordinary way, which is to seek to become "masters and possessors" through equalization and identification.[6] This means recognizing not-knowing as a condition of life, just as Friedrich Nietzsche says we must *"recognise untruth as a condition of life."*[7] It means not to harden or tense up but to rest, relax, and release by leaning toward and going into a state that refuses to yield to our way of knowing. Not to meet resistance with yet another resistance or withdrawal (which is resistance's other face) but to inquire and learn about resistance. This entails learning anew to inquire, learning to ask relevant questions.

Our habitual way tells us to avoid difficult situations of unstable equilibrium. Descartes advises us to move swiftly away from them—to retreat into the safe haven of theory, where the intellect/soul affirms *universal invariance* through "clear and distinct" ideas,[8] so we may do away with unknowable and dangerous experiences that present *particular variants* always in flux through the body and the "fluctuating testimony of the senses."[9] He instructs us to stick with theory's tried and proven method and cast away unreliable and error-prone experience.

To pass from theory to experience is tantamount to passing from known to unknown, intellect to body, reason to heart, in such a way that *the latter does not cut away the former*. And this is the crucial point. Cartesian reasoning forms the basis of our thinking in a tenacious way and instructs us to proceed by exclusion rather than inclusion. The analytic method of division, enumeration, and ordering—or "dissection," "one of the most highly developed skills in contemporary Western civilization"—has been so successful and prized that "we often forget to put the pieces back together again," writes Alvin Toffler.[10] Can we learn to put things together not against analytic method, but *with* it as an ally? Can we mobilize more of our being in relating to the world—our intellect and its theoretical thinking and analytical skills; our body with its senses and emotions; our experiences of myriad things, situations, people? Can we hold all of our selves in ourselves and see the world from there? Can we *live* our knowledge?

Beauty asks us not only to know (intellectually) but also to embody and experience what we know with our entire being.[11] "Most philosophies ... restrict our experience on the side of feeling and will at the same time that they indefinitely prolong it on the side of thought," Henri Bergson observes, discovering an affinity between his philosophy and William James's pragmatism. For Bergson, "what James asks of us" is "to accept experience wholly" and "not to mutilate it" because "our feelings are a part of it by the same right as our perceptions, consequently, by the same right as 'things.'" Bergson says that for James "the whole man counts": "And certainly the importance of human reason is diminished. But the importance of man himself—the whole of man, will and sensibility quite as much as intelligence—will thereby be immeasurably enhanced."[12] "The whole man counts"—such is not the way the Cartesian "minimal I" counts and measures. The conceptual perfection of minimum existence puts Descartes' "I" in a position of poverty and duality with respect to the universe. Living in scarcity—I am not given enough here and now—the "I" orients itself toward elsewhere and future in a stance offensive and defensive.

By the way we hold our selves—*not* holding back—we enter a new way of being in the world. We inquire in a different way. When all of our self participates, knowledge is not a maximum accumulation of solid truths, but that which validates the maximum of our own experience. "Rejecting—for any reason—what you recognize to be significant invalidates your own experience, your own power, and the impulses of your own heart," Gary Zukav says. "I suggest that you decide for yourself whether what stirs you is worthy of your interest. Do not look for footnotes in matters of the heart and the soul. Look inside yourself. You will find an answer. If you do not find it immediately, be patient and know that it will come. Your answer may be 'Yes,' 'No,' or 'Look more closely.' It may be specific to your experience. Will you listen to it? If not, you will always be looking for references, and longing to know from others how they know what they know."[13]

Poetry and Beauty ask us to live by firsthand experience—to live life like an experiment. Turning to others' experiences and to "footnotes" rather than to our own experience makes us live life at one remove, just as the hashish eaters, relying on an external substance to trigger inner experience, wallow in "secondhand paradise" in Baudelaire's "Le poème du hachisch." When we dismiss our own experience—because it does not "fit" with what is prescribed and expected by others and by ourselves—and override it with what "should be," we live at a far distance from ourselves, abandoning our selves to please others, as "secondhand human beings."[14]

When our knowledge activates and accepts our experiences, all of them, turning "experience upon itself to deepen and intensify its own qualities," it becomes, as John Dewey writes, "the wisdom by which men live."[15] Rainer Maria Rilke writes: "But only someone who is ready for everything, who doesn't exclude any experience, even the most incomprehensible, will live the relationship with another person as something alive and will himself sound the depths of his own being."[16] Experience is never a given and cannot be known in advance because it is what gives itself each moment in the present, requiring us to be right here, now, to receive it each time anew. Beauty comes to us precisely as an experience that we do not comprehend but that refuses to be excluded.

In "Hymne à la Beauté," the poet chooses "life and experience" and chooses to "deepen and intensify" both; the poem presents how he comes to do so. The poet's deep experience, finally, is one not of equality/identity but of difference. Suddenly, universe and time break out of their circle of self-sameness and undergo double subtraction: universe becomes "*less* hideous" and time "*less* heavy," each escaping from the pull of habit, the force of inertia. The poet realizes that it is okay not to know and that difference and questions are allowed simply to *be*, that is, to remain unidentified, unidentifiable, and hence open-ended.

Such realization, as abundant question and exclamation marks show us, is profoundly liberating and vitalizing. The poet experiences Beauty as opening to difference. From wanting to "master and possess" *conceptual difference* regarding Beauty's place of origin, or her *cause*, the poet comes to *experience* difference through her *effects*. He no longer approaches difference from without, as mere concept, while standing separate from Beauty, but instead becomes affected by Beauty and experiences difference from within, in his life. Life feels different. *Beauty makes a difference in life and to life.*

Inquiry into Beauty leads to insight on life. Questions on the origin of Beauty concerned with the representation of the other become, at the end, questions about life for the poet and also for us, that is, questions of the experience of the self—how to live *life as experience,* "less hideous[ly]" and "less heav[ily]," more openly, more deeply, more freely, and with more unhindered energy and joy.[17] "Hymne à la Beauté" celebrates Beauty as a gift that opens to genuine experience of life for those who are willing to listen to and answer her call. She "open[s] the door," the poet says, to "an Infinite that [he] love[s] and ha[s] never known." Beauty is a passage, a "door," to a life more abundant—in questions, feelings, and insights.

The poet, in "Hymne à la Beauté," goes through this passage, moving from aesthetico-philosophical stance of conceptual inquiry to ethical stance of felt/lived experience. At the end, difference, experienced as a lessening and relief of burden, compels the poet, and us as well, to see the pull of acquiescence to answer and the rigidity of the conceptual mold, which bind us and which define the position according to which we live and relate to people, things, and the environment. Insight is sudden illumination and awareness of the fixed patterns and conditionings—our thick "lens of the ego," as Henry Miller says—that underlie and form our thought, emotion, speech, and act.[18]

Learning anew is less about learning new contents or even new forms than about learning to see clearly all our habits of learning. In his book *On Creativity,* the physicist David Bohm writes:

> I have discovered in my scientific work that in the long run it is less important to learn of a particular new way of conceiving structure abstractly, than it is to understand how the consideration of such new ideas can liberate one's thought from a vast network of preconceptions absorbed largely unconsciously with education and training and from general background.... For by becoming aware of preconceptions that have been conditioning us unconsciously we are able to *perceive* and to

understand the world in a fresh way. One can then "feel out" and explore what is unknown, rather than go on, as has generally been one's habit, with mere variations on old themes, leading to modifications, extensions, or other developments within the framework of what has already been known.[19]

The poet's two questions to Beauty reflect such habit, pattern, and conditioning. The poet wants to know whence Beauty originates—do you come from A or B? C or D? Questions on origin are metaphysical in their "leading back . . . to the ground in order to lead . . . to certainty" and in their *"belief in antithesis of values."*[20] The poem "Hymne à la Beauté" contains many pairs of opposing "values" from beginning to end: "sky"/"abyss," "infernal"/"divine," "blessing"/"crime," "sunset"/"dawn," "cowardly hero"/"courageous child," "gulf"/"stars," "joy"/"disaster," "everything"/ "nothing," "heaven"/"hell," "Beauty"/"monster," "Satan"/"God," "Angel"/ "Siren." The last two pairs, "Satan"/"God" and "Angel"/"Siren," appear in capital letters in the final stanza. This emphasis goes hand in hand with the shift and intensification of energy at the poem's end.

The poet's intellectual inquiry seeks to *define* Beauty and delineate her by "clear and distinct" idea. To de-fine is to de-limit. Do you come from A or B? C or D?—this means that she must be from one or the other but not from both. We do not want blurry boundaries, but indubitable, separate, clear-cut ones that can hold Beauty in a "complete definition, which lets nothing escape,"[21] in one solid block. Such a conceptual approach amounts to quantification. We want to know where she stands in space; we want to measure her spatial extension and trace her outer limits—is she from "the depths of the sky" or "the abyss," "the black gulf" or "the stars," "heaven or hell"? In short, is she from the space above or below, left side or right? We want to go back to her ground and survey the land of her origin. Our inquiry starts with the geo-metry of Beauty, measuring her magnitude, equating it with known measures in an attempt to evaluate her.[22]

The conceptual approach takes as its premise the principles of sufficient reason (everything has a reason why it is) and bivalence (a statement is either true or false). Binary logic rules with its subtending laws of excluded middle and noncontradiction. Questions posed from such a perspective have firm and exact structures, and they mold, in turn, the answers they admit. They are not open and do not open, because they contain prescriptions that (de)limit Beauty's expanse. Even before any answers, the questions themselves already have closed Beauty in seeking a close-up.

Beauty's own proclamation in "La Beauté" (Baudelaire's sonnet that precedes "Hymne à la Beauté" by four poems in *Les fleurs du mal*[23]) invites such a "hard science" type of inquiry:

> I am beautiful, o mortals! like a dream of stone,
> And my bosom, where each man has bruised himself in turn,
> Is made to inspire in the poet a love
> Eternal and mute as matter.
>
> I reign in the azure like a sphinx no one comprehends;
> I unite a heart of snow to the whiteness of swans;
> I hate movement that displaces lines,
> And never do I weep and never do I laugh.
>
> Poets, in front of my grand attitudes,
> Which I seem to borrow from the proudest monuments,
> Will consume their days in austere studies;
>
> For I have, to fascinate these docile lovers,
> Pure mirrors that make all things more beautiful:
> My eyes, my large eyes of eternal clarities!
>
> *(Je suis belle, ô mortels! comme un rêve de pierre,*
> *Et mon sein, où chacun s'est meurtri tour à tour,*
> *Est fait pour inspirer au poète un amour*
> *Eternel et muet ainsi que la matière.*
>
> *Je trône dans l'azur comme un sphinx incompris;*
> *J'unis un cœur de neige à la blancheur des cygnes;*
> *Je hais le movement qui déplace les lignes,*
> *Et jamais je ne pleure et jamais je ne ris.*

> *Les poètes, devant mes grandes attitudes,*
> *Que j'ai l'air d'emprunter aux plus fiers monuments,*
> *Consumeront leurs jours en d'austères études;*
>
> *Car j'ai, pour fasciner ces dociles amants,*
> *De purs miroirs qui font toutes choses plus belles:*
> *Mes yeux, mes larges yeux aux clartés éternelles!)*
>
> [1: 21]

"La Beauté," considered the most Parnassian among Baudelaire's poems, presents Beauty as eternal, immutable, and impassible—the ideal of pure white marble as in Théophile Gautier's poem "L'art."[24] Beauty is likened to a "sphinx" and her great poses to "monuments." Neither motion ("I hate movement that displaces lines" [Je hais le mouvement qui déplace les lignes]) nor emotion ("And never do I weep and never do I laugh" [Et jamais je ne pleure et jamais je ne ris]) disturb her "eternal clarities" (clartés éternelles). "I am beautiful," Beauty states, "like a dream of *stone.*" Beauty is the ideal of solidity, of "clear and distinct" lines with indubitable borders—a Cartesian dream. She is the beloved object of the intellect of poets, absorbed in "austere studies," ideally resting on its "crystal rock" as in the poem "Les bijoux" ("The Jewels") [1: 158]—"crystal rock / Where, calm and alone, [my soul] had settled itself" (rocher de cristal / Où, calm et solitaire, elle [mon âme] s'était assise).

The poet's "hard" questions in "Hymne à la Beauté" thus have their grounds. But the lines that follow, describing Beauty's effect, constantly undo this (intellectual) ground(ing), just as in "Les bijoux" the seat of "crystal rock" ceases to provide a secure ground for the poet's reason in the presence of his beloved's sinuously undulating and sensuous body. While questions to Beauty separate with their disjunctive *or,* descriptions of Beauty unite opposing entities with their conjunctive *and.* With Beauty, it is not A *or* B, but A *and* B: "your gaze, infernal *and* divine, / Pours confusedly blessing *and* crime, / And one can for that compare you to wine." Each word describing Beauty systematically blurs and exceeds the boundary that the questions draw. Uniting is Beauty's main activity: in the sonnet "La Beauté," Beauty says, "I *unite* a heart of snow to the whiteness of swans" (J'unis un cœur de neige à la blancheur des cygnes).

The first verb for Beauty's actions in "Hymne" is "to pour" (*verser*). It is liquid, not solid. The adverb modifying "to pour" is "confusedly" (*confusément*). The French term *confusément* contains *fusion*. At the end of the first stanza, Beauty is explicitly "compare[d] to wine," and the association with liquid is pushed further: wine, one could say, is liquid that "confuses" the mind. Metaphors of liquid that fuses boundaries continue in the second stanza. Beauty's "kisses are a philter" that "make[s] the hero cowardly and the child courageous." Antithetical values united by *and* literally fuse into each other to become oxymorons. In "le héros lâche" (cowardly hero) and "l'enfant courageux" (courageous child), even the conjunction *and* dissolves. Cowardice and heroism (and courage and child) make direct contact, infusing their traits into each other, as in an osmosis.

Both "wine" and "philter" are not inert but potent fluids. It is as if some ethereal substance emanating from them has produced effects beyond the boundary of their material substance. Beauty is not a solid state, but liquid, almost evaporating into and expanding as a gas. She "diffuse[s] perfumes," notorious, in Baudelaire, for defying all spatial constrictions, as in the poem "Le parfum"—"this grain of incense that fills a church" (Ce grain d'encens qui remplit une église).[25] She is neither immutable nor eternal, but constantly changes like time and weather: "sunset," "dawn," "stormy evening." She "rules everything," yet "at random," with no rules. She has no coherence, no consistency, defying all *stereotypes*, or solid-types—"*stereo* means *solid*" in Greek, as Roland Barthes observes.[26] Nothing can be farther away from the ideal of solidity, from the "dream of stone"—our "ideal knowledge," in Serres' terms, of "solid crystal."[27]

Hard metaphysics of Beauty's origin meets fluid phenomenology of Beauty's appearance and effects. Beauty's "super-fluous" and "exuberant splendor" ungrounds the questions' ground, their dualistic conception, as a river erodes earth and human constructions. "Hymne à la Beauté" reverses Descartes' trajectory. If the Cartesian "I" of "clear and distinct" idea and solid knowledge reduces dubiousness into duality, the poetic "I" in "Hymne à la Beauté" opens up duality to dubiousness not only at the level of content and image—liquid, gas, union-fusion-confusion through conjunctive *and* versus solid, separation through disjunctive *or*—but also at the level of form: spatial order and the position of words.

Throughout the poem, all the pairs of opposing values appear in chiasmic inversion, constantly switching sides from right to left and vice versa. The first three stanzas perform careful and constant permutation: "depths of sky"/"abyss," "infernal"/"divine," "blessing"/"crime," "sunset"/"dawn," "black gulf"/"stars," "joy"/"disasters." The last two stanzas continue the inversion: "heaven"/"hell," "Satan"/"God," "Angel"/"Siren." Through chiasmus, opposing sides become reversals of each other, meet and touch each other, and cross over to each other's side.[28] The poem produces syntactic—literally spatial—blurring of sides, countering quantification, which aims to chisel out clear-cut dimension and separation of space. There is oscillation between two sides without definite/definitive settling—Beauty is a state of being of/in two: *duo-habere, dubitare*. She resists a Cartesian and geometrical approach.

Even the indubitable duality of the *or* questions starts to destabilize. The poet's first question, "Do you come from the depths of the sky or out of the abyss[?]" (Viens-tu du ciel profond ou sors-tu de l'abîme), becomes rearticulated as "Do you come out of the black gulf or descend from the stars?" (Sors-tu du gouffre noir ou descends-tu des astres?), with a chiasmic inversion: we go from "depths of the sky"/"abyss" to "black gulf"/"stars."

The same verb, "to come out" (*sortir*), modifies both "abyss" and "black gulf," placing them on equal grounds. This, in turn, aligns "depths of the sky" with "stars." But here, the match is not as strongly reinforced, since different verbs are used: "to come" (*venir*) for "sky" and "to descend" (*descendre*) for "stars." The notion of height implied by the verb "to descend," logically placing "stars" high up in the sky, is counterbalanced by the coupling of "depths" with "sky" ("ciel profond"). Instead of being alongside the "stars," "sky" now seems more to range itself with "black gulf," with which it shares other similarities. Both "black gulf" and "depths of the sky" come first in the series and are modified by adjectives—"black" (*noir*) and "deep/profound" (*profond*)—that are closely related.

"Abyss" and "stars" are not modified or linked to each other through adjectives. But with the rhyme, or even the homonymy, in French between *des astres* (stars) and *désastres* (disasters), a disaster is imminent in the sky: "sky" and "stars" may possibly, even probably, collapse into "abyss" and "gulf." The disaster of the profound abyss is contained in the stars of the sky. "Sky" (or "stars") and "abyss" (or "gulf") are not as distinct and far apart as *or* would like them to be. The disjunctive *or* is not effective in keeping things separate.

The indubitable *or* opens to the dubitable *and*. The founding structure of the poet's questions—seeking spatial distinction and definition: are you from above or below, left or right?—is abrogated not only by surrounding descriptions cast in *and* with chiasmic inversion, which (con)fuse spaces, but also from within, by its own formulation of questions, the spacing of its own language. "Ciel profond" (depths of the sky), the first term of distinction in the first question, already puts height and depth in close proximity, giving them almost similar dimensions. The antitheses in the poem correspond to the tension between two uses of language: one that prescribes, as Stengers articulates, by "*judging* phenomena [and] submitting them to a rational ideal"[29] and norms (questions in *or*) and one that describes phenomena as they are by submitting ourselves to them (description in *and*). There is gradual erosion of the first type of use, culminating in implosion/explosion at the end of the poem.

The poet's first question in the first stanza, for example—"Do you come from the depths of the sky or out of the abyss, / O Beauty?"—is taken up in the sixth stanza: "That you may come from heaven or hell, what does it matter, / O Beauty!" Rather than using two different verbs, "to come" (*venir*) and "to come out" (*sortir*), as he did at first, the poet now uses the same verb, "to come" (*venir*), for both "heaven" and "hell." He makes less differentiation.

Question mark changes into exclamation marks. Conceptual question gives way to felt experience. What is felt is a loosening of the grip of conceptual, binary, exclusive thinking. There is realization of incommensurability between our intellectual frame, on the one hand, and our experience of phenomena of Beauty and the universe, on the other. The world cannot be measured according to our rule(r) of the normative ideal. "That you may come from heaven or hell, what does it matter, / O Beauty! enormous, frightening, ingenuous monster!" the poet exclaims. "Enormous," therefore outside the norm—from the Latin *enormis*, with *ex-* (out of) and *norma* (a carpenter's square for measuring right angles, hence pattern, rule)—Beauty exceeds all limits. A "monster," like the "sphinx" in the poem "La Beauté," she unites entities that the norm separates. Monsters, as mythology shows (the Minotaur or Chimera, for example), are beings of impossible conjunction, mixture, and confusion. With her dubitable borders and composite/confusing nature, Beauty is anything but the Cartesian ideal. The "dream of stone" of "La Beauté" turns out to be Descartes' nightmare.

At the end of the poem, each of the three normative *ors* is conjoined with "what does it matter": "That you may come from heaven *or* hell, *what does it matter*"; "From Satan *or* from God, *what does it matter*"; "Angel *or* Siren, / *What does it matter.*" *Or* becomes less disjunctive, and the separate categorization it creates and maintains even irrelevant.

"What does it matter" (*qu'importe*), the counterpoint to "or" (*ou*), appears for the first time in the sixth stanza:

> That you may come from heaven or hell, what does it matter,
> O Beauty! enormous, frightening, ingenuous monster!
> If your eye, your smile, your foot, open for me the door
> To an Infinite that I love and have never known?

> (*Que tu viennes du ciel ou de l'enfer, qu'importe,*
> *O Beauté! monstre énorme, effrayant, ingénu!*
> *Si ton œil, ton souris, ton pied, m'ouvrent la porte*
> *D'un Infini que j'aime et n'ai jamais connu?*)

In French, *qu'importe* rhymes with *porte*—"door," the first word literally containing the second. The rhyme brings out the door that has remained embedded and hidden so far, making it present, and opens it, creating a passageway through *qu'importe*. A door opens walls, connects spaces, and allows passage without completely collapsing the spaces it links. As opposed to a wall, which only separates, a door creates a range of different possibilities of spatial relation: it can close, or open, or be anywhere in-between.

The disjunctive *où* (or) functions like a wall imposing only one relation, of separation and antagonism. It is the hard and impenetrable wall of binary opposition. *Qu'importe* (what does it matter) is a door, opening "sky" to "abyss," "joy" to "disaster," left side to right side, above to below, and indubitable *or* to dubitable *and*. It is a term of conjunction and passage between *or* and *and*, between separation and connection, exclusion and inclusion.

Beauty's "eye," "smile," and "foot" open the door for the poet. Beauty is opening. The poet's exclamation, "qu'importe," which, too, opens, hence follows Beauty's opening. His "qu'importe" resonates with Beauty—with her *porte*. Beauty moves (inside) the poet's words. "Qu'importe" is his word to Beauty, his "hymn to Beauty."

"I am beautiful, o mortals! like a dream of stone" (Je suis belle, ô mortels! comme un rêve de pierre)—Beauty addresses the poets and us in "La Beauté." To respond to her call and say "Yes, you are beautiful" means to speak as "mortals." To say yes to Beauty, we must assume our mortal nature. Beauty calls us to respond with full awareness and bearing of our own death. Just as the rhyme between *qu'importe* and *porte* brings out the door, which has hitherto been unrecognized and yet has always been there, Beauty's words "o mortals!" call us to recognize our own "fragility and perishability," to move closer to our true mortal nature.

The "*astringent effects*" I spoke of, which bring about the poet's transformation and final realization in "Hymne à la Beauté," are the shock of death. This happens in the fifth stanza, between the first four (where the poet asks his two questions in *or* and follows them with descriptions in *and*) and the last two (where he drops his questions in a triple exclamation, "what does it matter"). It is a crucial stanza of transformation, which makes the poem and the poet tip over to a new state:

> The dazzled dayfly flies toward you, candle,
> Crackles, flares, and says: Let us bless this torch!

The lover panting bent over his beautiful one
Seems like a dying man caressing his tomb.

*(L'éphémère ébloui vole vers toi, chandelle,
Crépite, flambe et dit: Bénissons ce flambeau!
L'amoureux pantelant incliné sur sa belle
A l'air d'un moribond caressant son tombeau.)*

This stanza stands out from the rest: it is the only one in the entire poem where the structure of address between the poet as "I" and Beauty as "you" changes. The relationship between first- and second-person singular governing the rest of the poem is transposed to a relationship between third-persons singular. Poet becomes a "dayfly" (éphémère), then a "lover" (amoureux) who looks like a "dying man" (moribond); and Beauty, first called "you" (toi), becomes a "candle" (chandelle), then "*his* [the lover's] beautiful one" (*sa* belle) and "*his* [the lover's] tomb" (*son* tombeau). Both poet and Beauty move toward death and toward each other in one and the same move.

In becoming an "éphémère," the poet assumes and lives his ephemeral, and hence mortal, nature. It is as if the poet had been carrying on, during the first four stanzas of "Hymne à la Beauté," the theoretical and "austere studies" he started in "La Beauté"; now, in the fifth stanza of "Hymne," he is belatedly waking up from his transfixed state (Beauty "fascinates" her "docile lovers" in "La Beauté") and responding to Beauty's first call—"I am beautiful, o mortals!"—dating back from "La Beauté." The poet finally hears his own calling; he hears his own death in Beauty's "o mortals!" He realizes his transient nature and experiences it as no different from that of a dayfly: "The dazzled dayfly flies toward you, candle, / Crackles, flares, and says: Let us bless this torch!" (L'éphémère ébloui vole vers toi, chandelle, / Crépite, flambe et dit: Bénissons ce flambeau!). Poet and words emerge ephemerally in the span of one stanza out of seven, as if living only for one day of the week.[30]

Hearing and answering Beauty is saying yes to our own death. In turning toward Beauty, we become *éphémère*. We are "a dying man." We "caress [our] tomb." The change in the personal pronoun, from "I"/"you" to "he"/"she"/"it," registers this death. Emile Benveniste says of the third person that it is a "non-person, being marked by the absence of what precisely qualifies the 'I' and the 'you.'"[31] Grammatically, death makes person disappear into non-person. Poetically, the disappearance of "I" and "you" abolishes the distance and separation between "I" and "you," allowing complete opening between the two. The difference between "I" and "not-I" disappears in a loving union. In one and the same move, poet-dayfly flies into Beauty-candle and burns into her-it, forming one flame, and poet-lover leans over his beloved, "caressing his tomb." There is total fusion and union that consume not just the poet's days in "austere studies" but his entire being. Poet-dayfly-lover is poet-Icarus, "burned by the love of the beautiful" (brûlé par l'amour du beau) ["Les plaintes d'un Icare" 1: 143].

Yet another change of voice occurs in the fifth stanza. A voice in the first-person plural—"Let us bless this torch!" (Bénissons ce flambeau!)—emerges from the third-person singular. A unified voice in exclamation springs forth, inaugurating the series of exclamations that leads to final insight in the subsequent stanzas. When poet-dayfly burns into Beauty-candle, living his death, the song of celebration and benediction emerges—"Bénissons ce flambeau!" It is the true moment of hymn within "Hymne à la Beauté." Poet and Beauty live and die in loving union and burning fusion in total transfusion. It is outburst—implosion and explosion—of poetic language within the poem. Poetic language comes to be and resonates beautifully in this stanza: the rhymes of *beau* and *belle* (masculine and feminine forms of the adjective *beautiful*)—"chandelle"/"belle," "flambeau"/"tombeau"—sing death, fusion, light, lightness all at once as beautiful—*beau* and *belle*.

Medusa becomes touchingly beautiful when Perseus lets her "fragility and perishability" show through her stony encasement. So it is with us, when we become aware of the hardness with which we have covered the truth of our mortality—our true nature—in order not to face the terror of our own death; we are able to experience our vulnerability and accept the genuine tenderness of our heart. To experience and embrace our mortal nature is to come back to ourselves here and now as body, heart, mind, and soul. It is to risk occupying all of our selves fully, saturating our own phenomena,[32] coming into full contact with life's intensity, fluidity, and preciousness. It is *opening to the contiguity and contingency of life.*

Weed twigs, touching Medusa and absorbing her power that is both deadly and life-giving, stiffen *and* blossom into coral.[33] Opening to death is opening to life. When life and death no longer battle and clash (through *or*) but touch each other (through *and*), when we "caress our tombs," when there is contiguity between life and death, our life feels "less hideous," "less heavy," and even perhaps touchingly beautiful. There is blossoming of life as "the dubitative and fragile marvel," to use Serres' words[34]—"les fleurs du mal." We are all Minerva and Medusa to ourselves. Beauty calls us to be Perseus, too, for ourselves.

The poet calls Beauty an "enormous, frightening, ingenuous monster!" (monstre énorme, effrayant, ingénu!). Beauty comes as the experience precisely of both terror ("frightening") and genuineness ("ingenuous"). Genuine experience and terror go together, because to feel genuinely means to feel our heart opening. Vulnerability feels terrifying. But this is the spot where Beauty holds us in *"Negative Capability"*[35] and asks us to go deep into the heart of our experience, acknowledging peril and taking risks, and thus to commit ourselves truthfully to the spirit of "experience" and the "peril" that lies at its heart (from the Latin *experiri*, with *ex-* + *peritus* [peril]). Such is the truth of life Beauty reveals to us. She tells us and reminds us, shows us and demonstrates to us—*monster* derives from the Latin *monere* and *monstrare* (to warn, to be an omen of, to show, to point out)—that "fear is a natural reaction to moving closer to the truth," as Pema Chödrön writes.[36] We must face fear: this is the rigorous and vigorous truth of life and death. It is not by covering up our vulnerable and mortal nature but by seeing clearly into it, discovering an opening where there seemed to be only a dead-end wall, and having the courage and trust to open and walk through that door of terror, that we truly enter the realm of experience and lived/felt knowledge. For only then do we wake up. Beauty calls us to open our doors and walk our own paths —she calls us to freedom.

"Not good, not bad, but *my* taste of which I am no longer ashamed and which I have no wish to hide," Nietzsche's Zarathustra announces. "'This is *my* way; where is yours?'—thus I answered those who asked me 'the way.' For *the* way—that does not exist."[37] Beauty does the same. She reflects back, through her eyes, which are like "pure mirrors," the questions we ask her: "What is your way, Beauty?"—"What is *your* way?" She does not provide us with "*the* way" or *the* theory; she does not even give us "footnotes." Her "eye," her "smile," her "foot" "open . . . the door / To an Infinite" that leads not to the absolute path. She does not lead; she simply opens us (to) here and now, and opens the question of "the path" itself.

When we receive knowledge—and knowledge of death, in particular—taking it into our bloodstream, so that it can imbue our whole being, letting it come in through the doors of our heart and mind to reach our soul, as Pascal says,[38] then knowledge blooms into, and as, our words, acts, emotions, and thoughts. It *is* what we say, do, feel, and think. It is *how* we live. Beauty asks us to know the hard fact of our death "not only through our reason but also through our heart,"[39] letting it sink into the deepest core of our being. The anchor we lift at the end of *Les fleurs du mal* we take into the inner ocean of the heart, and thus we enter into life's stream and embark on our truest journey:

> O Death, old captain, it is time! let us lift anchor!
> This country wearies us, o Death! let us prepare to leave!
> If the sky and the sea are as black as ink,
> Our hearts, which you know, are filled with rays of light!
>
> Pour us your poison and let it comfort us!
> We want, so strongly does the fire burn our brains,
> To plunge into the depths of the abyss, Hell or Heaven, what does it matter?
> To the depths of the Unknown to find something *new!*[40]
>
> (*O Mort, vieux capitaine, il est temps! levons l'ancre!*
> *Ce pays nous ennuie, ô Mort! Appareillons!*
> *Si le ciel et la mer sont noirs comme de l'encre,*
> *Nos cœurs que tu connais sont remplis de rayons!*

Verse-nous ton poison pour qu'il nous réconforte!
Nous voulons, tant ce feu nous brûle le cerveau,
Plonger au fond du gouffre, Enfer ou Ciel, qu'importe?
Au fond de l'Inconnu pour trouver du nouveau!
["Le voyage" 1: 134, original emphasis]

The hymn to death that closes *Les fleurs du mal* is also a hymn to Beauty: "To plunge into the depths of the abyss, Hell or Heaven, what does it matter? / To the depths of the Unknown to find something *new!*" has a deep resonance with "Hymne à la Beauté"'s "That you may come from heaven or hell, what does it matter, / O Beauty! . . . / If your eye, your smile, your foot, open for me the door / To an Infinite that I love and have never known?" Death is to "plunge" to "the depths of the Unknown to find something *new*," and Beauty "opens the door" to "an Infinite that I love and have never known."[41]

Death—Beauty—Unknown—New—Infinite—Love.

Death and Beauty open to the unknown and new, to an infinite—"an Infinite that I love," the poet says. Beauty, through Death, and also Death, through Beauty, call us to love, because love, not just knowledge, opens us to the unknown, the new, and the infinite. Love—an experiential relation of opening, surrendering, and offering of total attention—which soaks, shocks, and wakes us up in our entire being (as in the poem "A une passante" ["To a Woman Passing By"]), is what matters deeply and truly. Poetry tells us this: "Here is my secret. It's quite simple," but "it's something that's been too often neglected." "People have forgotten this truth," but "you mustn't forget it." "The only things you learn are the things you tame."[42]

To live poetically in the world means to listen to and take into our hearts this "simple secret" that the fox tells the Little Prince. "To tame" (*apprivoiser*) is "to create ties" (*créer des liens*), the fox says: "For me you're only a little boy just like a hundred thousand other little boys. . . . For you I'm only a fox like a hundred thousand other foxes. But if you tame me. . . . You'll be the only boy in the world for me. I'll be the only fox in the world for you."⁴³ "Taming" between the fox and the Little Prince, and between the Little Prince and his rose, is love between the poet and Beauty. At the end of "Hymne à la Beauté," the poet calls Beauty "o my *only* queen!" He realizes Beauty's secret—"the only things you learn are the things you [love]." Both taming and loving "force us to turn around the *principium identitatis indiscernibilium* [principle of the identity of indiscernibles] and affirm the opposite, namely, the *principium de discernendo identico* [principle of the discernment of identicals]," as José Ortega y Gasset writes.⁴⁴ Love, like Beauty, makes a difference.

"Whilst in speaking of human things, we say that it is necessary to know them before we can love them, which has passed into a proverb, the saints on the contrary say in speaking of divine things that it is necessary to love them in order to know them, and that we only enter truth through charity, from which they have made one of their most useful maxims."⁴⁵ What Pascal says here of "divine truth" holds true for poetic truth. Love does not come at the end; it must be there at the beginning. It is not reason's Tower of Babel that joins us to the divine, but our open heart.

Poetry calls us to pass from knowing to learning—from craving knowledge and clinging to it through battling and solidifying, to loving to learn and receive and also to release and dissolve what we learn into our beings and into the world. Poetry proposes a different way of "knowing." From the structure of war and of subject/object dichotomy, in which the former dominates the latter, we pass into a relation of love—what James calls "intimacy," Bergson "sympathy," and Einstein "friendliness."⁴⁶ Poetry opens a door to remind us that we *have a choice* to step out of the centripetal force field of the known that pulls us to inertia, security, and sleep. It asks us to venture beyond the rigid lines of equations that quantify, reduce, and bind the world to human measure, to experience the incommensurability of life and the universe in all its terror and joy. Poetry's lines—verse (from the Latin *vertere*, "to turn")—turning, swirling, gathering momentum to burst (out of) the constricting circle of sufficient reason, fear, and slumber, remind us, as Miller says, of "a great work of art, . . . of all that is fluid and intangible. Which is to say, *the universe.*"⁴⁷ Of *our* universe, the *only one* that is given to us.

In "Hymne à la Beauté," Beauty "pours" (*verser*) out her phenomenal abundance, and the poet turns toward (*vers*) her finally to embrace the "universe." *Verser, vers, univers*—poetry's verse and universe. Miller continues: "It [the universe] cannot be understood; it can only be accepted or rejected. If accepted we are revitalized; if rejected we are diminished. Whatever it purports to be it is not: it is always something more for which the last word will never be said."⁴⁸ "Hymne à la Beauté" shows the poet's trajectory from trying to "understand" Beauty, from an oppositional stance, to "accepting" her and saying "yes" to her and to the whole universe. At the end, the poet is "revitalized" not because he has "understood" Beauty or found the answers to his questions but because he has *learned* that to accept and to love are the only way to true affirmation in/of life.

"To affirm is to create," Gilles Deleuze writes of Nietzsche's philosophy: "*to affirm is not to take charge, to take upon oneself, but to deliver, to discharge what lives.* To affirm is to make light: not to load life with the weight of higher values, but *to create* new values that are those of life, that make of life the light and the active.*"⁴⁹ "To make light" and "active," "to discharge," "to create," "to affirm": all of this happens in the *triple affirmation of "what does it matter"* in the last two stanzas of Baudelaire's "Hymne à la Beauté." "What does it matter" discharges life from "the weight of higher values"—"heaven" over "hell," "God" over "Satan," "Angel" over "Siren"—and "creates new values which are those of life, that make of life the light and the active." At the end of the poem, life is "light" (there is double subtraction: "less hideous" and "less heavy") and "active" (there is discharge, release, and hence abundance of life's energy).

"Almost in the cradle are we apportioned with heavy words and worths: 'good' and 'evil'—so calls itself this dowry. For the sake of it we are forgiven for living." "Heavy onto him are earth and life, and so *wills* the spirit of gravity! But he who would become light, and be a bird, must love himself:— thus do *I* teach." So Nietzsche writes in the section of *Thus Spake Zarathustra* entitled "The Spirit of Gravity." Lightness, love, and life converge: "He who will one day teach men to fly will have shifted all landmarks; to him will all landmarks themselves fly into the air; the earth will he christen anew—as 'the light body.'"[50] For the poet in "Hymne à la Beauté," the universe does he bless anew—as "the light body."

Of the universe, Miller writes: "Whatever it purports to be it is not: it is always something more for which the last word will never be said." So, too, is Beauty in Baudelaire. In "La Beauté," Beauty's seeming solidity does not produce solid knowledge; on the contrary, it makes her inaccessible. She is like a "sphinx no one comprehends" (sphinx incompris). Her hardness stands in the way, resisting our understanding. Poets "consume their days in austere studies," being "bruised" by her heart of stone, without figuring her out. But her hardness is only a cover: "my grand attitudes, / Which I seem to borrow from the proudest monuments" (mes grandes attitudes, / Que j'ai l'air d'emprunter aux plus fiers monuments). Her monumental solidity and immobility are a semblance.

"I am beautiful" (Je suis belle), begins Beauty, who at the end says: "Pure mirrors that make all things more beautiful: / My eyes, my large eyes of eternal clarities!" (De purs miroirs qui font toutes choses plus belles: / Mes yeux, mes larges yeux aux clartés éternelles!). The poem begins with "beautiful" (belle) and ends with "more beautiful" (plus belle). However beautiful she may be, she is always "more" beautiful. Her eyes are "pure mirrors that make all things more beautiful." A mirror, especially a "pure" one, ought to reflect back the identical image of what stands in front of it. But Beauty's enigma lies in her trespassing all identifications. She possesses no measure whereby we can mimic her magnitude; no equations can be written. More than in the adjective *belle*, Beauty's essence resides in the adverb *plus*. She is a passage to "more," a "door" to abundance. Her "pure-self" is always her "plus-self."

"She is beautiful, and more than beautiful; she is astonishing" (Elle est belle, et plus que belle; elle est surprenante), Baudelaire writes in the prose poem "Le désir de peindre" ("The Desire to Paint") [1: 340]. Here, "her eyes are two caves scintillating vaguely with mystery, and her gaze illuminates like lightning: it is an explosion in the darkness" (Ses yeux sont deux antres où scintille vaguement le mystère, et son regard illumine comme l'éclair: c'est une explosion dans les ténèbres). The "I" speaks of the beautiful woman's "laughter," "burst[ing]," which makes us "dream of the miracle of a splendid flower blossoming in a volcanic ground" (au bas de ce visage . . . éclate . . . le rire . . . qui fait rêver au miracle d'une superbe fleur éclose dans un terrain volcanique).

Beauty comes as the experience of sudden "illumination"—like "lightning" (*l'éclair*), "explosion," "burst[ing]" (*éclate*), and "blossoming" (*éclose*). The words in French begin with similar sounds—*éclair, explosion, éclate, éclose*—emphasizing the close connections among the movements they denote. The final release of energy into exclamation in "Hymne à la Beauté"; the bursting of laughter in "Le désir de peindre"; the explosion, this time, of the soul, in another prose poem of Baudelaire, "Any Where Out of the World: N'importe où hors du monde" [1: 357], and also of the artworks of the painter Constantin Guys, which Baudelaire admired as "luminous explosion[s] in space" (explosion lumineuse dans l'espace) [2: 700] in his essay *Le peintre de la vie moderne*—all constitute the underlying energetics of Baudelaire's poetry. It is *Les fleurs du mal* as the "miracle of a splendid flower blossoming in a volcanic ground."[51]

Poetry as insight, an experience of the "Infinite" as both explosion *and* (*et*) implosion, extensive *and* (*et*) intensive, breaks open the circle that separates the former from the latter, so that explosion *is* (*est*) implosion and extensive *is* (*est*) intensive—*a sun within a sun.*

"We know to give our entire life every day" (Nous savons donner notre vie entière tous les jours), Arthur Rimbaud writes in the prose poem "Matinée d'ivresse" ("Drunken Morning").[52] When the poet, in Baudelaire's "Hymne à la Beauté," suddenly turns into a "dayfly" in the span of one stanza out of seven, burns into Beauty's flame, and says "Let us bless this torch!" he learns, at that moment, to "give [his] entire life." Poetry emerges in that giving. "'*Emergence*' is understood as the appearance of the unanalyzable totality of a new entity that renders irrelevant the intelligibility of that which produced it," Isabelle Stengers writes.[53] The apparition of *éphémère* in the fifth stanza, which dislodges the logic of Baudelaire's poem and precipitates a new state in the following stanzas, is "emergence." The "intelligibility" that guided the inquiry and "produced" questions in *or* is "render[ed] irrelevant" with *qu'importe*.

After the fifth stanza, the poem resumes its prior structure of address —"I"/"you"—in the subsequent two stanzas. We seem to be back to "before," and yet life itself has shifted in its entirety. The universe offers true meaning—the *only* one (*uni*-verse)—and becomes "the light one" because the poet now "knows to give his entire life." When we withhold ourselves in a defensive stance and launch attacks in order to crack open Beauty's secret and submit her to our knowledge, Beauty, as a mirror, returns to us our own acts of aggression. She, too, withholds herself, retreating into her monumental fortress, against which we bruise ourselves to death. Beauty proclaims in "La Beauté" that at her "bosom," "each man has bruised himself" (Et mon sein, où chacun s'est meurtri). The verb *meurtrir* in French means both "to bruise" and "to kill." Nothing comes forth from this situation of deadlock. But when we open ourselves to the experience of the unknown, willing to be with questions without answers, learning to love Beauty as she is—an eternal enigma—then she, too, in turn, opens to us, blessing and transforming our life.

Miller writes that "understanding is not a piercing of mystery, but an acceptance of it, a living blissfully with it, in it, through and by it."[54] Rilke urges us "to love *the questions themselves*": "Don't search for the answers, which could not be given to you now, because you would not be able to live them. And the point is, to live everything. *Live* the questions now. Perhaps then, someday far in the future, you will gradually, without even noticing it, live your way into the answer."[55] Intimacy with the unknown—to love and live the questions of the moment—this "love's knowledge" is poetic knowledge.[56]

We realize that it is not outer conquests but inner insight that frees us and the universe, because "inner" insight precisely steps out of the inner/outer dichotomy. "You do not need to leave your room. Remain sitting at your table and listen. Do not even listen, simply wait. Do not even wait, be quite still and solitary. The world will freely offer itself to you to be unmasked, it has no choice, it will roll in ecstasy at your feet," Franz Kafka writes.[57] "The world" "has no choice" but to "freely offer itself" to us and "roll in ecstasy" at our feet, when we "know to give our entire life every day," because when we give ourselves fully, we dissolve the hard line that separates us from the world, and what we do, the universe does too: "it has no choice."

"We know to give our entire life every day"—this means dying every day as *éphémère* and, thereby, waking up and discovering *éternité* anew every day. This is living poetically in the world. Rimbaud's poem "L'éternité" begins and ends with this:

> She is found again.
> What?—Eternity.
> It is the sea gone
> With the sun.
>
> (*Elle est retrouvée.*
> *Quoi?—L'Éternité.*
> *C'est la mer allée*
> *Avec le soleil.*)[58]

A poem lives and dies, rises and sets, as a sun within a sun.

EPILOGUE

"Emotion-in-Syntax"

"We are unknown to ourselves, we men of knowledge—and with good reason." So Friedrich Nietzsche begins his preface to *On the Genealogy of Morals*. "We have never sought ourselves—how could it happen that we should ever *find* ourselves? . . . Whatever else there is in life, so-called 'experiences'— which of us has sufficient earnestness for them? Or sufficient time? Present experience has, I am afraid, always found us 'absent-minded': we cannot give our hearts to it—not even our ears! . . . So we are necessarily strangers to ourselves, we do not comprehend ourselves, we *have* to misunderstand ourselves, for us the law 'Each is furthest from himself' applies to all eternity— we are not 'men of knowledge' with respect to ourselves."[1]

Poetry calls us to awaken, this moment, from being "absent-minded," to "give our hearts" or "even our ears!" as Nietzsche says—"our entire life," in Rimbaud's words[2]—to "present experience." Poetry offers the possibility of deeper intimacy with life, but intimacy, and the joy and lightness it brings, comes about only when we inquire genuinely into the state of our "absent mind," observing honestly how we bypass experience by withdrawing, withholding, and keeping ourselves at a distance. Our willingness to acknowledge our difficulties in staying present is already an act of presence of mind and of intimacy.

"Every man, when he gets quiet, when he becomes desperately honest with himself, is capable of uttering profound truths."[3] Henry Miller's statement is poetry's imperative: to become "quiet" and "desperately honest" with ourselves in order to see the "profound truths" at the core of our being. There are joy and love but also fear, anger, doubt, gloom, pain, shame, guilt, hatred. Poetry demands that we acknowledge all of these, with exactitude and kindness, that we notice how we relate to each habitually, clinging to pleasure and seeking to avert pain, selecting, segregating situations, people, and things according to our preference, establishing binary oppositions or rigid hierarchies, making judgments, excluding what we don't want. Most often, ridding ourselves of what we dislike lies beneath the threshold of consciousness, and we do not realize that our strategies to curtail pain lead to greater suffering. Like the drunkard in Antoine de Saint-Exupéry's *The Little Prince*, who drinks to forget that he is "ashamed of drinking,"[4] we live trapped in the logic and circle of addiction, denial, and hypocrisy.

Baudelaire exposes and denounces this pattern of "holding back" and the hypocritical and narcotic relationship we tend to hold with the world. His experimental poetry of *Les fleurs du mal, Les paradis artificiels*, and *Le spleen de Paris* demands that we practice clear-seeing and awareness of the addiction and inertia that govern our life, in which we, "absent-minded," get by with minimum effort. Poetry asks us not to retreat into absence but to offer our presence fully to ourselves and to the world. Poetry shifts us from minimal to maximal living. It offers the most authentic and precious of gifts: the chance to know our selves intimately. "We *know to give* our entire life every day." Rimbaud's words move us to experience poetry's way of knowing as giving—a practice of offering life in infinite generosity.

Poetry delivers the shock of Beauty. We have no choice but to face its presence. "Studying the beautiful is a duel in which the artist shrieks with fright before being defeated" (L'étude du beau est un duel où l'artiste crie de frayeur avant d'être vaincu), Baudelaire ends his prose poem "Le *confiteor* de l'artiste" [1: 278].[5] Rilke's "Duino Elegies," too, opens with an overwhelming intimacy with Beauty and terror:

> Who, if I cried out, would hear me among the angels'
> hierarchies? and even if one of them pressed me
> suddenly against his heart: I would be consumed
> in that overwhelming existence. For beauty is nothing
> but the beginning of terror, which we still are just able to endure,
> and we are so awed because it serenely disdains
> to annihilate us. Every angel is terrifying.[6]

> *(Wer, wenn ich schriee, hörte mich denn aus der Engel*
> *Ordnungen? und gesetzt selbt, es nähme*
> *einer mich plötzlich ans Herz: ich verginge von seinem*
> *stärkeren Dasein. Denn das Schöne ist nichts*
> *als des Schrecklichen Anfang, den wir noch grade ertragen,*
> *und wir bewundern es so, weil es gelassen verschmäht,*
> *uns zu zerstören. Ein jeder Engel ist schrecklich.)*[7]

Poetic experience speaks the encounter with Beauty and the terror of absolute surrender Beauty demands. In poetry's voice—in its "shriek[ing]" ("Wenn ich schriee")—we hear, as angels do, the "beginning" (Anfang) of "Beauty" (Schöne) and "terror" (Schrecklichen, schrecklich).

Rilke's beautiful angel, "pressing" us "suddenly against his heart," "presses" us to the heart of our experience, to the experience of the heart. The heart-to-heart encounter with Beauty is "consum[ing]," "overwhelming," and "terrifying." But if we stay present and open to the terrifying pressure, in that intimacy of fear and pain, we discover what we have never known before: the angel does *not* strike us; he "serenely disdains to annihilate us." It is neither the angel nor the pressure but *we* who annihilate ourselves by shutting down, withdrawing, becoming absent from our own emotions.

Self-annihilation and self-abandonment are our habitual pattern and primal addiction in life. We live farthest from ourselves, as Nietzsche observes, in "all eternity."[8] We live death and life as though they were routine. We live eternity as though it were routine. When poetry makes us aware, we begin to see that what has been serving us only robs us, and doubly so: self-annihilation robs our selves of ourselves, and it abducts the angel as well. Every poem asks—"Do you feel your heart and the angel's?" "Can you bear Beauty, and life's awesomeness, surpassing all the measures we know?" "Can you bear terror that does not end in annihilation?" "Can you live with 'Negative Capability' and rest with questions that have no answers?" "Will you stop turning in the circle of addiction to comfort and security and break out?" "Will you stop living 'eternity' as routine and discover 'eternity' as breaking out of that endless confining circle?" Poetry gives us a choice: continue in a narcotic relationship to the world or break the habit, wake up, and engage in a poetic relationship to the world in order to achieve a relationship of unity and Beauty.

Miller writes: "Every day we slaughter our finest impulses. This is why we get a heart-ache when we read those lines written by the hand of a master and recognize them as our own, as the tender shoots which we stifled because we lacked the faith to believe in our own powers, our own criterion of truth and beauty."[9] Half-asleep and narcotized, running away from pressure and pain, we suffer heart-ache. Rilke's angel, or a beautiful poem, "pressing" us deep, asks: "Do you see the tender shoots which you stifled in yourself?—of hopes and dreams of the spring of your life, but also, paradoxically, of despair, pain, terror, and death?" For the shoots of pain, too, remain vulnerable, as "fragile and perishable" as the severed head of Medusa, which Perseus lays *delicately,* Ovid says, on the soft bed of weed twigs. Shoots of pain and horror are all the *more* "tender," all the more in need of tending, because we do not permit pain and even horror to manifest themselves in their "exuberant splendor."[10] We crush or pull them out as weeds. Tender shoots, whether of flower or weed, may be new seeds. Rimbaud writes that poetry is an act of opening, "every day," to our "entire life." In binary thinking that denies half of our self we deny poetry.

For all that sprouts and shows itself (up) in our life—even our monsters, in the etymological sense of the Latin *monstrum,* an omen of God (from *monere*, "to warn," and *monstrare*, "to show")—we have a choice between being absent, denying, repressing, or condemning what is, and being present, in stillness, acknowledging and opening to what is. Miller writes: "If accepted we are revitalized; if rejected we are diminished."[11] The monsters become "Ennui" (Boredom), "le monstre délicat" "smoking his houka," whom Baudelaire denounces at the end of his poem "Au lecteur" ("To the Reader") [1: 6]. With each rejection, "Ennui" grows, perpetuating our narcotic relationship to the world. But the monsters we dare to accept are transformed into Beauty, the "monstre énorme, effrayant, ingénu" that Baudelaire celebrates in his "Hymne à la Beauté" [1: 25]. With each acceptance, "the universe [becomes] less hideous and the instants less heavy": we create and engage in a poetic relationship to the world. Perseus is the "hero of lightness," Calvino says, because he accepts and treats Medusa, *the monster* par excellence, with a "gesture of refreshing courtesy" that touches and reaches into Medusa's original "exuberant splendor," allowing her to manifest herself in all her awe-full beauty. Beneath our stony and stoned protective cover *we* are tender shoots.

"Why do we have to read this morbid stuff?" Ross Chambers reports an "earnest delegation of students" asking him about Baudelaire's *Les fleurs du mal*.[12] There are tremendous violence, depression, anger, hatred, fear, and pain. Yet, there are, or can be, at the same time, energy, release, liberation, an opening up of breathing space, an abundance, an "exuberant splendor." Giving voice to all that we stifle is possible because we have, Miller writes, "the faith to believe in our own powers, our own criterion of truth and beauty." Baudelaire had the courage to tend to the "tender shoots" and let them flower. Flowers of evil—flowers of beautiful monsters—tender shoots emerge as roses of pure contradiction. Poetry requires tending to, attention toward, and tenderness.

We are, perhaps, like the panther Rilke describes in his poem:

> His gaze has been so worn by the procession
> Of bars that it no longer makes a bond.

Around, a thousand bars seem to be flashing,
And in their flashing show no world beyond.

The lissom steps which round out and re-enter
That tightest circuit of their turning drill
Are like a dance of strength about a center
Wherein there stands benumbed a mighty will.

Only from time to time the pupil's shutter
Will draw apart: an image enters then,
To travel through the tautened body's utter
Stillness—and in the heart to end.

(Sein Blick ist vom Vorübergehn der Stäbe
so müd geworden, daß er nichts mehr hält.
Ihm ist, als ob es tausend Stäbe gäbe
und hinter tausend Stäben keine Welt.

Der weiche Gang geschmeidig starker Schritte,
der sich im allerkleinsten Kreise dreht,
ist wie ein Tanz von Kraft um eine Mitte,
in der betäubt ein großer Wille steht.

Nur manchmal schiebt der Vorhang der Pupille
sich lautlos auf—. Dann geht ein Bild hinein,
geht durch der Glieder angespannte Stille—
und hört im Herzen auf zu sein.)[13]

We pace in the "tightest circuit" of a "turning drill," our "gaze" "so worn by the procession of bars"—thousands of them surrounding us in an infinite expanse like the bars of rain in Baudelaire's "Spleen"—we cannot hold anything, not even ourselves. But, at times, an "image enters" us, hitting us with *"astringent effects"*[14] to "travel through [our] tautened body's utter stillness—and in the heart to end": like lightning—poetry strikes.

To be "worthy of what happens," to "[extract] something gay and loving in what happens, a light, an encounter, an event, a speed, a becoming,"

Gilles Deleuze describes the "Stoical way."[15] To be "worthy of what happens," we need first to be present for "what happens," open to that happening. Reading poetry—encountering a poem—is an event. As readers and also as critics of poetry, we must "be worthy of" the poems that befall us. We open our "worn" eyes like the panther drawing his "pupil's shutter" "apart." We take the risk of being present to/for poetry. Being present is the first, and the fundamental, responsibility. We offer, as Perseus did to Medusa, a "gesture of refreshing courtesy," our presence and our attention.[16]

A "live hypothesis" is, for William James, one that "scintillates" with real possibilities. We face a "genuine option," as James defines it, when we are forced to choose, on the spot—the opportunity will pass, never to return—among several "live" hypotheses.[17] Every poem is a "genuine option." The last line of Rilke's poem "Archaic Torso of Apollo"—"You must change your life" (Du mußt dein Leben ändern)—offers a choice between reading *absent-mindedly*, letting the words go by as addressing only others and as mere representation of the other, or reading *genuinely*, seeing the words "scintillate," opening to their "travel[ing] through" "[our] heart," receiving them as genuine options for an experience of the self.[18]

Are we willing to read a poem genuinely, this moment? Does it make a difference in our lives? Are we willing to take the risk the poem and the poet took to manifest themselves in the world? Maurice Blanchot writes of an "essential risk" in Rilke—to "risk language" and to "risk being"—which Orpheus takes in turning to see Eurydice: "Everything is risked, then, in the decision to look."[19] Bruno Latour writes in his foreword to Isabelle Stengers' book *Power and Invention: Situating Science* that "every species forces the natural historian to take as much risk to account for its evolution through an innovative form of narration as it took the species to survive"[20] As readers and critics of poetry, are we willing to put the world and our own words at risk in order to create living scholarship? The risk and choice belong to us, bequeathed by the poet who took the original risk.

The poet and critic Michel Deguy asks: "Now, in these times of *our* modernity, when knowledge no longer reckons with poetry . . . in what way can the practice of poetry, reading and writing, interest our *savoir-vivre* . . . ?"[21]

Poetry's "*savoir-vivre*" is to *vivre le savoir*, to live knowledge. Through the words that plunge into our depths, we come to touch our life and set ourselves free. We "*give* our entire life" to poetry in every "single sitting"[22] and learn to release ourselves into the flow and rhythm of life, "emotion-in-syntax," as Mary Oliver writes.[23]

If the poem is to reveal itself, to give its self, and to happen, so, too, is the reader to show the self and happen, for to receive the poem of deep transformative power means receiving, recognizing, and embracing our ephemeral, "fragile and perishable" self, risking our own being to hear and respond to poetry's imperative. "What is reading?" Bubjung Seunim asks. "Through the voice of another to hear/listen to my own deep original voice."[24] Reading occurs when the words written by others break out of their eternal, selfsame circle to come into us and echo our "original voice." At such moments, the poems we read emerge deep within our being like a luminous sun on the sea's horizon—just like "Eternity" in Rimbaud's poem:

> She is found again.
> What?—Eternity.
> It is the sea gone
> With the sun.
>
> (*Elle est retrouvée.*
> *Quoi?—L'Éternité.*
> *C'est la mer allée*
> *Avec le soleil.*)[25]

Eternity, unchanging and outside of the moment by definition, gets lost and "found again," "is . . . gone" and comes back. It is as momentary as the rising and falling of "the sea gone / With the sun." When we read, we live eternity's ephemeral emergence (from the Latin *ex*, "out of," and *mergere*, "to plunge into water").

William Blake writes in his poem "Eternity":

> He who binds to himself a joy
> Does the winged life destroy;

> But he who kisses the joy as it flies
> Lives in eternity's sun rise.[26]

Icarus's wings unbind; he falls from sun to sea and goes with "the sea gone with the sun," in "eternity's sun rise" and sunset. Open but do not hold onto the motion, emotion, and commotion of life—rising, falling, and flowing with no wings into "emotion-in-syntax"; let beauty and joy ignite our ephemeral being every day; "kiss joy as it flies."

NOTES

Prologue. A Sun within a Sun

1. "Icarus," *The Dictionary of Classical Mythology*, Pierre Grimal, trans. A. R. Maxwell-Hyslop (New York: Blackwell, 1986) 227.

2. *Anthologie de la poésie française*, ed. Georges Pompidou (Paris: Hachette [Livre de poche], 1961) 100–101.

3. All references to Baudelaire's works are to the *Œuvres complètes*, ed. Claude Pichois, 2 vols. (Paris: Gallimard [Pléiade], 1975–76); and *Correspondance*, ed. Claude Pichois and Jean Ziegler, 2 vols. (Paris: Gallimard [Pléiade], 1973), and appear in the text with volume and page numbers. *Correspondance* is abbreviated as *Corr.* Unless otherwise indicated, the translations are my own.

4. Maurice Blanchot, *The Space of Literature*, trans. Ann Smock (Lincoln: U of Nebraska P, 1982) 247.

5. Elie Wiesel, *The Fifth Son*, qtd. by Jean-Luc Nancy, *A Finite Thinking*, ed. Simon Sparks (Stanford: Stanford UP, 2003) 255.

6. "The question is not so much how you can mimic a science . . . but how much risk one can take in allowing one's words to be modified by the world." Bruno Latour, foreword, *Power and Invention: Situating Science*, by Isabelle Stengers, trans. Paul Bains (Minneapolis: U of Minnesota P, 1997) xvii.

7. Stengers 19, 5.

8. Latour xiii.

9. Latour xiv.

10. Latour xviii–xix.

11. Stengers 5, original emphasis.

12. Stengers 6.

13. Paul Valéry, "Poésie et pensée abstraite," *Œuvres*, ed. Jean Hytier, 2 vols. (Paris: Gallimard [Pléiade], 1957) 1: 1324, original emphasis. Valéry speaks of "les vers" as "étranges discours" in plural; I use it in the singular.

14. Maurice Blanchot, *Le livre à venir* (Paris: Gallimard [Folio], 1959) 10.

15. *Charles Baudelaire: Selected Poems*, trans. Carol Clark (New York: Penguin, 1995) 145. I render in verse form Clark's prose translation.

16. Henry Miller, *Henry Miller on Writing*, ed. Thomas Moore (New York: New Directions, 1964) 208.

17. Henry Miller, *The Rosy Crucifixion. Book One. Sexus* (New York: Grove, 1965) 26.

18. Stengers 19.

Chapter 1. Surrender of Freedom and Surrender to Freedom

1. For "Le poème du hachisch," which is in volume 1, only page numbers are given in chapter 1. Here, I have made singular the original quote, which is plural. Orpheus also appears in an earlier version, "Du vin et du hachisch" [1: 384], and is associated with the talent of a Spanish musician who performs drunk and inspired by wine. I refer to the speaker of "Le poème du hachisch" as Baudelaire.

2. Ernest Pinard, the prosecutor who indicted Baudelaire for "outrage to public morality and good morals," used the term "poison" in his prosecution speech [1: 1207].

3. Jacques Derrida explores and destabilizes hierarchical oppositions between writing/speech, poison/remedy, and original/copy in "La pharmacie de Platon," *La dissémination* (Paris: Seuil, 1972) 71–191.

4. "What are we doing when we speak of Baudelaire? Some are 'Baudelaireans,' research specialists . . . scholars, experts on Charles Baudelaire's lifework and 'searching' to know it better. Others—as in my case—like to speak 'in the interest of poetry' so that, at the end of the next century, there will continue 'to be poetry.'" Michel Deguy, "To Spear It on the Mark, of Mystical Nature," trans. Wilson Baldridge, *Baudelaire and the Poetics of Modernity*, ed. Patricia A. Ward (Nashville: Vanderbilt UP, 2001) 187. Gilles Deleuze offers a similar alternative for philosophy: "Who is a Spinozist? Sometimes, certainly, the individual who works 'on' Spinoza, on Spinoza's concepts, provided this is done with enough gratitude and admiration. But also the individual who, without being a philosopher, receives from Spinoza an affect, a set of affects, a kinetic determination, an impulse, and makes Spinoza an encounter, a passion." *Spinoza: Practical Philosophy*, trans. Robert Hurley (San Francisco: City Lights, 1988) 129–30.

5. I borrow the formulation from Richard Terdiman: "The prose poem needs reexamination *from the side of prose*." *Discourse/Counter-Discourse: Theory and Practice of Symbolic Resistance in Nineteenth-Century France* (Ithaca: Cornell UP, 1985) 261, original emphasis.

6. Michel Butor, *Répertoire I* (Paris: Minuit, 1960) 119, 117.

7. Gilles Deleuze, *Negotiations, 1972–1990*, trans. Martin Joughin (New York: Columbia UP, 1995) 23, slightly revised translation.

8. Gilles Deleuze and Félix Guattari, *A Thousand Plateaus*, trans. Brian Massumi (Minneapolis: U of Minnesota P, 1987) 166, slightly revised translation.

9. Gilles Deleuze and Clair Parnet, *Dialogues* (Paris: Flammarion, 1996) 67, my translation.

10. Valéry, "Poésie et pensée abstraite" 1: 1321.

11. Baudelaire calls hashish "poison" several times in the poem [410, 412, 426].

12. This quote appears twice in Baudelaire: in *Hygiène* [1: 674] and in *L'œuvre et la vie d'Eugène Delacroix* [2: 761].

13. Only page numbers are given for subsequent references to *Le peintre de la vie moderne*.

14. See Barbara Spackman, *Decadent Genealogies: The Rhetoric of Sickness from Baudelaire to D'Annunzio* (Ithaca: Cornell UP, 1989) 33–104, for a comparative study of the convalescent in Baudelaire.

15. See Walter Benjamin for a reading of fencing in Baudelaire as "designed to open a path through the crowd," from "the phantom crowd of the words, the fragments, the beginnings of lines from which the poet, in deserted streets, wrests the poetic booty." "On Some Motifs in Baudelaire," *Illuminations*, trans. Harry Zohn, ed. Hannah Arendt (New York: Schocken, 1968) 165.

16. The French *congestion* alone, as it appears in the text, doesn't mean "stroke," although *cerebellum* at the end of the sentence reconstructs the expression *congestion cérébrale*, which does mean "stroke." See Kevin Newmark for an analysis of *congestion* as "strokes of violence that can enable and always interrupt any given system of representation." "Off the Charts: Walter Benjamin's Depiction of Baudelaire," Ward, *Baudelaire and the Poetics of Modernity* 72–84.

17. For "shock" and "trauma" in Baudelaire, see Benjamin, "On Some Motifs" 160–80; Kevin Newmark, "Traumatic Poetry: Charles Baudelaire and the Shock of Laughter," *Trauma: Explorations in Memory*, ed. Cathy Caruth (Baltimore: Johns Hopkins UP, 1995) 236–55.

18. Walter Benjamin, "Theses on the Philosophy of History," *Illuminations* 257. Eugene Holland discusses the process of "intensification" in Baudelaire in *Baudelaire and Schizoanalysis: The Sociopoetics of Modernism* (Cambridge: Cambridge UP, 1993).

19. In "Du vin et du hachisch," published in 1851, Baudelaire writes that hashish "interrupts digestive functions," whereas wine "activates digestion" [1: 397].

20. On pain and Baudelaire, see Vaheed Ramazani, "Writing in Pain: Baudelaire, Benjamin, Haussman," *Boundary 2* 23.2 (1996): 199–224. Pierre Klossowski analyzes in Nietzsche the relations among pain, body, convalescence, voluptuousness, thought, and the vicious circle (or the eternal return) in *Nietzsche et le cercle vicieux* (Paris: Mercure de France, 1969).

21. The "soul of [Baudelaire's] choosing," or the laboratory guinea pig who will

undergo the hashish "experiment," is a specimen of "the *banal form of originality*" (la *forme banale de l'originalité*) [429–30, original emphasis], in contrast to the "literary hero," who is "immutably concentrated."

22. Baudelaire writes the following in a letter to his mother dated December 30, 1857: "If morality can cure the body, a violent continuous work will cure me, but one must will, with a weakened will;—vicious circle" (Si le moral peut guérir le physique, un violent travail continu me guérira, mais il faut vouloir, avec une volonte affaiblie; —cercle vicieux) [*Corr* 1: 438].

23. For a study of literalization and incorporation in "Le poème du hachisch," see Joshua Wilner, "'Le Bonheur Vomitif': Incorporation and Figuration in Baudelaire's 'Poème du Hachisch,'" *Feeding on Infinity: Reading in the Romantic Rhetoric of Internalization* (Baltimore: Johns Hopkins UP, 2000) 95–108.

24. Another proverb Baudelaire associates with hashish intoxication that has the same centripetal configuration as the Rome proverb is "passion relates everything back to itself" (la passion rapporte tout à elle) [436].

25. Benjamin, "On Some Motifs" 183.

26. Paul de Man, "Anthropomorphism and Trope in the Lyric," *The Rhetoric of Romanticism* (New York: Columbia UP, 1984) 242.

27. Ross Chambers, "The Classroom versus Poetry; or, Teaching Transportation," *Approaches to Teaching Baudelaire's* Flowers of Evil, ed. Laurence Porter (New York: MLA, 2000) 173.

28. Chambers, "The Classroom" 174.

29. Benjamin, "On Some Motifs" 163.

30. Walter Benjamin, "The Work of Art in the Age of Mechanical Reproduction," *Illuminations* 217–51. Subsequent references to this article appear in the text.

31. Although Baudelaire and Benjamin make similar distinctions between unique experience and reproducibility, they do not express similar (degrees of) preference. Baudelaire strongly favors the former, placing poetry above hashish and painting above photography; Benjamin is more ambiguous, open, perhaps even favorable toward reproducibility.

32. For a discussion of space, distance, and immensity in Baudelaire, see Gaston Bachelard, "Intimate Immensity," *The Poetics of Space*, trans. Maria Jolas (Boston: Beacon, 1994) 183–210; Jean-Pierre Richard, "Profondeur de Baudelaire," *Poésie et profondeur* (Paris: Seuil, 1955) 93–162.

33. Hashish hallucination abolishes all distance. What is "only a natural comparison" for the poet becomes reality for the addict [420]. Hashish goes against the metaphorical distance of poetry. It is a force of contiguity. Barbara Johnson traces the

passage from the metaphor of poetry to the metonymy of prose poetry in Baudelaire in *Défigurations du language poétique: La seconde révolution baudelairienne* (Paris: Flammarion, 1979). Holland, in *Baudelaire and Schizoanalysis*, argues that the shift from metaphor to metonymy occurs earlier, between the two poetry editions (1857 and 1861) of *Les fleurs du mal*. "Le poème du hachisch," published between the two poetry editions (in 1858 as an article, "De l'idéal artificiel: Le hachisch," in *La revue contemporaine*; in 1860 as the first of part of *Les paradis artificiels*), stages the tension between metaphor and metonymy in the battle between poetry and hashish and offers different inflexions in the dynamic between the two figures.

34. Ovid, *Metamorphoses*, trans. Frank Justus Miller, 3rd ed. (1977; Cambridge: Harvard UP, 1999) 8.224, vol. 3 of *Ovid* (6 vols., 1916–99). Subsequent references to Ovid appear in the text.

35. Latour xvii.

36. Chambers, "The Classroom" 181.

37. See Jean-Luc Nancy, "Le rire, la présence," *Une pensée finie* (Paris: Galilée, 1990) 297–324, for a beautiful reading of the prose poem "Le désir de peindre."

38. Jorge Luis Borges, "The Fearful Sphere of Pascal," *Labyrinths: Selected Stories and Other Writings* (New York: New Directions, 1964) 192. For stories of circles, see Ralph Waldo Emerson, "Circles," *The Essential Writings of Ralph Waldo Emerson* (New York: Modern Library, 2000) 252–62; Rudy Rucker, *Infinity and the Mind* (Boston: Birkhäuser, 1982) 17. See Georges Poulet's discussion of the circle in Baudelaire in *Les métamorphoses du cercle* (Paris: Flammarion, 1961) 407–37.

39. In the poem "Chant d'automne" ("Autumn Song") [1: 56–57], death and departure mingle: "It seems to me, lulled by this monotonous shock, / That someone hastily nails down a coffin somewhere. / For whom?—summer was yesterday; autumn is here! / This mysterious sound rings like a departure" (Il me semble, bercé par ce choc monotone, / Qu'on cloue en grande hâte un cercueil quelque part. / Pour qui? —c'était hier l'été; voici l'automne! / Ce bruit mystérieux sonne comme un départ).

40. The last word of *Les fleurs du mal* is "*new*": "To the depths of the Unknown to find something *new*!" (Au fond de l'Inconnu pour trouver du *nouveau*!) [1:134, original emphasis]. The known opens to the unknown, and the old to the new.

41. Benjamin, "On Some Motifs" 191, 194.

42. Benjamin, "On Some Motifs" 179.

43. Benjamin, "On Some Motifs" 179, original emphasis.

44. Hashish takes over the thought process and makes it "rhapsodic"—an expression Baudelaire borrows from De Quincey's *Confessions* that defines "a train of ideas

suggested and dictated by the external world and circumstantial chance" (un train de pensées suggéré et commandé par le monde extérieur et le hasard des circonstances) [428]. In hashish hallucination, "the train of ideas is *infinitely more* accelerated and more *rhapsodic*" (le train de pensées est *infiniment plus* accéléré et plus *rhapsodique*) [428, original emphasis].

45. Michael Grant and John Hazel, "Fates," *Who's Who in Classical Mythology* (New York: Oxford UP, 1973) 175.

46. Blanchot, "Orpheus's Gaze," *The Space of Literature* 173, 172, original emphasis. Subsequent references to "Orpheus's Gaze" appear in the text.

47. Ovid uses the adjective *audax* for "bold"—"the boy began to rejoice in his bold flight" (puer *audaci* coepit gaudere volatu) [8.223]—which means both "courageous"/"daring" and "rash"/"foolhardy."

48. Maurice Blanchot, "Rilke and Death's Demand," *The Space of Literature* 142, original emphasis.

49. Blanchot, "Rilke and Death's Demand" 142. Smock translates as *circulation* the original French term *cercle* (see *L'éspace littéraire* [Paris: Gallimard (folio), 1955] 183). I have revised it to *circle.*

50. Blanchot, epigraph to *The Space of Literature.*

51. Maurice Blanchot, "The Song of the Sirens: Encountering the Imaginary," *The Gaze of Orpheus and Other Literary Essays,* trans. Lydia Davis (New York: Station Hill, 1981) 106.

52. Maurice Blanchot, "The Original Experience," *The Space of Literature* 236, 238.

53. Blanchot, "The Song of the Sirens" 106–07.

54. Blanchot, "The Song of the Sirens" 107.

55. Michel Foucault, "Maurice Blanchot: The Thought from Outside," *Foucault/ Blanchot,* trans. Brian Massumi (New York: MIT P [Zone], 1990) 43–44.

56. Blanchot, "Orpheus's Gaze" 175.

57. *Selected Poems* 145. I render in verse form Clark's prose translation.

58. Max Milner compares the rigor of Baudelaire's poetic hygiene in *Les paradis* to that of Poe's "poetic principle." "Le paradis se gagne-t-il?" *Baudelaire: Figures de la mort, figures de l'éternité,* ed. John E. Jackson and Claude Pichois, *L'année Baudelaire* 2 (Paris: Klincksieck, 1996) 22. Jean-Paul Sartre's *Baudelaire* (Paris: Gallimard [Folio], 1947) opened up exchanges and discussions on bad faith, ethics, responsibility, free will, freedom, and evil between Blanchot and Georges Bataille, among others. See Maurice Blanchot, "L'echec de Baudelaire," *La part du feu* (Paris: Gallimard, 1949) 133–51; Georges Bataille, "Baudelaire," *La littérature et le mal* (Paris: Gallimard [Folio], 1957) 17–47.

59. Blanchot, "Orpheus's Gaze" 173–74.

60. Benjamin, "On Some Motifs" 194.

Chapter 2. The "Frivolous" Other and the "Authentic" Self

1. All references to Mallarmé's works are to the *Œuvres complètes,* ed. Bertrand Marchal, 2 vols. (Paris: Gallimard [Pléiade], 1998–2003), and appear in the text with volume and page numbers. For *La dernière mode,* which is in volume 2, only page numbers are given in chapter 2. A facsimile edition renders the original layout of the magazine: *Stéphane Mallarmé. La dernière mode: Gazette du monde et de la famille,* ed. Jean-Paul Amunategui (Paris: Ramsay, 1978). For an English translation, see *Mallarmé on Fashion: A Translation of the Fashion Magazine* La Dernière mode, *with Commentary,* trans. P. N. Furbank and Alex Cain (Oxford: Berg, 2004). Unless otherwise indicated, the translations are my own.

2. Rosemary Lloyd, *Mallarmé: The Poet and His Circle* (Ithaca: Cornell UP, 1999) 233.

3. Lloyd 228.

4. Edgar Allan Poe, "The Poetic Principle," *The Portable Poe,* ed. Phili van Doren Stern (New York: Penguin, 1977) 574, original emphasis. See Philippe Lacoue-Labarthe, "The Echo of the Subject," *Typography: Mimesis, Philosophy, Politics,* ed. Christopher Finsk (Stanford: Stanford UP, 1989) 139–207, for a reflection on rhythm and Mallarmé's statement that "every soul is a rhythmic knot" (toute âme est un nœud rythmique).

5. Gilles Deleuze and Félix Guattari, "Of the Refrain," *A Thousand Plateaus* 314.

6. For the history of *La dernière mode,* see Jean-Pierre Lecercle, *Mallarmé et la mode* (Paris: Séguier, 1989) 19–33.

7. The name "Zizi" is spelled in two ways: "Zizi" (597) and "Zizy" (608). The term *bonne* in "bonne mulâtre de Surate" could be translated either as the adjective *good* ("good mulatto of Surat") or as the noun *maid* ("mulatto maid of Surat"). I will use the first translation.

8. *Fugue,* as absence and music, would be a kind of "Musicienne du silence" (Musician of silence) in the poem "Sainte" [1: 27].

9. See "Observation relative au poème *Un coup de dés jamais n'abolira le hasard*" [1: 391].

10. *Mallarmé in Prose,* ed. Mary Ann Caws (New York: New Directions, 2001) 79, slightly revised translation.

11. See Jean-Paul Amunategui's introduction to the Ramsay facsimile edition of *La dernière mode.*

12. Mallarmé's initials, "SM," appear only once in *La dernière mode:* in the "Conseils sur l'éducation" of the third issue [555]. Apart from this, Mallarmé's name appears in full twice in each issue: on the list of possible literary contributors on the inside cover and at the end of the "Gazette et programme de la quinzaine" as the addressee to which all books and inquiries should be sent (see the Ramsay edition). The surreptitious appearance of his initials in the third issue perhaps prepares for the chiasmic reading of the initials "MS/SM" in the next, the fourth, issue.

13. Mary Lydon also notes the chiasmic crossing of the two initials into the pseudonym "Ix" and the consequent "withdrawal of identity into anonymity" in "Skirting the Issue: Mallarmé, Proust, and Symbolism," *Skirting the Issue: Essays in Literary Theory* (Madison: U of Wisconsin P, 1996) 85. Incidentally, the symbol "X" is often used as a signature by people who cannot write their names.

14. *Mallarmé in Prose* 82.

15. *Mallarmé in Prose* 83, slightly revised translation.

16. *Mallarmé in Prose* 84.

17. Roger Dragonetti, *Un fantôme dans le kiosque: Mallarmé et l'esthétique du quotidien* (Paris: Seuil, 1992) 91.

18. This is quoted from the Ramsay edition. This passage appears in each issue, just before the "Correspondance avec les abonnées."

19. The literary section is otherwise described as being "always Parisian" (toujours parisienne) [612].

20. The *Robert* dictionary gives Tsia-Toung, and *Webster's* gives Quanzhou. Both trace the etymology of *satin* back to Chinese via the Arabic *zaitun*. *The Oxford English Dictionary* notes the following concerning the Chinese etymology of *satin*: "The word cannot be connected etymologically with the app. synonymous Arab. zaituni, f.Zaitun name of a city in China (the locality of which is disputed). Fr. Hirth (Archit. Stud. neu, Spr. LXVLL, 1882, p.204) suggests that the Arabs may have confused the name of the town with the Cantonese sze-tün = Mandarin ssu-tuan, Satin; but the conjecture that the Cantonese form is the source of Ital. setino is extremely improbable."

The *Oxford English Dictionary*'s contestation of the Chinese etymology does not invalidate my reading, since Mallarmé believed in the Chinese origin of the word.

21. Although *Les mots anglais* was published in 1877, Mallarmé most likely wrote it in 1875 and seems to have had it in mind as least as early as 1872, when he started to teach English at the Lycée Fontanes. Bertrand Marchal, the editor of the *Œuvres complètes*, makes a link between the education column of *La dernière mode* ("Conseils sur l'éducation") and Mallarmé's pedagogical writings on the English language, of which *Les mots anglais* forms a part [editorial notes 2: 1798]. For a study of *Les mots anglais*, see Jacques Michon, *Mallarmé et les* Mots anglais (Montreal: Presse Universitaire de Montréal, 1978) 42–46.

22. The name of *satin*'s country of origin, China, means "the country of the middle" in Chinese. Expressions such as "l'empire du milieu" and "the middle kingdom" refer to China.

23. This is according to the original layout of the magazine that the Ramsay edition renders.

24. "Satin" closely links fetishism and translation and thus can be read in conjunction with Guy Rosolato's chapter "Le fétichisme dont se *dérobe* l'objet," *La relation d'inconnu* (Paris: Seuil, 1978) 19–30. Rosolato's reading of Freud's article "Fetishism" underlines the fundamental role of translation and therefore of the mother tongue. Rosolato focuses on the necessary move toward the mother tongue, which, in the case Freud discusses, is the move from German to English, from the "Glanz auf der Nase" to the "glance at the nose." In this process, he distinguishes two ways in which meaning can "change" or "slip" (*glissement*): through homonyms (*Glanz* to *glance*) and translation (*Nase* to *nose*). What is preserved in the slippage from *Glanz* to *glance* is the phoneme *glans*, which both German and English adopted from Latin (*gland, penis*). The maternal penis then, as a phoneme, circulates between languages, and Rosolato affirms that "these relationships of translation constitute the fetish; they cannot be separated. Their distortions form it and drive it" [23]. According to Rosolato, the mother tongue substitutes for the maternal phallus through an upward displacement. In our case, the ways in which "Satin" points to the name/space of the mother—to her tongue or organ—and circulates freely among different tongues through translation makes her an exemplary fetish. For an analysis of fetishism in Mallarmé's "Hérodiade," see Charles Bernheimer, "Fetishism and Decadence: Salomé's Severed Heads," *Fetishism as Cultural Discourse*, ed. Emily Apter and William Pietz (Ithaca: Cornell UP, 1993) 62–83.

25. See Lydon's "Skirting the Issue" for her reading of the mother tongue, the fetish, "la Chose," and "Rien" in *La dernière mode*, and of how Mallarmé's poetry "[makes] *la langue maternelle* strange to the native ear" [90–95]. Barbara Johnson analyzes "what is maternal in Mallarmé" in her essay "Mallarmé as Mother," *A World of Difference* (Baltimore: Johns Hopkins UP, 1987) 137–43.

26. "Margaret," Eric Partridge, *Origins: A Short Etymological Dictionary of Modern English* (New York: Greenwich, 1983) 381.

27. Jacques Derrida, "The Double Session," *Dissemination*, trans. Barbara Johnson (Chicago: U of Chicago P, 1981) especially 209–26. Miss Satin deploys remarkably the Derridean "logic of the hymen" [212] "as a cloth, a tissue, a medium" (*milieu*) [215]: "the hymen ... produces the effect of the medium (a medium as element enveloping both terms at once; a medium located between the two terms). It is an operation that *both* sows confusion *between* opposites *and* stands *between* the opposites 'at once'" [212]. "Rightly or wrongly," Derrida says, "the etymology of 'hymen' is often traced to a root *u* that can be found in the Latin *suo, suere* (to sew) and in *huphos* (tissue). *Hymen* might then mean a little stitch (*syuman*) (*syuntah*, sewn, *siula*, needle; *schuh*, sew; *suo*). . . . Both words [hymen, hymn] would have a relation with *uphainô* (to weave, spin—the spider web—machinate), with *huphos* (textile, spider web, net, the text of a work—

Longinus), and with *humnos* (a weave, later the weave of a song, by extension a wedding song).... The hymen is thus a sort of textile. Its threads should be interwoven with all veils, gauzes, canvasses, fabrics, moires, wings, feathers, all the curtains and fans that hold within their folds all—almost—of the Mallarméan corpus" [213].

28. *Mallarmé in Prose* 47–48.

29. The expression "obnubilation des tissus" is from "L'action restreinte" [2: 215]. It is also the title chosen by Amunategui for the preface to the Ramsay facsimile edition of *La dernière mode*. As both an "obnubilation des tissus" and a "tissu d'obnubilation" —a surface that exposes and hides itself through its reflective brilliance—"Miss Satin" functions as a mirror. According to Rosolato, the mirror is "a fetishistic object par excellence": "it veils itself, since the better it reflects, *the better it is forgotten*, and if it seems to be hollowed by the images it takes in, it is in order better to dissimulate its impassable, *unpenetrated* surface as an object; it reflects back without growing weak, while giving the illusion of receiving an imprint, or of opening itself; hence, among other reasons, the fascination it exerts" [25, original emphasis]. Incidentally, Mallarmé writes "clouding of fabrics and liquefaction of mirrors" (obnubilation des tissus et liquéfaction de miroirs) ["L'action restreinte" 2: 215].

30. For a discussion of the image and theme of clouds in Mallarmé, see Jean-Pierre Richard, *L'univers imaginaire de Mallarmé* (Paris: Seuil, 1961) 387–90.

31. Jean-Luc Steinmetz, *Mallarmé: L'absolu au jour le jour* (Paris: Fayard, 1998) 271.

32. Steinmetz 372.

33. Steinmetz 444.

34. Steinmetz 474.

35. *Mallarmé in Prose* 109.

36. Gilles Deleuze, "Preface to the French Edition," *Essays Critical and Clinical*, trans. Daniel W. Smith and Michael A. Greco (Minneapolis: U of Minnesota P, 1997) lv, original emphasis. Proust's original is as follows: "Les beaux livres sont écrits dans une sorte de langue étrangère." Marcel Proust, "Notes sur la littérature et la critique," *Contre Sainte-Beuve*, ed. Pierre Clarac (Parris: Gallimard [Pléiade], 1971) 305.

37. *Œuvres complètes*, ed. Henri Mondor and G. Jean-Aubry (Paris: Gallimard [Pléiade], 1945) 1581.

38. Paul Valéry, "*Le coup de dés*. Lettre au directeur des *Marges*," *Œuvres* 1: 626, original emphasis.

39. Blanchot, "Orpheus's Gaze" 176, 175. "Tout se joue donc dans la décision du regard": Blanchot, *L'espace littéraire* 231.

Chapter 3. "Vise of Stone" and Open Air

1. Italo Calvino, *Six Memos for the Next Millennium: The Charles Eliot Norton Lectures 1985–1986*, trans. Patrick Creagh (New York: Vintage, 1993). Subsequent references appear in the text.

2. Italo Calvino, *The Uses of Literature: Essays*, trans. Patrick Creagh (New York: Harcourt Brace, 1986) 146–61.

3. Calvino, *Uses of Literature* 147, 160.

4. Medusa was the mortal of the three Gorgons.

5. Calvino, *Six Memos* 4.

6. Chambers, "The Classroom" 170.

7. Calvino, *Six Memos* 26, 3, 5. For a reading of melancholy as "the intimate company" of Baudelaire, see Jean Starobinski, *La mélancolie au miroir: Trois lectures de Baudelaire* (Paris: Julliard, 1989).

8. Ross Chambers, *The Writing of Melancholy: Modes of Opposition in Early French Modernism*, trans. Mary Seidman Trouille (Chicago: U of Chicago P, 1993) 26.

9. Jonathan Culler, "Teaching the Devil," Porter, *Approaches to Teaching* 144. See also his "Baudelaire's Satanic Verses," *Diacritics* 28.3 (1998): 86–100.

10. Ross Chambers, "Poetry in the Asiatic Mode," *The Writing of Melancholy* 130.

11. Calvino, *Six Memos* 4.

12. Arden Reed, *Romantic Weather: The Climates of Coleridge and Baudelaire* (Hanover: UP of New England [published for Brown UP], 1983) 290. Reed gives an extensive and rich study of the "spleen" weather in various aspects, including its link to oppressive time (the two *temps* in French).

13. Walter Benjamin, *Paris, capitale du XIXe siècle: Le livre des Passages*, trans. Jean Lacost [from German to French] (Paris: Cerf, 1993) 126; Walter Benjamin, *The Arcades Project*, trans. Howard Eiland and Kevin McLaughlin [from German to English] (Cambridge: Harvard UP, 1999) 101–02; Walter Benjamin, *Gesammelte Schriften*, ed. Rolf Tiedemann and Hermann Schweppenhäuser (Frankfurt: Suhrkamp, 1982) 5: 156–57. I am taking the liberty to translate from French to English, checking it against Eiland and McLaughlin's translation. I have kept the term *most suave* from the French translation, instead of the *most genial* offered by the English translation, for the German original *lindesten*.

14. Chambers, "Poetry" 130.

15. Calvino, *Six Memos* 10.

16. In the prose poem "Chacun sa chimère" ("To Each His Chimera") [1: 282–83], the narrator encounters several men walking "under the cupola of splenetic sky," bent

with the weight of an "enormous Chimera" each of them is carrying on his back. Another mythological monster presses down with a weight that is "as heavy as a bag of flour or coal" and "envelops and oppresses" each man with its "elastic and powerful muscle," digging its "claws" into his chest. The narrator notices that none of the men seems "irritated" by the "ferocious animal" and seems even to consider it "as forming part of himself." At the end, the narrator, who at first was eager to understand the "mystery," is overcome by an "irresistible indifference" that is heavier than the weight of the Chimera carried by these men. Hans-Jost Frey's reading of the prose poem points out that "indifference," or "apathy"/"ennui," is "a burden heavier than the chimera" and that "the highest lucidity is not what claims to eliminate the chimeralike but rather what recognizes it." *Studies in Poetic Discourse: Mallarmé, Baudelaire, Rimbaud, Hölderlin,* trans. William Whobrey (Stanford: Stanford UP, 1996) 105, 110.

17. For a critique of the danger, violence, and trap of aesthetic formalization and education in terms of "gracefulness," "weightlessness," "fall," and "rise," see Paul de Man, "Aesthetic Formalization: Kleist's *Uber das Marionettentheater*," *The Rhetoric of Romanticism* 263–90.

18. Benjamin, *Paris, capitale du XIXe siècle* 126.

19. Walter Benjamin has noted the "correspondence between antiquity and modernity" in Baudelaire. "Zentralpark: Fragments sur Baudelaire," *Charles Baudelaire: Un poète lyrique à l'apogée du capitalisme,* trans. Jean Lacost [from German to French] (Paris: Payot, 1979) 236. The translation from French to English is mine.

20. Benjamin, "On Some Motifs" 168. Also see Ross Chambers, "Baudelaire's Street Poetry," *Nineteenth-Century French Studies* 13.4 (1985): 244–59.

21. See Ross Chambers, "The *Flâneur* as Hero (on Baudelaire)," *Australian Journal of French Studies* 28.2 (1991): 142–53.

22. Benjamin, "On Some Motifs" 165. Subsequent references to "On Some Motifs in Baudelaire" are in the text.

23. In *Le peintre de la vie moderne,* the process of painterly creation is depicted in terms of a "duel" between the synthetic faculty, which abbreviates into an "arabesque of contour," and the "riot of details, which all demand justice with the fury of a crowd enamored with absolute equality" (une émeute de détails, qui tous demandent justice avec la furie d'une foule amoureuse d'égalité absolue) [2: 698–99].

24. "Brumes et pluies" [1: 100–01] is the title of a poem in "Tableaux parisiens" in the 1861 edition. In the first edition of *Les fleurs du mal,* it was in the first section and came just after the four "Spleen" poems.

25. For compelling readings of "A une passante," see Ross Chambers, "The Storm in the Eye of the Poem: Baudelaire's 'A une passante,'" *Textual Analysis: Some Readers Reading,* ed. Mary Ann Caws (New York: MLA, 1986) 156–66; Rainer Nägele, "Transla-

tions of Eros: Sophocles/Hölderlin, Baudelaire/Benjamin," *Echoes of Translation: Reading between Texts* (Baltimore: Johns Hopkins UP, 1997) 112–16.

26. Calvino, *Six Memos* 6.

27. Benjamin's sentence is: "The delight of the urban poet is love—not at first sight, but at last sight. It is farewell forever which coincides in the poem with the moment of enchantment" ["On Some Motifs" 169].

28. Chambers, "The Storm in the Eye" 159–61.

29. This glimpse of the woman passing by is the fulgurant shock of the "memory of the present" [*Le peintre de la vie moderne* 2: 696].

30. Victor Hugo, in a *lettre-préface* to Baudelaire's essay on Théophile Gautier, says: "You endow the sky of art with something of a macabre ray. You create a new shiver" (Vous dotez le ciel de l'art d'on ne sait quel rayon macabre. Vous créez un frisson nouveau) [editorial notes 2: 1129].

Chapter 4. Beyond Hell and Paradise

1. Calvino, *Six Memos* 4, slightly revised translation.
2. Calvino, *Six Memos* 5, 6.
3. John Dewey, *Art as Experience* (New York: Perigee, 1934) 299.
4. Dewey 303.
5. Deleuze, "To Be Done with Judgment," *Essays Critical and Clinical* 135.
6. There is a slight inconsistency regarding the exact date of publication of *Les fleurs du mal*, or its availability for sale (*mise en vente*). Claude Pichois gives two dates in his Pléiade edition: June 21 in the editorial notes [1: 809, 1177] and June 25 in the chronology at the beginning [1: xl]. Other editions give one or the other date.
7. In reality, editions of *Les fleurs du mal* containing the condemned pieces started to appear earlier, after only sixty years, without being legally pursued. This happened in 1917 as Baudelaire's work entered the public domain. See Marcel Ruff, ed., *Baudelaire: Œuvres complètes* (Paris: Seuil [l'Intégrale], 1968) 734.
8. Jean Delabroy, ed., *Charles Baudelaire: Les fleurs du mal* (Paris: Magnard, 1993) 636, my translation.
9. Bourdin was the son-in-law of the director of *Le figaro*, Villemessant. For documentation of the trial, see also Pichois' editorial notes [1: 1176–1224] and Baudelaire's notes to his attorney [1: 193–96].
10. Delabroy 637.
11. The verdict was published the day after the trial in *La gazette des tribunaux*.
12. Baudelaire did not appeal the decision but wrote to Empress Eugénie on November 6, 1857, to ask if she would intervene in his favor to reduce the fine [*Corr* 1:

432]. On January 20, 1858, his request was partially granted, the fine reduced to fifty francs. The six condemned poems were: "Les bijoux," "Le léthé," "A celle qui est trop gaie" ("To a Woman Who Is Too Gay"), "Femmes damnées: Delphine et Hippolyte," "Lesbos," and "Les métamorphoses du vampire." On Baudelaire's trial and censorship in poetry, see Richard Sieburth, "Poetry and Obscenity: Baudelaire and Swinburne," *Comparative Literature* 36.4 (1984): 343–53; E. S. Burt, "'An Immoderate Taste for Truth': Censoring History in Baudelaire's 'Les Bijoux,'" *Poetry's Appeal: Nineteenth-Century French Lyric and the Political Space* (Stanford: Stanford UP, 1999) 188–220.

13. Dominick LaCapra, "1857: Two Trials," *A New History of French Literature*, ed. Denis Hollier (Cambridge: Harvard UP, 1989) 727, 729.

14. Dominick LaCapra, *Madame Bovary on Trial* (Ithaca: Cornell UP, 1982) 30.

15. This is according to Charles Boullay, whom Pichois cites and who published the judiciary writings of Ernest Pinard, the prosecutor of Baudelaire [1: 1180 n. 1].

16. Delabroy 651–52. For the trial records, see Ruff 734.

17. For Flaubert's trial, see LaCapra, *Madame Bovary on Trial*.

18. LaCapra, *Madame Bovary on Trial* 37. For records of Flaubert's trial, see the Pléiade edition: Flaubert, *Œuvres*, ed. Albert Thibaudet and René Dumesnil (Paris: Gallimard [Pléiade], 1951) 1: 615–83.

19. LaCapra, *Madame Bovary on Trial* 39. Part of the reason why Flaubert was acquitted and Baudelaire condemned, LaCapra suggests, is that Baudelaire's lawyer, Gustave Chaix d'Est-Ange, was not as "eloquent" as Flaubert's (Antoine-Jules Sénard). LaCapra also points out that Pinard seems to have won the case (against Baudelaire) in which he was less invested personally. Pinard, for whom Christian morality constituted the "foundation of modern civilizations," considered *Madame Bovary* more devoid of Christian faith than *Les fleurs du mal* and thus more offensive. See LaCapra, "1857" 727. As I indicate earlier, Pinard did not insist on the religious immorality charges against Baudelaire.

20. Pichois gives an account of the exchange between Baudelaire and Flaubert in his editorial notes to Baudelaire's article on *Madame Bovary* [2: 1120–21]. Flaubert's letters to Baudelaire are gathered in *Lettres à Charles Baudelaire*, ed. Claude Pichois, *Etudes baudelairiennes*, vols. 5–6 (Neuchâtel: Baconnière, 1973) 149–59. Subsequent references to this book will use the abbreviation *LAB*.

21. Baudelaire wrote to his mother on December 25, 1857, that he "almost was prosecuted for his article on *Madame Bovary*" (j'ai failli être poursuivi pour mon article sur *Madame Bovary*, livre poursuivi, mais acquitté) [*Corr* 1: 436]. Pichois writes in the notes to Baudelaire's article on Flaubert that the authorities had difficulties prosecuting an article on a book that had been acquitted [2: 1121].

22. Parts of this "Notes nouvelles" of 1857 concerning morality would eventually be incorporated verbatim into the essay on Gautier written beginning in September 1858 (when "Le poème du hachisch" appeared in *La revue contemporaine*) and published in March 1859.

23. Flaubert's letter of January 20, 1857, qtd. in LaCapra, *Madame Bovary on Trial* 15. LaCapra begins *Madame Bovary on Trial* with this quote and states that "over a hundred years after the trial, the mystery still remains."

24. The dossier contained articles from Edouard Thierry, Frédéric Dulamon, J. B. d'Aurevilly, and Charles Asselineau in support of Baudelaire, which are reproduced in the editorial notes [1: 1187–1205].

25. LaCapra, "1857" 687.

26. Benjamin, "On Some Motifs" 155.

27. Flaubert, *Œuvres* 1: 631–32.

28. Calvino, *Six Memos* 4.

29. The four prefaces appear in the Pléiade edition [1: 181–86].

30. It is found in the second one, according to the Pleiade edition's classification. See the editorial notes [1: 1168, 1373].

31. *Les paradis artificiels* was published in May 1860, and the second edition of *Les fleurs du mal* in February 1861. The letter of July 14, 1860, to Poulet-Malassis, written just two months after the publication of *Les paradis artificiels*, shows that Baudelaire had already written three (out of the four) "plans for prefaces" by then ("I have made three drafts of preface. We will see about it together" [J'ai fait trois essais de préface. Nous verrons cela ensemble] [*Corr* 2: 67]).

32. In the letter of July 9, 1857, to his mother, quoted earlier, in which Baudelaire writes that arts and literature are "foreign" to morality, he mentions his piece on opium, which would become the second part of *Les paradis artificiels*. In another letter to his mother, of January 7, 1860, Baudelaire writes: "Malassis is demanding the *preface* to the new *Fleurs du mal* and the *dedication* of the *Paradis artificiel (opium and hashish)*" (Malassis réclame la *préface* des nouvelles *Fleurs du mal* et la *dédicace* du *Paradis artificiel* [opium et haschisch] [sic]) [*Corr* 1: 653].

33. LaCapra, *Madame Bovary on Trial* 7–8.

34. See Martha C. Nussbaum, *Poetic Justice: The Literary Imagination and Public Life* (Boston: Beacon, 1995), for a discussion of the intersection of law and literature and the role emotion and literature have in the faculty of judgment.

35. I borrow the expression "poetry's appeal" from the title of E. S. Burt's book *Poetry's Appeal: Nineteenth-Century French Lyric and the Political Space*. "Le poème du hachisch" has an early and quite different version entitled, "Du vin et du hachisch, comparés

comme moyens de multiplication de l'individualité" [1: 377–98], published in *Le messager de l'Assemblée* in March 1851. A second version, close to the final one that would be part of *Les paradis artificiels* in 1860, appeared in September 1858 in *La revue contemporaine* under the title "De l'idéal artificiel: Le haschisch." Between submission of the manuscript of *Les fleurs du mal* to his publisher in February 1857 and its publication in June, the studies on opium and hashish surface in Baudelaire's letters as ongoing projects. Baudelaire's first mention of the opium piece (a translation of De Quincey's *Confessions*) occurs in his letter to Poulet-Malassis of March 18, 1857 [*Corr* 1: 385]. In another letter to his publisher of April 27, 1857, he mentions the project in plural (*Excitations artificielles* [*Corr* 1: 397]), suggesting his plan to rework the earlier hashish piece. Constant references in his letters to the hashish study, between April 1857 and its publication in *La revue contemporaine* in September 1858, indicate that Baudelaire was writing the piece before, during, and after the trial, when the issue of morality in literature was in the air and in his own life.

36. The differences between "Le poème du hachisch" and its initial version of 1851, "Du vin et du hachsich," can be seen, in this light, to "register" the change in Baudelaire's political orientation and his experience of confronting the political regime through the trial. In "Du vin et du hachisch," Baudelaire had already condemned hashish—it incapacitates and isolates, whereas wine fortifies and promotes work and sociability—but this was motivated, as Pichois notes, primarily by his "democratic convictions" at the time [1: 1360]. Later, it is the censored poet who writes in "Le poème du hachsich," "reading" his own trial in the trial against hashish.

37. Walter Benjamin, "Baudelaire," *Walter Benjamin: Selected Writings, Volume 1: 1913–1926*, ed. Marcus Bullock and Michael W. Jennings (Cambridge: Harvard UP, 1996) 362.

38. In France, opium was prohibited in 1908, and hashish in 1916. Claude Pichois and Robert Kopp, "Baudelaire et le haschisch: Expérience et documentation," *Revue des sciences humaines* (July–September 1967): 467.

39. The historical accounts come from the editorial notes of the Pléiade edition [1: 1358–68]; Claude Pichois and Robert Kropp, "Baudelaire et l'opium: Une enquête à reprendre," *Europe* (April–May 1967): 61–79; Pichois and Kropp, "Baudelaire et le haschisch"; and Angélique Kinini, "Genèse de la toxicomanie dans l'imaginaire romantique et médical (1800–1860): Les étranges alliances des substances hallucinatoires dans le temps et l'espace," *Sciences et techniques en perspective* 1.1 (1997): 5–84.

40. Baudelaire refers to Moreau de Tours in a footnote at the end of "Du vin et du hachisch" [1: 397]. Dorvault's book, reedited in 1847, 1850, 1855, and 1858, was the principal source for the second section of "Le poème du hachisch," on the pharmacology of hashish. The 1858 version, "De l'idéal artificiel: Le haschisch," contains at

the end of the first section a footnote to Dorvault, which Baudelaire deleted for the final version of 1860. Baudelaire's letters to Poulet-Malassis (April 22 and 27, and May 1 and 3, 1860) [*Corr* 2: 28, 32, 36, 37] indicate that Dorvault wanted to use the footnote as publicity for his practice and proposed to sell *Les paradis artificiels* at his pharmacy in exchange. After some hesitation, Baudelaire decided against it, anticipating accusations of immorality, and took the footnote out altogether.

41. Egypt was one of the providers of hashish. Egypt was the object of French military and intellectual conquest during the first half of the nineteenth century, beginning with Napoleon's Egyptian expedition of 1798–1801. François Champollion deciphered the hieroglyphics in 1821, and in 1836, an Egyptian obelisk was erected in the middle of Paris at the Place de la Concorde.

42. "Une *étude* sévère et minutieuse sur les jouissances et les dangers contenus dans les *Excitants*" [letter to Abel Villemain, December 11, 1861, *Corr* 2: 193–94, original emphasis].

43. His defense article, dated July 24, 1857, was refused by *Le pays* but included as one of the four articles in Baudelaire's defense dossier. See the editorial notes [1: 1191–96].

44. *Le pays*, August 28, 1860, reprinted in Jules Barbey d'Aurevilley, *Les œuvres et les hommes: XXIII poésies et poëtes* (Genève: Slatkine, 1968) 113, 114.

45. See Baudelaire's letter to Paul Dalloz, June 26, 1860, *Corr* 2: 53. The letters of May 13, 1858, to his mother and May 14, 1858, to Poulet-Malassis inform us of *Le moniteur*'s hesitation in publishing "Un mangeur d'opium" [*Corr* 1: 495–96]. The opium piece was eventually published in *La revue contemporaine*, where the hashish article also appeared in September 1858.

46. *LAB* 155, original emphasis.

47. Blaise Pascal, *Pensées*, trans. A. J. Krailsheimer (New York: Penguin, 1979) 247, slightly revised translation.

48. Flaubert to Baudelaire, June 25 1860, *LAB* 155, original emphasis.

49. The pages Flaubert admired in "Le poème du hachisch" are 409–12, 419–21, and 429–30.

50. *LAB* 156, original emphasis.

51. *LAB* 155–56.

52. *LAB* 150.

53. Kristin Ross, *The Emergence of Social Space: Rimbaud and the Paris Commune* (Minneapolis: U of Minnesota P, 1988) 53–54; Blanchot, "Orpheus's Gaze" 176.

54. None of his fellow writers who wrote about drugs condemns them so severely. The moralistic condemnation of "Le poème du hachisch" stands out as "different,"

too, from Baudelaire's own general poetics, in which he conceives art and poetry to be "foreign" to morality. Baudelaire's writings offer two ready explanations. There is morality for the arts, which is different ("tout autre") from "positive and practical" morality, which everyone follows ["Notes pour mon avocat" 1: 194], and "the right to contradict oneself" (le droit de se contredire) [1: 709].

55. Pichois and Kopp, "Baudelaire et le haschisch" 475–76.

56. Gilles Deleuze, "Preface to the English Edition," *Difference and Repetition*, trans. Paul Patton (New York: Columbia UP, 1994) xv.

57. Gilles Deleuze, "Preface," *Difference and Repetition* xx.

58. Ross 53.

59. Deleuze, "Difference in Itself," *Difference and Repetition* 50–51.

60. Blanchot, "The Song of the Sirens" 106.

61. Philippe Lacoue-Labarthe and Jean-Luc Nancy both trace *expérience* back to its etymology in discussing the experience of poetry and freedom. See Lacoue-Labarthe's *La poésie comme expérience* (Paris: Christian Bourgois, 1986) 30–31 and Nancy's *L'expérience de la liberté* (Paris: Galilée, 1988) 25.

62. Deleuze, "Avant-propos," *Différence et répétition* xxi (Paris: PUF, 1972) 4, original emphasis, my translation.

63. *Selected Poems* 145. I render in verse form Clark's prose translation.

64. Deleuze, *Spinoza* 40.

65. Deleuze, "Difference in Itself" 51.

66. Calvino, *Six Memos* 10.

67. Deleuze, "Preface to the English Edition," *Difference and Repetition* xvi.

68. Deleuze, "Difference in Itself" 29.

69. *LAB* 187. Hugo refers to Baudelaire's article on Théophile Gautier published in *L'artiste* on March 13, 1859. The sentence quoted earlier, "I say that if the poet has pursued a moral goal he has diminished his poetic power," which was originally part of the essay on Poe ("Notes nouvelles sur Edgar Poe," of January 1857), is repeated verbatim in the article on Gautier, which Baudelaire thought of publishing as a preface to the second edition of *Les fleurs du mal*.

70. Deleuze, "Difference in Itself" 29; Octavio Paz, *The Other Voice: Essays on Modern Poetry*, trans. Helen Lane (New York: Harcourt Brace, 1990) 153.

71. Calvino, *Six Memos* 6.

72. Calvino, *Six Memos* 5.

73. "The work of art leaves the domain of representation in order to become 'experience'" [Deleuze, "Difference in Itself" 56].

74. See Pascal's fragment "Justice, Force," *Pensées, Œuvres complètes*, ed. Louis Lafuma (Paris: Seuil, 1963) 512.

75. In "Le poème du hachsich," the addict at the height of delusionary self-glorification "admires his face of Narcissus" (admire sa face de Narcisse) [1: 440].

76. LaCapra, "1857" 728.

77. Ross Chambers, "Poetry in the Asiatic Mode: Baudelaire's 'Au lecteur,'" *Yale French Studies* 74 (1988): 111. Chambers developed the article into the chapter "Poetry in the Asiatic Mode," in *The Writing of Melancholy*. See 141–43 for an extended analysis of the "involuntary tear."

78. Ross Chambers, "Nervalian Mist and Baudelairean Fog," *The Shaping of Text: Style, Imagery, and Structure in French Literature*, ed. Emanuel J. Mickel Jr. (Toronto: Associated UP [Bucknell UP], 1993) 102.

79. Suzanne Guerlac, *The Impersonal Sublime: Hugo, Baudelaire, Lautréamont* (Stanford: Stanford UP, 1990) 94, my emphasis.

80. In the second part of *Les paradis artificiels*, "Un mangeur d'opium," Baudelaire experiments further with the process of "amalgamation" [1: 399] of *fondre* by fusing De Quincey's writing with his own and taking to a new level his practice of poetic monograph. There is a difference between hashish as intoxication and addiction, which Baudelaire never celebrates, and opium/wine as inebriation and inspiration of the creativity of the (child-)genius, which he does celebrate in his "wine" poems and in Wagner's music. The opposition stands for difference in *modes* of being in the world, poetic versus narcotic, more than a real difference in the substances per se. Opium, although a drug, seems to stand for Baudelaire (via De Quincey) for states of intensity and risk—depth, pain, difficulty—for writing as practice of freedom. See Alina Clej, *A Genealogy of the Modern Self: Thomas De Quincey and the Intoxication of Writing* (Stanford: Stanford UP, 1995) and Guerlac's *The Impersonal Sublime* [85–93] for studies linking De Quincey and Baudelaire. The alliance between alchemist and blacksmith is a mythic archetype. See Mircea Eliade, *Forgerons et alchimistes* (Paris: Flammarion, 1956), and Joseph Campbell, *The Mythic Image* (Princeton: Princeton UP, 1974) 484–99.

81. In the "tragic circle" [1: 429] of the poetic monograph, there are tension and play between the Dionysian and the Apollonian, the two principles Nietzsche saw as forming an intimate pair in Greek tragedy. See Friedrich Nietzsche, "The Dionysiac World View," *The Birth of Tragedy and Other Writings*, ed. Raymond Geuss and Ronald Speirs, trans. Ronald Speirs (Cambridge: Cambridge UP, 1999) 117–38.

82. Dewey 299.

83. Calvino, "Ovid and Universal Contiguity," *The Uses of Literature* 146–61; Calvino, *Six Memos* 8; "Au fond de l'Inconnu pour trouver du *nouveau!*" ["Le voyage" 1: 134, original emphasis].

84. Miller, *Henry Miller on Writing* 203, 201.

85. Benjamin, *The Arcades Project* 101, slightly revised translation.

86. Miller, *Henry Miller on Writing* 197.

87. Miller, *Henry Miller on Writing* 181, 183.

88. Miller, *Henry Miller on Writing* 189.

Chapter 5. Quantum Elegance

1. Baudelaire's first translation of Poe ("Révélation magnétique") appeared in the journal *La liberté de penser* on July 15, 1848.

2. The first volume of the translation, *Histoires extraordinaires*, with the first preface, "Edgar Poe, sa vie, et ses œuvres," was published a year before, in March 1856.

3. Poe, "The Poetic Principle" 568. Subsequent references to Poe's works appear in the text.

4. Baudelaire translated "The Philosophy of Composition," but not "The Poetic Principle."

5. John Pawson, *Minimum* (London: Phaidon, 1996) 7.

6. Qtd. in Banesh Hoffman and Helen Dukas, *Albert Einstein, Creator and Rebel* (New York: Viking, 1972) 18.

7. Brain Greene, *The Elegant Universe: Superstrings, Hidden Dimensions, and the Quest for the Ultimate Theory* (New York: Vintage, 2000).

8. Stengers 5, original emphasis.

9. Cf. Honoré de Balzac, *Traîté de la vie élégante: Suivi de théorie de la démarche* (Paris: Arléa, 1998).

10. *The Parisian Prowler: Le Spleen de Paris. Petits Poèmes en Prose*, trans. Edward K. Kaplan (Athens: U of Georgia P) 129.

11. Almost all the versions of the frontispiece Baudelaire wanted for the second edition of *Les fleurs du mal*, in 1861, and for *Les epaves* (a collection of the condemned and excised pieces of *Les fleurs* appearing in Amsterdam), in 1866, show a serpent wrapping around the skeleton/trunk of the tree of knowledge. The second edition of *Les fleurs* was published without a frontispiece; *Les epaves* was published with one. See the editorial notes [1: 812–13]; Claude Pichois and François Buchon, eds., *Iconographie de Charles Baudelaire* (Geneva: Pierre Cailler, 1960) figs. 108–12.

12. Baudelaire's poetics of modernity echoes Rimbaud's poetics of the *voyant:* "I say you have to be a visionary, make yourself a visionary. A Poet makes himself a visionary through a long, boundless, and systematized *disorganization* of *all the senses*" [Rimbaud to Paul Demeny, May 1871, *Complete Works*, trans. Paul Schmidt (New York: Harper and Row, 1975) 102]. "Je dis qu'il faut être voyant, se faire voyant. Le Poète se fait voyant par un long, immense et raisonné *dérèglement* de *tous les sens*" [*Œuvres complètes*, ed. Antonin Adam (Paris: Gallimard [Pléiade], 1972) 251, original emphasis].

13. Paul Valéry, "Situation de Baudelaire," *Œuvres* 1: 613. Subsequent references to Valéry's work appear in the text.

14. See Valéry: "ce n'était point là autre chose que se défendre, jusque dans le détail et le fonctionnement élémentaire de la vie mentale, *contre l'automatisme*" ["Je disais quelquefois à Stèphane Mallarmé" 1: 658, original emphasis].

15. Gilles Deleuze, "Literature and Life," *Essays Critical and Clinical* 5.

16. Paul de Man writes that Mallarmé asks us "to increase clarity and insight within our mind." See "The Double Aspect of Symbolism," *Romanticism and Contemporary Criticism: The Gauss Seminar and Other Papers*, ed. E. S. Burt, Kevin Newmark, and Andrzej Warminski (Baltimore: Johns Hopkins UP, 1993) 163. Jean-Paul Sartre titled his book on Mallarmé *Lucidité face à son ombre*.

17. Mallarmé to Maurice Guillemot, qtd. in Jacques Scherer, *L'expression littéraire dans l'œuvre de Mallarmé* (Paris: Droz, 1947) 79.

18. See Pascal Durand, "Du sens des formes au sens du jeu: Itinéraire d'un apostat," *Actes du colloque Mallarmé* (Cerisy, 1997), ed. Bertrand Marchal and Jean-Luc Steinmetz (Paris: Hermann, 1998).

19. See the "Observation relative" to "Un coup de dés": "subdivisions prismatiques de l'Idée" [1: 391].

20. Julia Kristeva, *La révolution du language poétique: L'avant-garde à la fin du XIXe siècle: Lautréamont et Mallarmé* (Paris: Seuil, 1974) 272.

21. Deleuze, "Preface to the French Edition," *Essays Critical and Clinical* v.

22. Auguste Comte, *Philosophie première: Cours de philosophie positive, leçons 1 à 45*, ed. Michel Serres, François Dagognet, and Allal Sinaceur (Paris: Hermann, 1975) 66, 70.

23. Stengers 26.

24. *Newton's Principia: The Central Argument*, trans. Dana Densmore and William H. Donahue (Santa Fe: Green Lion, 1996) 3.

25. Michel Serres, *The Troubadour of Knowledge*, trans. Sheila Faria Glaser with William Paulson (Ann Arbor: U of Michigan P, 1977) 123.

26. Gottfried Wilhelm Leibniz, "Principles of Nature and of Grace, Founded on Reason," *The Monadology and Other Philosophical Writings*, trans. Robert Latta (New York: Garland, 1985) 418.

27. Stengers 29.

28. Gaston Bachelard writes that determinism is a "mechanics of solid": *Le nouvel esprit scientifique* (Paris: PUF, 1968) 106. Albert Einstein observes that Euclidean geometry presupposes a world of "practically-rigid body": "Geometry and Experience," *Sidelights on Relativity* (New York: Dover, 1983) 34.

29. René Descartes, *Discours de la méthode* (Paris: Bordas, 1965) 53, 62–65, my emphasis.

30. Michel Serres, "The Algebra of Literature," *Textual Strategies: Perspectives in Post-Structuralist Criticism*, ed. Josué V. Harari (Ithaca: Cornell UP, 1979) 274.

31. I borrow the expression ("elegant universe") from Brian Greene's *The Elegant Universe*.

32. Descartes, *Discours* 146.

33. John Keats to his brothers, George and Thomas Keats, December 21, 27(?), 1817, *Selected Letters of John Keats*, ed. Grant F. Scott (Cambridge: Harvard UP, 2002) 60, original emphasis.

34. Jean-Luc Marion, *Being Given: Toward a Phenomenology of Givenness*, trans. Jeffrey L. Kosky (Stanford: Stanford UP, 2002) 10, 9, original emphasis.

35. Calvino, *Six Memos* 6; Marion, *Being Given* 201.

36. Calvino, *Six Memos* 6.

37. Deleuze, "Difference in Itself" 50–51.

38. Calvino, *Six Memos* 8.

39. Marion, *Being Given* 201.

40. William James, "The Sentiment of Rationality," *The Will to Believe and Other Essays in Popular Philosophy* (New York: Dover, 1956) 109–10.

41. Calvino, *Six Memos* 56.

42. Deleuze, *Negotiations* 100–01, slightly revised translation.

43. Henri Focillon, *La vie des formes* (Paris: PUF, 1990) 17.

44. Stengers 5; Kristeva 272; Valéry, "*Le coup de dés*. Lettre au directeur des *Marges*" 1: 626.

45. "There is rhythm as soon as style is emphasized" [Lloyd 228] (rythme dès que style [s'accentue]) ["Crise de vers" 2: 205].

46. Poe, *The Portable Poe* 574, original emphasis.

47. Michel Butor, *Histoire extraordinaire: Essai sur un rêve de Baudelaire* (Paris: Gallimard [Folio], 1961) 46. Baudelaire's body is also, as Butor notes [89], the poison that contaminates his mistress, Jeanne Duval, with his incurable disease. Baudelaire's body literally becomes the "auteur du mal" (author of evil).

48. Calvino, *Six Memos* 56.

49. *Uncollected Poems: Rainer Maria Rilke*, trans. Edward Snow (New York: Farrar, Strauss and Giroux, 1996) 224–25.

50. A poetics of elegance and exactitude leads to a poetics of perfect and pure contradiction in which contraries—minimum and maximum, brevity and length—do not annihilate but enhance and give sharper focus to each other. My referring to (the last part of) "Le voyage," one of the longest poems of Baudelaire, in a chapter on "brevity" participates, perhaps, in this poetics of contradiction.

51. Calvino, *Six Memos* 56.

Chapter 6. The Eternal Enigma of Beauty

1. Baudelaire personifies "Beauty" as a feminine entity. I refer to "Beauty" as she/her and to the "I" of the poem as "the poet."
2. Marion, *Being Given* 201.
3. Stengers 5, original emphasis.
4. Serres, *The Troubadour of Knowledge* 123.
5. Stengers 26.
6. Descartes, *Discours* 146.
7. Friedrich Nietzsche, *Beyond Good and Evil*, trans. Helen Zimmern (Buffalo: Prometheus, 1989) 9, original emphasis.
8. Descartes, *Discours* 110.
9. "Fluctuantum sensuum fidem": René Descartes, *Regulae ad directionem ingenii*, ed. Adam and Tannery (Paris: Vrin, 1930) 10; "Rules for the Direction of the Mind," *The Philosophical Works of Descartes*, trans. Elizabeth S. Haldane and G. R. T. Ross (London: Cambridge UP, 1973) 1: 7.
10. Alvin Toffler, foreword, *Order out of Chaos: Man's Dialogue with Nature*, by Ilya Prigogine and Isabelle Stengers (New York: Bantam Books, 1984) xi.
11. See William Waters, *Poetry's Touch: On Lyric Address* (Ithaca: Cornell UP, 2003), and Elaine Scarry, *On Beauty and Being Just* (Princeton: Princeton UP, 1999), for examples of scholarship that experiments with, and engages in, a new mode of writing that is consonant with my approach to poetry's and Beauty's demands.
12. Henri Bergson, "On the Pragmatism of William James: Truth and Reality," *The Creative Mind*, trans. Mabelle L. Andison (New York: Philosophical Library, 1946) 251, 250–51.
13. See Gary Zukav's Web site: http://www.zukav.com (accessed March 2003).
14. I borrow the expression from Jiddu Krishnamurti, *Freedom from the Known*, ed. Mary Lutyens (New York: Harper and Row, 1969) 17.
15. Dewey 34.
16. Rainer Maria Rilke, *Letters to a Young Poet*, trans. Stephen Mitchell (New York: Random, 1984) 90.
17. I borrow the formulation "life as experience" from Dewey's *Art as Experience*.
18. Henry Miller, "Obscenity and the Law of Reflection," *Henry Miller on Writing* 188.
19. David Bohm, *On Creativity*, ed. Lee Nichol (London: Routledge, 1998) 39, original emphasis.
20. Marion, *Being Given* 7; Nietzsche, *Beyond Good and Evil* 7, original emphasis.
21. Stengers 29.

22. The term *geometry* comes from the Greek *geometrein*, "to measure land," with *geo* (land) and *metrein* (to measure). See Michel Serres for an account of geometry's origin in Egypt: *Les origines de la géometrie: Tiers livre des fondations* (Paris: Flammarion, 1993).

23. This is the order in the second edition of 1861.

24. Théophile Gautier, *Emaux et Camées* (Paris: Gallimard, 1981) 148–50.

25. The poem "Le parfum" is the second sonnet of an ensemble of four entitled "Un fantôme" [1: 39].

26. Roland Barthes, *Roland Barthes par Roland Barthes* (Paris: Seuil, 1995) 61, original emphasis.

27. "The ideal of knowledge is crystalline solid": Michel Serres, "Solide, fluides, flammes," *Hermès V: Le passage du nord-ouest* (Paris: Minuit, 1980) 43.

28. Rodolph Gasché discusses different models of chiasmus and their functioning in his introduction to Andrzej Warminski's *Readings in Interpretation: Hölderlin, Hegel, Heidegger* (Minneapolis: U of Minnesota P, 1987) ix–xxvi.

29. Stengers 22, original emphasis.

30. *Ephémère* comes from the Greek *ephêmeros*, with *epi* (during) and *hêmera* (day). The life span of one (or half) stanza of the *éphémère*, in a poem of seven stanzas, seems to play on this meaning.

31. "The non-person, which possesses as its sign the absence of that which specifically qualifies the 'I' and the 'you'": Emile Benveniste, "Relationships of Person in the Verb," *Problems in General Linguistics*, trans. Mary Elizabeth Meek (Coral Gables: U of Miami P, 1971) 200.

32. I borrow the expression from Jean-Luc Marion's book title *In Excess: Studies of Saturated Phenomena*, trans. Robyn Horner and Vincent Berraud (New York: Fordham UP, 2002).

33. Medusa has two veins: one gives life and the other death.

34. Michel Serres with Bruno Latour, *Conversations on Science, Culture, and Time*, trans. Roxanne Lapidus (Ann Arbor: U of Michigan P, 1995) 42.

35. The expression, again, is from Keats. See chapter 5.

36. Pema Chödrön, *When Things Fall Apart: Heart Advice for Difficult Times* (Boston: Shambhala, 2000) 1.

37. Friedrich Nietzsche, *Thus Spoke Zarathustra*, trans. Walter Kaufmann (New York: Viking, 1966) 195, original emphasis.

38. "The mind and the heart are like doors through which [truths within our reach] are received by the soul": Blaise Pascal, "De l'art de persuader," *Œuvres complètes*, 355.

39. "We know truth not only through our reason but also through our heart" [Pascal, *Œuvres complètes* 512].

40. The last two lines are from *Selected Poems* 145. I render in verse form Clark's prose translation.

41. Both poems were added to the second edition of *Les fleurs du mal*, of 1861. There are other overlapping images: the poet calls out "o Death," as he did "o Beauty"; the verb "to pour" appears in both ("pour us your poison"; "your gaze . . . / Pours confusedly blessing and crime") and so, too, does the image of flame/fire. Here, fire "burn[s] our brains," and in "Hymne," the poet, as "éphémère," burns into Beauty's "torch."

42. Antoine de Saint-Exupéry, *The Little Prince*, trans. Richard Howard (New York: Harcourt, 2000) 63, 59, 64, 60.

43. Saint-Exupéry 59.

44. José Ortega y Gasset, *What Is Knowledge?* ed. and trans. Jorge García-Gómez (Albany: State U of New York P, 2002) 35.

45. *Blaise Pascal: Thoughts, Letters, Minor Works*, trans. W. F. Trotter, M. L. Booth, and O. W. Wight (New York: P. F. Collier and Son, 1910) 406.

46. William James, *Essays in Radical Empiricism and a Pluralistic Universe*, ed. Ralph Barton Perry (New York: E. P. Dutton, 1971) 273; Henri Bergson, *Œuvres* (Paris: PUF, 1959) 1362. I heard Einstein's statement in a lecture by Tara Brach.

47. Miller, "Why Don't You Try to Write? (*Sexus*)," *Henry Miller on Writing* 23, original emphasis.

48. Miller, "Why Don't You Try to Write?" 23, original emphasis.

49. Gilles Deleuze, *Nietzsche et la philosophie* (Paris: PUF, 1973) 212, original emphasis.

50. Friedrich Nietzsche, *Thus Spake Zarathustra*, trans. Thomas Common (New York: Modern Library, 1982) 214, original emphasis, slightly revised translation.

51. This is especially the case in "Any Where out of the World: N'importe où hors du monde" [1: 356–57]: "Finally, my soul explodes, and wisely she tells me, 'Anywhere! anywhere! so long as it is out of this world!'" (Enfin, mon âme fait explosion, et sagement elle me dit: "N'importe où! n'importe où! pour vu que ce soit hors de ce monde").

52. Rimbaud, *Œuvres complètes* 131.

53. Stengers 12, original emphasis.

54. Henry Miller, "Reflections on Writing," *The Creative Process: A Symposium*, ed. Brewster Ghiselin (New York: New American Library, 1952) 181.

55. Rilke, *Letters to a Young Poet* 34–35, original emphasis.

56. I borrow the phrase "love's knowledge" from the title of Martha C. Nussbaum's book *Love's Knowledge: Essays on Philosophy and Literature* (Oxford: Oxford UP, 1990). To live/love the questions as opposed to die/kill for the answer—might the sphinx-like Beauty, here, be proposing a model of knowledge (question/answer) that

is different from the ancient mythology of Œdipus and the Sphinx, where finding the answer to the riddle has fatal consequences for both Œdipus and the Sphinx? Maurice Blanchot writes: "The poem is the answer's absence. The poet is one who, through his sacrifice, keeps the question open in his work." See *The Space of Literature* 247.

57. Franz Kafka, "Reflections on Sin, Pain, Hope, and the True Way," *The Great Wall of China: Stories and Reflections,* trans. Willa Muir and Edwin Muir (New York: Schocken, 1946) 307.

58. Rimbaud, *Œuvres complètes* 79. The "triple affirmation" of *et* (and) in the phonetic resemblance/echo between *éphémère* and *éternité* is striking.

Epilogue. Emotion-in-Syntax

1. Friedrich Nietzsche, *On the Genealogy of Morals and Ecce Homo,* trans. Walter Kaufmann (New York: Vintage, 1989) 15, original emphasis.

2. "We know to give our entire life every day" (Nous savons donner notre vie toute entière tous les jours): Arthur Rimbaud, "Matinée d'ivresse," *Œuvres complètes* 131.

3. Miller, *Henry Miller on Writing* 25.

4. Saint-Exupéry 34–35.

5. *The Parisian Prowler* 4.

6. Rainer Maria Rilke, "Duino Elegies," *The Selected Poetry of Rainer Maria Rilke,* ed. and trans. Stephen Mitchell (New York: Vintage, 1989) 151.

7. Rainer Maria Rilke, *Duiniser Elegien: Die Sonette an Orpheus* (Frankfurt: Insel, 1974) 11.

8. Nietzsche, *On the Genealogy of Morals* 15.

9. Miller, *Henry Miller on Writing* 25.

10. Marion, *Being Given* 201.

11. Miller, *Henry Miller on Writing* 23.

12. Chambers, "The Classroom" 170.

13. Rainer Maria Rilke, "The Panther" ("Der Panther"), *The Best of Rilke,* trans. Walter Arndt (Hanover: UP of New England, 1989) 68–69.

14. Stengers 5, original emphasis.

15. Deleuze and Parnet, *Dialogues* 66.

16. See Hans Ulrich Gumbrecht, "To Be Quiet for a Moment," *Production of Presence: What Meaning Cannot Convey* (Stanford: Stanford UP, 2004) 133–52 for a scholarly journey toward presence and silence in "reconnecting with the things of the world" [144].

17. James, "The Will to Believe," *The Will to Believe* 2–3.

18. Rilke, "Archaic Torso of Apollo," *The Best of Rilke*, 102–03.

19. Blanchot, *The Space of Literature* 238, 175.

20. Latour xvi.

21. Deguy 192, original emphasis.

22. See the aesthetics of "a single sitting" in Poe's "The Philosophy of Composition," *The Portable Poe* 552.

23. "Language is almost no more than a compression, or elaboration—an exactitude, declared emphasis, emotion-in-syntax—not at all essential to the message. And therefore, as an elegance, as something superfluous, it is likely (because it is *free* to be so used) to be carefully shaped, to take risks, to begin and even prolong adventures that may turn out poorly after all—and all in the cause of the crisp flight and the buzzing bliss of the words, as well as their directive—to make, of the body-bright commitment to life, and its passions, including (of course!) the passion of meditation, an exact celebration, or inquiry, employing grammar, mirth, and wit in a precise and intelligent way. Language is, in other words, not necessary, but voluntary." Mary Oliver, "Three Songs," *West Wind: Poems and Prose Poems* (Boston: Houghton Mifflin, 1997) 17, original emphasis.

24. Bubjung Seunim, "The Book I Read That Summer," *No Possession* [in Korean] (Seoul: Bumwoosa, 2001) 69.

25. Arthur Rimbaud, "L'éternité," *Œuvres complètes* 79.

26. William Blake, "Eternity," *The Complete Poetry and Prose of William Blake*, ed. David V. Erdman (Berkeley: U of California P, 1982) 470.

INDEX

"A une passante" ("To a Woman Passing By") (Baudelaire), 90–93
"Abel et Caïn" (Baudelaire), 96
acceptance, 3, 6, 7, 157, 173, 176
addiction. *See* intoxication/addiction
affirmation, 118, 173, 212n58
alchemy/ chemistry, 12, 14
"Alchimie de la douleur" ("Alchemy of Suffering") (Baudelaire), 14, 126
"All roads lead to Rome," 23–25, 34, 38, 119
"Any Where Out of the World: N'importe où hors du monde" (Baudelaire), 175
art criticism. *See* critics/criticism
Asselineau, Charles (friend of Baudelaire), 101
"*astringent effects*," 5, 136, 154, 166, 183
attention, 153, 182; Baudelaire's, to appearance (as a Dandy), 146; Mallarmé's, to poetic form, 138–41; of reader, 131, 149
"Au lecteur" ("To the Reader") (Baudelaire), 82–85, 102–3, 107
aura, 28
authenticity, 41
automatism: of daily life, 138; versus literature, 147
awareness, 6, 87

Bachelard, Gaston, 207n28
Balzac, Honoré de, 71, 109–10
Barbey d'Aurevilly, Jules, 71, 110–12
Baudelaire, Charles, vii, 1; "A une passante" ("To a Woman Passing By"), 90–93; "Abel et Caïn," 96; "Alchimie de la douleur" ("Alchemy of Suffering"), 14, 126; "Any Where Out of the World: N'importe où hors du monde," 175; "Au lecteur" ("To the Reader"), 82–85, 102–3, 107; "La Beauté," 160–62, 166–67, 174, 176; and Beauty, 91–94, 151–54, 157–76; "Bénédiction," 26; "Les bijoux" ("The Jewels"), 97, 105–6, 161; "Chacun sa chimère," 197–98n16; "Une charogne" ("Carrion"), 127; "Le *confiteor* de l'artiste," 179–80; *Conseils aux jeunes littérateurs* (Advice to Young Men of Letters), 15; on contradiction, 149; "Correspondances," 26; *De l'essence du rire* (*On the Essence of Laughter*), 27; "Le désir de peindre" ("The Desire to Paint"), 31, 174; "Epilogue," 12, 127; and fashion, 68, 71, 148; "Femmes damnées," 97; Flaubert and, 99–100, 111–12, 115–17; *Les fleurs du mal* (*The Flowers of Evil*), 10, 11, 31, 41, 81–91, 96–108, 110, 119, 125–27, 129, 131–32, 145, 182, 200n19; and form, 136–38; and hashish, 110; "Hymne à la Beauté" ("Hymn to Beauty"), 151–54, 157–75; "Les litanies de Satan," 96; "Les métamorphoses du vampire," 97; and modernity, 148; on morality, 100–101, 107–8; *Les paradis artificials: Opium et hachisch*, 11, 40–41, 108, 110–15; *Le peintre de la vie moderne* (*The Painter of Modern Life*), 17–21, 68, 77, 92; "Les plaintes d'un Icare" ("The Laments of an Icarus"), 2–3, 29–30, 38; and Poe, 11, 100, 131–32; "Le poème du hachisch," 5, 9, 11–17, 21–34, 38–39, 41, 107–8, 110–15, 125–28, 136, 157, 201–2n35; on poetry, 6, 9–10, 131–33, 135–36; "Le reniement de saint Pierre" ("Saint Peter's Denial"), 96; *Salon de 1845*, 89; *Salon de 1846*, 88, 116; *Salon de 1859*, 28; and self-knowledge, 179;

Baudelaire, Charles *(cont.)*,
"Le soleil" ("The Sun"), 19; "Spleen I," 85; "Spleen II," 81; "Spleen III," 81, 85–86; "Spleen IV," 81; *Le spleen de Paris*, 136–37; "Spleen et Idéal," 81–82, 85–87; "Tableaux parisiens," 89–90; and thought, 120–22; trial of, 9, 96–108, 110, 125, 129, 200n19; "Le voyage," 119, 145, 170–71

"La Beauté" (Baudelaire), 160–62, 166–67, 174, 176

beautiful: love of, 2,3,4; modern, 92

Beauty: approach to, 151–77; Baudelaire and, 91–94, 151–54, 157–76; death and, 167, 170–71; and difference, 157–58, 172; and experience, 8, 156–58, 164–65; explosion of, 93–94, 150, 175; as fluid, 161–65; and freedom, 169; and hardness, 160–61; as opening, 166; poetry and, 4, 6, 132, 156, 179–81; and risk, 168–69; shock of, 93–94, 150, 175, 179;and terror, 91–94, 169, 180

"Bénédiction" (Baudelaire), 26

Benjamin, Walter: on distance, 32–33; on ennui, 109; on *Les fleurs du mal*, 26; "On Some Motifs in Baudelaire," 89–92, 94, 102–3; on shock of poetry, 27; on weather, 86; "The Work of Art in the Age of Mechanical Reproduction," 28

Benveniste, Emile, 168

Bergson, Henri, 156, 172

"Les bijoux" ("The Jewels") (Baudelaire), 97, 105–6, 161

binary opposition, 10, 88, 128–29, 179. *See also* opposition/negation

Blake, William, 185–86

Blanchot, Maurice, 3, 6, 36–41, 72, 184

body: Baudelaire and Mallarmé and, 148; of child, 17–18; of convalescent, 17–18; poetry and, 18–20; wholeness of self and, 156. *See also* "corporeal mechanism"

Bohm, David, 158

boredom. *See* "Ennui"

Bourdin, Gustave, 96

brevity, 93, 131–34, 135. *See also* minimum

Broise, Eugène de, 97

Bubjung Seunim, 185

Burroughs, William, 10

Butor, Michel, 10, 148, 208n47

cadence, 7

Calvino, Italo: on exactitude, 147; on fluidity, 146; on lightness, 73–74; on Ovid's *Metamorphoses*, 78; on Perseus and Medusa, 74–77, 78–80, 95, 122, 182; on poetry, 149, 150

catastrophe, 94

cause and effect, 132, 134, 136, 142

"celestial mechanism," 16–18, 30–31, 86–87

censorship. *See* morality: literature and

certainty, 4–7, 24, 40, 119–20, 142, 155. *See also* knowledge; known/unknown

"Chacun sa chimère" (Baudelaire), 197–98n16

Chambers, Ross, 26, 31, 82, 84, 93, 125–26, 182

chance, 7, 144–45, 146–47. *See also* contingency

"Une charogne" ("Carrion") (Baudelaire), 127

chiasmus, 59, 163–64, 210n28

child: creativity and, 17–18; inspiration and, 30–31

Chödrön, Pema, 169, 210n36

circle, 5, 21, 157, 172; of hashish, 22–23, 31–32, 136; of poetry, 31, 126, 136; of the serpent, 137–38

clash, 75, 81, 88, 169. *See also* touch

Comte, Auguste, 141

concentration, in creative works, 5, 14–16, 21–22, 95, 126, 133, 138; and love, 94

conceptual approach, 146, 157–60

Confessions of an English Opium Eater (De Quincey), 40, 109, 205n80

"Le confiteor de l'artiste" (Baudelaire), 179–80

congestion, 19–20

Conseils aux jeunes littérateurs (Advice to Young Men of Letters) (Baudelaire), 15; content and form: in mathematical proof, 134–35; in poetry, 132–34, 135–40

contiguity, 78, 79, 81, 89, 94, 169; and contingency, 78, 144

contingency, 72, 77–78, 89, 94, 169. *See also* chance; contiguity
contradiction, 27, 149–50, 182
convalescence, 17–18, 30
coral, 75–81; and petrifaction, 79
"corporeal mechanism," 16–18, 30–31, 86–87
"Correspondances" (Baudelaire), 26
correspondences: between opposing elements, 88–89; between "Spleen" and "Ideal," 86
cosmic forces, 86
courage, 1–2, 36, 182
"Un coup de dés" ("A Throw of Dice") (Mallarmé), 71–72, 139–40, 144–45, 150
creativity, 15, 19–20, 158–59. *See also* inspiration; poetry
critics/criticism: Baudelaire on, 116; characteristics of ideal, 95–96, 118, 128–29. *See also* readers
crossing of boundaries: in *La dernière mode*, 52–59; in Medusa myth, 76–77
crowd, 89–91
Culler, Jonathan, 83

Daedelus, 1, 36
De l'essence du rire (*On the Essence of Laughter*) (Baudelaire), 27
De Man, Paul, 26, 198n17
De Quincey, Thomas, 40, 109, 205n80
death, 31, 76–77, 91–93, 145, 166–71
definition, 159; ideal of complete, 142
Deguy, Michel, vii, 10, 184
Delacroix, Eugène, 15–16, 21, 109–10
Deleuze, Gilles: on affirmation, 173; on difference, 46, 117–18, 120–22, 128, 144; on experimentation, 120; on intoxication, 10–11; on judgment, 95–96; on literary language, 71, 141; on Stoicism, 183–84; on style, 147; on thought, 120–21; on writing and knowledge/ignorance, 119
denial of unknown/feared/mysterious, 103–7, 130, 137, 143, 182
depth, 38–39, 68, 118
La dernière mode, gazette du monde et de la famille (The Latest Fashion, Gazette of the World and of the Family) (magazine), 42–72; authorship in, 52, 63–64; contents of, 47; and "Un coup de dés," 71–72 doubling and crossing in, 52–59; foreignness in, 57–60; and *fugue*, 46–50, 70–71; Ix in, 53–56, 59; jewelry in, 51, 65; journalistic versus literary writing in, 47–48, 53–54, 67–68; language of, 71; Madame du Ponty in, 58, 59, 61–62, 64–65; Mallarmé on, 43–44; Mallarmé's translation in, 52, 63; the maternal in, 61–65; Miss Satin in, 52–53, 56–61, 65–68; MS/SM (play of initials) in, 52–54, 59, 66, 69–70, 193n12; music in, 49–50; on Paris, 54–58; publication schedule of, 48–51; status of, 43–45; time in, 49–51, 52 and vacation as theme, 55–56, 64 Derrida, Jacques, 195–96n27
Descartes, René, 142–43, 155–56, 162, 165
"Le désir de peindre" ("The Desire to Paint") (Baudelaire), 31, 174
Desportes, Philippe, 2
devil. *See* Satan
Dewey, John, 95, 128, 157
difference: Beauty and, 157–58, 172; Deleuze on, 117–18; judgment versus, 128–29; versus negation, 117; and originality, 115–16; Perseus and, 122–25, 144; poetry and, 157–58; thinking and, 120–22
digestion, 17, 19–20
discernment, 128
disposition, 139
distance, 28–29, 32, 33
Dragonetti, Roger, 55
duality, 143, 162

Einstein, Albert, 135, 172, 207n28
Elegance: and life, 136; in mathematics/physics, 134–35, 141–43; in poetry, 136, 138, 147, 148, 150. *See also* brevity; exactitude
The Elegant Universe (Greene), 135
embrace. *See* openness
emergence, 95, 153, 175

Index (217

Emerson, Ralph Waldo, 14, 16, 32
emotion, 55
"emotion-in-syntax," 185–86, 213n23
encounter, 88, 93, 149
energy, 5, 15, 16, 20, 139, 150, 154, 182
"Ennui," 83–88, 107, 109, 121, 125–26, 182, 197–98n16
entropy, 14, 15, 19, 41, 127
equation, 134–35, 141–42, 155
eternity, 181, 185–86
ethics and poetics, 138
Eurydice, 34–38, 72, 94, 184
event, 184
evil, 82–83, 89
exactitude, 133–34, 135, 139, 143–47, 148, 150, 179
experience, 155–58, 164–65, 168–69; of Beauty, 132, 136; lived, 143; poetry's, 6, 12, 118; of the present, 178–79
experiment, 6, 12, 118
expertise, 118–20
"exuberant splendor," 5–6, 25, 31, 34, 94, 118

failure, 7, 24, 26, 30, 35, 41, 88
falling, 7, 8, 38, 137
fashion: form and, 147–49; Mallarmé and, 42–72; poetry and, 46, 51, 68–69
fate, 34–36
fear, 79, 85, 143, 147, 169, 180
"Femmes damnées" (Baudelaire), 97
fetishism, 63, 195n24, 196n29
Le figaro (newspaper), 96
Flaubert, Gustave: Baudelaire and, 99–100, 111–12, 115–17; and hashish, 115; *Madame Bovary*, 98–101, 105, 108, 125, 200n19; trial of, 98–101, 105, 108, 125, 200n19
Les fleurs du mal (*The Flowers of Evil*) (Baudelaire), 10, 11, 31, 41, 96, 119, 125–27, 131–32, 145, 182; reviews of, 96; themes of, 81–91; trial concerning, 96–108, 110, 125, 129, 200n19; fluidity, 145–47, 162–65
Focillon, Henri, 148
fondre, 126–27, 205n80
form: Baudelaire's experiments with, 126–27, 136–38; and content, 135, 140; formation and, 126–27; Mallarmé and, 138–41; poetry and, 131–34, 136–41, 147, 163; relationship to world through, 149. See also syntax; rhythm
Foucault, Michel, 40–41, 147
fragility, 6, 75, 166
Fraisse, Armand, 131, 133, 136
freedom: addiction opposed to, 9–10, 23–26; poetry and, 5–6, 10, 25, 31, 34, 41, 94, 118–20
Frey, Hans-Jost, 197–98n16
frivolity, 86–87
fugue, 46–50, 70–71

Gautier, Théophile, 82, 109–10, 161
generosity, poetry as practice of, 179
gift / to give, 38, 94, 175–76
Goethe, Johann Wolfgang von, 32
gravity, 8, 25, 37, 38, 117, 126, 146, 173; of form in Mallarmé, 138–41; in mathematics and physics, 141–42
Greene, Brian, 135
Grimal, Pierre, 1
Guattari, Félix, 46
Guerlac, Suzanne, 126
Guillemot, Maurice, 139
Gumbretch, Hans Ulrich, 212n16

habit, 5, 137, 159
hardening, 75–77, 79
hashish: addiction to, 38–39; chemistry of, 12; dangers of, 22–23, 27–28, 108–9; Flaubert and, 115; intoxication from, 5, 9–10, 13–16, 87, 108–9; popularity of, 109–10
"Hérodiade" (Mallarmé), 139
heroism of modern life, 88, 89
Holland, Eugene, 189n18, 191n33
Houssaye, Arsène, 137
Hugo, Victor, 122
humors, theory of, 82
hymen, 66, 195n27
"Hymne à la Beauté" ("Hymn to Beauty") (Baudelaire), 151–54, 157–75
hypocrisy: etymology of, 128; in literary trials,

102; morality and, 102–3, 129–30; of readers, 84–88, 93, 103

Icarus, 1–3, 7–8, 29–31, 32, 36, 38, 93, 94, 186
identity, 124–25. *See also* difference
ignorance, writing and, 119
inertia, 15, 137, 157; Newton's law of, 142
inexhaustibility, 29–30
infallibility, 24
ingestion, 17, 19
insight, 154, 158, 175
inspiration, 17, 19, 30–31, 37. *See also* creativity
intensification/intensity, 94, 95, 136, 138, 159
intimacy, 178–79
intoxicants, French popularity of, 109–10
intoxication/addiction: Baudelaire's examination of, 127–28; contradiction versus, 27; freedom opposed by, 9–10, 23–26; hashish, 5, 9–10, 13–16, 87, 108–9; poetry and, 10–11, 14–15, 21–31, 87, 108–9; strength of, 39–40

James, William, 146, 156, 172, 184
Jean-Aubry, G., 72
jewelry, 50–51, 64–65
Johnson, Barbara, 191n33
journalism, literature versus, 42, 47–48, 53–54, 67–68
joy, 6, 7, 8, 10, 17, 172, 178, 186
judgment, 95–96, 120, 128–30

Kafka, Franz, 177
Keats, John, 143
knowledge: and certainty versus doubt, 162–63; conceptual approach, 146, 157–60; in Descartes, 142–43; learning versus, 172–73; living, 146, 156; love and, 172, 211n56; in mathematics and physics, 135; poetry and, 118, 119, 129, 145, 172, 176; self-knowledge, 178–81, 184–85; writing and, 119. *See also* certainty
known/unknown, 41, 141–47, 151–57, 170–71, 176. *See also* thought
Kristeva, Julia, 140

LaCapra, Dominick, 97, 102, 108, 125, 130, 200n19
language: and crossing, 59; literary, 6, 67, 71, 141; Mallarmé on, 42–43; mother tongue, 63–64; Oliver on, 213n23; poetic, 6, 37–38, 138
L'artiste (journal), 99
Latour, Bruno, 4–5, 184
laughter, 27
learning, 172–73
Leibniz, Gottfried Wilhelm, 142
lightness, 8, 38, 72, 73–81, 173, 178, 182
liquid. *See* fluidity
"Les litanies de Satan" (Baudelaire), 96
literary criticism. *See* critics/criticism
literature: journalism versus, 42, 47–48, 53–54, 67–68; morality and, 97, 100–101, 103–6, 108, 110–15. *See also* language; poetry
Little Prince, 171–72
The Little Prince (Saint-Exupéry), 179
love, 3, 4, 5, 94, 171–72, 176, 211n56
lucidity, 10, 26–27, 138, 197–98n16
Lucretius, 146
Lydon, Mary, 194n13, 195n25

Madame Bovary (Flaubert), 98–101, 105, 108, 125, 200n19
Mallarmé, Geneviève, 69
Mallarmé, Stéphane, vii; and boating, 43–44, 69–70; "Un coup de dés" ("A Throw of Dice"), 71–72, 139–40, 144–45, 150; and dreams, 43–45; as fashion journalist, 42–72, 148; and *fugue*, 46–50, 70–71; "Hérodiade," 139; and jewelry, 51; on language, 42–43; as Miss Satin, 52–53, 59, 64, 66, 70, 148; and music, 50–51; poetic experiments of, 71–72, 138–41, 150; poetic themes of, 67; on poetry, 149; and style, 148; translation of Tennyson by, 52, 63; on types of writing, 43–45
Marchal, Bertrand, 71, 194n21
"Mariana" (Tennyson), 52
Marion, Jean-Luc, 143–44, 146

Index (219

mathematics, 133–34, 138, 141–43
Medusa, 74–81, 85, 89, 92–93, 122–24, 138, 144, 168–69, 181–82, 184
melancholy, 82, 85–86
melding, 126–27
metal, 126, 136
"Les métamorphoses du vampire" (Baudelaire), 97
Metamorphoses (Ovid), 78
metaphor, 23–25, 32, 38
metaphysics, 143, 162
Miller, Henry, 7, 10–11, 129–30, 157–58, 172–73, 176, 179, 181, 182
Minerva, 123–24, 144
minimum, 134–35, 143
modernity, 85, 88, 89, 93, 148; and antiquity, 85, 89, 93
Mondor, Henri, 72
Le moniteur (journal), 111, 113
monstrous, 169, 181–82. *See also* Medusa
morality: Baudelaire on, 100–101, 107–8; and censorship, 107; ennui and, 85, 107; fallibility and, 24; *Les fleurs du mal* trial, 96–108, 110, 125, 129, 200n19; literature and, 97, 100–101, 103–6, 108, 110–15, 129–30; *Madame Bovary* trial, 98–101, 105, 108, 125, 200n19; relativity of, 113–14; *The Tropic of Cancer* incident, 129–30. *See also* hypocrisy
Moreau de Tours (physician), 109–10
mother: figure of, 61–65; tongue, 63, 195nn24–25
music, in *La dernière mode*, 49–50

Nancy, Jean-Luc, 191n37
Narcisssus, 124
narcotic relation to the world, 86–88, 107, 181
negation. *See* opposition/negation
"Negative Capability," 143, 169, 181
Newmark, Kevin, 189nn16–17
Nietzsche, Friedrich, 155, 169–70, 173, 178, 180
Nussbaum, Martha, C., 201n34, 211n56

obscenity, 97–98, 104, 123, 125, 129–30
Oliver, Mary, 185, 213n23

"On Some Motifs in Baudelaire" (Benjamin), 89–92, 94, 102–3
openness, 3, 30–32, 37, 145, 154–55, 157, 165–66, 169–72, 176, 181, 182, 184–86. *See also* acceptance
opium, 109, 205n80
opposition/negation, 10, 88, 117–20, 123–25, 128–29, 144, 159–60, 166, 179, 181
order and chaos, 93–94
orgy, 15
Orientalism, 110
originality, 115–16
Orpheus, 9–10, 33–41, 72, 87, 93–94, 106, 184
Ortega y Gasset, José, 172
Ovid, 30, 38, 74–75, 77–78, 89, 122–24, 146, 181

pain, 6, 179–80
Les paradis artificiels: Opium et hachisch (Baudelaire), 11, 40–41, 108; reception of, 110–15
Paris, 54–56
Pascal, Blaise, 113–14, 116, 170, 172
Pawson, John, 134
Paz, Octavio, 122
Le peintre de la vie moderne (*The Painter of Modern Life*) (Baudelaire), 17–21, 68, 77, 92
perception, 96, 129
peril, 118
perishability, 6, 75, 166
Perseus, 74–76, 78, 80, 89, 95, 122–25, 138, 144, 168–69, 181–82, 184
petrifaction, 74, 79. *See also* coral
phantasmagoria, 127–28
phenomenology, 162
"The Philosophy of Composition" (Poe), 132, 134
physics, 142; and string theory, 135. *See also* mathematics
Pichois, Claude, 98, 101, 111
Pinard, Ernest, 98–99, 101, 103–7, 125, 130, 200n19
"Les plaintes d'un Icare" ("The Laments of an Icarus") (Baudelaire), 2–3, 29–30, 38
Poe, Edgar Allan, 11, 46, 100, 131–35, 148, 149;

"The Philosophy of Composition,"
132, 134; "The Poetic Principle," 132
"Le poème du hachisch" (Baudelaire), 5, 9,
11–17, 21–34, 38–39, 41, 107–8, 110–15,
125–28, 136, 157, 201–2n35
poet: and Beauty, 171–72; function of, 12,
16–17; Icarus as, 2–3, 29–31; Orpheus
as, 34–39; Perseus as, 74–75, 95; and
self, 149. *See also* poetry
"The Poetic Principle" (Poe), 132
poetic relation to the world, 6, 41, 88, 89, 107,
118, 120, 181–82
poetry: Baudelaire on, 6, 9–10; and Beauty, 6,
132, 179–81; and body, 18–20; and contradiction, 27; and correspondence, 89;
demands of, on reader, 6, 8, 25, 39, 119,
179, 184–86; and depth, 38–39, 118; and
difference, 122, 157–58; and distance,
28–29, 32; exactitude in, 143–47; and
experience, 156–58; and failure, 7, 36;
fashion and, 46, 51, 68–69; fashion
writing and, 42–48; and fluidity,
145–47; and form, 127, 131–34, 136–41,
147, 163; and freedom, 10, 25, 41,
118–20; versus hypocrisy, 88; and inexhaustibility, 29–30; intoxication and,
10–11, 14–15, 21–31, 87, 108–9; jewelry
and, 51; and knowledge, 119, 129, 172,
176; language of, 6, 37–38, 138; length
of, 131–34; and life, 88–89, 136, 146,
178–80, 185; and lucidity, 10, 26–27;
Mallarmé on, 149; mathematics/science versus, 141–47; morality and,
100–101, 108; music and, 51; and otherness, 43; as passage, 20, 22, 118, 145, 147,
154, 155, 158; and purity, 7; and responsibility, 6, 7, 25, 41, 184; and risk, 3–8,
41, 118–20, 146–47, 184; and selfknowledge, 178–81, 184–85; and sobriety, 10; and transport, 25–26; and unity,
132–33. *See also* concentration; creativity;
literature; poet
point of view, 116–17
Poulet-Malassis, Auguste, 97
La presse (journal), 137

proofs, mathematical, 134–35
prose poetry, 136–37
Proust, Marcel, 71, 141

questions, 3–4, 146, 151–55, 157, 159–60, 164,
170, 176, 211n56; relevant, 146, 155

rain, 85–87
readers: attention of, 149; Baudelaire's, 102–3;
demands of poetry on, 6, 8, 25, 39, 119,
179, 184–86; hypocrisy of, 84–88, 93,
103. *See also* critics/criticism; reading
reading, 184–85
realism, obscenity and, 98, 99
reason: Cartesian, 155–56; morality of literature and, 104–6; opposition of, to
difference, 120–24, 129; principle of
sufficient, 142, 159; and senses, 104–6;
and war, 123–24. *See also* certainty;
Minerva; opposition/negation; thought
Reed, Arden, 85
"Le reniement de saint Pierre" ("Saint
Peter's Denial") (Baudelaire), 96
repression. *See* denial of
unknown/feared/mysterious
La revue contemporaine (journal), 11
rhythm, 7, 46–47, 55–56, 64, 149
Rilke, Rainer Maria, 149–50, 157, 176, 179–80,
182–83, 184
Rimbaud, Arthur, 177, 178, 179, 185, 196n29
risk: avoidance of, 7; Beauty and, 168–69;
Mallarmé and, 72; Orpheus and,
39–41; poetry and, 3–8, 41, 118–20,
146–47, 184; safety versus, 39–41;
significance of, 7
"risky construction": in science, 4; in poetry,
4–6
Rosolato, Guy, 195n24, 196n29
Ross, Kristin, 116

Saint-Exupéry, Antoine, 179
Salon de 1845 (Baudelaire), 89
Salon de 1846 (Baudelaire), 88, 116
Salon de 1859 (Baudelaire), 28
Satan, 82–83, 127–28

"satin," 59–60, 63, 194n20
Scarry, Elaine, 209n11
science, 4–5
self-annihilation, 179–80
self-knowledge, 178–81, 184–85
Semaine théâtrale (newspaper), 100
sens, 24, 34, 35, 38. *See also* metaphor
senses, morality of literature and, 103–6
serpent, 137, 206n11
Serres, Michel, 142, 162
shock, 6, 27, 93–94, 150, 159, 166, 175, 179
Six Memos for the Next Millennium (Calvino), 73, 147
sobriety, 10–13, 147
"Le soleil" ("The Sun") (Baudelaire), 19
sonnets, 136
spleen, moral numbness and, 82–86
"Spleen I" (Baudelaire), 85
"Spleen II" (Baudelaire), 81
"Spleen III" (Baudelaire), 81, 85–86
"Spleen IV" (Baudelaire), 81
Le spleen de Paris (Baudelaire), 136–37
"Spleen et Idéal" (Baudelaire), 81–82, 85–87
Steinmetz, Jean-Luc, 69–70
Stengers, Isabelle, 4–5, 141–42, 164, 169, 175
style, 71, 147–48, 149, 150
subtraction, 73, 134, 143, 157, 173
sufficient reason, 142, 159
"sun within a sun," 5, 8, 16, 29, 87, 118, 147, 175, 177
surrender, 10, 41, 180
synesthesia, 18
syntax: "emotion-in-syntax," 185–86, 213n23; Mallarmé and, 139–41, 150; poetic versus mathematical, 141–42

"Tableaux parisiens" (Baudelaire), 89–90
taming, 171–72. *See also* love
tenderness, 168, 182
Tennyson, Alfred, Lord, 52, 63
terror, 6, 145, 169, 172. *See also* fear
theory, 155
thought, 120–23, 158–59. *See also* certainty; known/unknown; reason
touch, 75–80, 145, 169. *See also* clash
translation, 52, 59–60, 64, 195n24
trial procedures, during Second Empire, 97–98
The Tropic of Cancer (Miller), 129
truth, 142

Ulysses, 40–41, 120, 130
unity, 132–33, 168

Valéry, Paul: on art, 29; on Baudelaire, 148; on Mallarmé, 70, 72, 138, 140, 141; on poetry, 6, 12
vaporization, 9, 14, 15, 84–85, 126. *See also* concentration
Verlaine, Paul, 43, 46
Villiers de l'Isle-Adam, Auguste, 51
"Le vin de l'assassin" ("The Murderer's Wine") (Baudelaire), 96
"Le voyage" (Baudelaire), 119, 145, 170–71
vulnerability, 168–69, 181

Wagner, Richard, 15–16
Waters, William, 209n11
weather, 85–87
weight, 73, 74, 78, 79, 81–82, 85–88, 126; of the soul, 8. *See also* lightness
wisdom, 6, 157
"The Work of Art in the Age of Mechanical Reproduction" (Benjamin), 28

Zukav, Gary, 156